CANADIAN VOICES

Volume Two

AN ANTHOLOGY OF PROSE AND POETRY

BY EMERGING CANADIAN WRITERS

To Elysia from her granddad
for her 2015 birthday

Published by:

BookLand Press
6021 Yonge Street
Suite 1010
Toronto, Ontario M2M 3W2
Canada
www.booklandpress.com

Project coordinator: Trade Architects (Canada) Inc.

Printed and bound in Canada.

Library and Archives Canada Cataloguing in Publication

Canadian voices: an anthology of prose and poetry by emerging Canadian writers.

ISBN 978-0-9784395-5-2 (v. 1). ISBN 978-0-9784395-8-3 (v. 2)

1. Canadian literature (English) -- 21st century.

PS8251.1.C36 2009   C810.8'006   C2009-905893-6

TABLE OF CONTENTS

PART ONE: PROSE

PART TWO: POETRY

PART ONE
PROSE

HOW TO RESUSCITATE ROSES
by Valerie Albemarle

AN ABSENCE SINCE SUMMER is long enough to miss the breakfasts of lightly salted salmon, smoked ham, and tea with chocolates. Back home with nobody to keep an eye on things Daria has a Starbucks coffee for breakfast. Wait... this *is* home, now become a holiday destination. It'll be a white and frosty New Year's Eve - finally, after many warm rainy ones. No need to go anywhere after breakfast and she can linger to her heart's content. She muses over green tea on why salmon comes in so few edible forms back in BC. Why there is no such tender, buttery, lightly salted variety available? Maybe it's thought to spoil easily; this fish isn't smoked, it's essentially raw, with only the fat and salt to preserve it. But here people are not protected from their food and accept the inherent risks of enjoying it. The pursuit of all-engulfing safety has not caught on here - yet.

"So tell me about your work. You never tell me anything, getting information out of you is like pulling a bucket out of a well. Your veterinary training - might it help you understand human medicine one day?" Mother is trying to find mitigating circumstances to this unspoken misfortune, Daria's engaging in a profession so unladylike and unworthy of her perceived talents.

"Well," Daria starts in a safe and wishy-washy key, "the animals have blood coursing through their veins, much like we do, and basically the same physiology. Some medications work very differently in different animals though. Some medications you give only to humans, I wouldn't know how those work." She must carefully avoid getting recruited as medical consultant only to be fired for giving unwelcome advice.

Presently, even a leisurely breakfast is over and they depart to their respective activities: mother to mark her students' papers, Daria to read short stories by Chekhov, her chosen author on this visit.

Daria is deprived of culture in her northern wilderness, and several trips to concerts and theatres have been planned during her visit. Finding the opera theatre is a challenge. Daria no longer recognizes the city where she grew up and spent her youth, the sky and the buildings she knows are obscured by what look like half-built skyscrapers housing brightly lit department stores. They turn for help to a man who has come from Central Asia to make a life in the big city by clearing snow in winter, and sweeping sidewalks and caring for flowerbeds in summer. He points them to the statue of Pushkin, they remember where they are in Russia and slowly recover their bearings. The opera is enjoyable, the lead singer is decent but not export grade according to mother. Not the kind they will invite to sing in Milan.

On the way home mother makes a sheepishly brazen stab at liberating Daria from the cat which is perceived to be a threat to peaceful sleep. "The cat is happy boarding at the clinic, maybe she will like to stay there for good?" The fact that Daria wanted a cat, and sleeps peacefully with the bedroom door closed, is irrelevant. But the seeds of doubt have been planted; or maybe previously sprouted seeds have been watered. Daria has little experience keeping animals and plenty leaving them alone; almost two years into her veterinary career she has not made up her mind about the whole idea of animals as pets. On difficult and sad days she perceives her work as that of a prison doctor in charge of making the inmates as happy and healthy as their condition permits.

The grapes mother has bought at the market are alive with flavour and tender, vulnerable: amber cabochons dripping with fragrant juice. They grew and ripened under the sun somewhere in Central Asia, now a foreign country since the crumbling of the Soviet Union. There is no room in the little fridge and the grapes are spread on a newspaper under the table. She falls into her habit of reading a paper, any old rag, before using it for lining. The page she opens advertises cats and dogs free to good homes. The animals are described in tender and playful terms with pictures attached. Will these animals be happy in their new homes? What, indeed, does Daria want with a cat? She can't even let her outside from her condo on the second floor, and the cat dissipates her exuberant energy by galloping around like a horse. After the animal ads comes the column with ads from witches offering to cast spells, undo spells put on a client by some less experienced professional, or cause a chosen person to fall in love with the client (the chosen person's photograph is usually

required for this). Witches are plenty in Russia but a good one is hard to find. Daria needs only one page of the newspaper for the grapes - she washes and eats half of them right away.

For dinner, mother makes pork chops with pan-roasted scalloped potatoes whose description does not exist in any cookbook. Daria has not been able to replicate them. "So, come tax time be sure to tell these tax collectors of yours that you are a veterinarian living in the remote north. If there's any justice, they must make allowances for a situation like that."

"I'm sure neither of these circumstances will inspire sympathy in these tax collectors of mine." Mother has fallen back onto her original perception of a veterinarian as a respected farm hand. The bear-infested wilderness where Daria lives is forty minutes outside Vancouver. It does look kind of far to the north on the map mother has. It doesn't have theatres, or the unbelievable variety of quality delicious foods that Moscow does - so there!

"Do you have any desire to live and work in Europe? You speak French and Spanish, you could learn Italian, you can cut open your dogs and cats in one of these countries." And sew them shut again, please don't forget that part.

"I love where I am, mother. I chose the place, I love the mountains and the ocean and the forests. I have no desire to move anywhere."

"But it's so FAR away!" *Not far enough!!!*

At night Daria sits on her bed thinking about what's involved in moving to Europe and when she would need to make this decision. It provides some relief to think that this doesn't need to happen for a few years. She studies the patterns of burl on the karelian birch wardrobe that must be one of the first things she saw in this world. She grew up in this room, slept in this bed on this same mattress, drew the same curtains over the large windows with the same wooden frames, lit the same gas range to make tea, and opened the door of the same fridge to get a snack. None of them have been decommissioned or replaced, they've all made it to their early forties.

She's right back in her room, with at least half her life gone by. The cotton wool stuffing in the mattress has become rock-hard over the years and Daria finds it difficult to fall asleep. She sneaks the foam mattress from its storage and sinks into grateful sleep as her bones finally find comfort, a soft layer between her and the past.

"Do you get to dress nicely for your job? I suppose not, you probably have to wear a white coat over your clothes."

No comment is needed or expected. But mother is right: Daria misses wearing pretty clothes.

"So do the owners bring you gifts for taking good care of their animals?"

"Not usually. Sometimes they bring flowers or a box of chocolates as a token of appreciation. But they pay good money for the care of their animals so I don't expect to be paid in gifts."

"Ah, so your work's not very *fertile*, as we would say here." Daria is getting vaguely alarmed about her lack of concern over not getting lavish gifts.

"Now, Alexander does lots of surgeries privately," mother continues.

Alexander is the husband of mother's friend since university.

"He is in high demand, an excellent oncologist. He uses the facility on weekends and off-days to do these surgeries." Daria dares not ask what happens if there are complications. That's probably unthinkable for an oncologist of his calibre.

"I bet your boss does surgeries like that too, where the clients pay him directly."

"My boss already works for himself. He owns the place. And how do you expect a surgery to happen without being recorded in the files - with all the drugs used, the anaesthetic record, the assistant's time?"

Petty and perfectly surmountable details that mother dismisses.

"How do you know he doesn't do it on days when you're off? There are lots of things I'm sure go on without your knowledge. It's not difficult to hide from an idiot like you."

Daria should gratefully jump on this as her universal defence. Instead, she makes some dumb remark about her boss writing off the cost of entire surgeries and hospital stays for pet owners in dire straits. But she gets up from the table feeling thoroughly stupid, and starts to wonder in earnest how her boss manages to fly under his own accountability radar and why he would want to. For the things she knows to be true back home have no weight in this reality, they've been unhinged and set to float in space that obeys very different laws of ontological gravity.

Mother's students give her flowers on the final day of exams: roses the colour of sunsets spiced up with baby's breath, and some oversized fleshy leaves which she discards on aesthetic grounds. The roses start to wilt quickly, but she fills the tub with cold water to an inch's depth and sets the roses floating there in the dark. After a day they're fresh and taut with moisture, and the treatment is repeated periodically. If she knows how to bring back roses, what if she's also right about..?

The journey from Moscow to Vancouver takes over twenty hours. The Aeroflot plane is named after a Russian painter but there's nothing

to watch. The Air Canada plane has no name but offers a variety of things to watch. There is plenty of time to separate love from blackmail and conviction from doubt.

In between Daria watches movies that she would not watch under any other circumstances and takes fitful unrefreshing naps. It takes a few days to realize she is back in Canada, and a week to get over jet lag. The cat is back in the apartment and galloping like a horse. At work Daria moves through her cases with confidence and authority that surprise her. Mother calls in a couple of days saying she misses Daria's voice. She reports that the roses are crisp and fresh, and asks if Daria is eating right and getting enough sleep.

THE CONDUCTOR
by Dahn Alexander Batchelor

ALL OF HIS LIFE, that is, up to the first thirty years of it, Donny Davis had one unfulfilled ambition — to conduct a large symphony orchestra in front of a large admiring audience.

There was one hurdle he had to cross, of course. He didn't have a symphony orchestra which was his to conduct. In fact, not only had he never played an instrument in a symphony orchestra or even a small band; he only went to grade four in his piano lessons.

Then one day he read in the local paper that anyone could make a bid to be a guest conductor at one of the city's symphony orchestra's open-air concerts held in the amphitheater in the city's main park during a summer evening, irrespective of his or her musical training. The highest bidder would be the conductor of the orchestra this upcoming summer. Donny bid four thousand dollars and since it was the highest bid received, he was told that he would be given the opportunity to conduct the orchestra for any piece he chose the orchestra to perform so long as the selection didn't last longer than ten minutes.

He met with the musical director of the orchestra to discuss what musical selection he would like the orchestra to play while he acted as its guest conductor.

While browsing through the list of the selections in the orchestra's manuscript library, his eyes suddenly opened wide when he saw that they had the music for Tchaikovsky's *Symphony No. 6*, the *Pathetique*. He handed the manuscript to the musical director who opened it and then said to Donny,

"It is a complicated piece to conduct but there is a part in it that is rather easy to conduct and it is very expressive. Its performance would be just under ten minutes." He added, "I suggest that you buy a recording of that piece so that you are familiar with the music."

Donny replied, "Oh, I am very familiar with that piece as I already have a recording of it and I have played it many times."

When Donny got home, he began playing the taped music as he looked down at the manuscript where the musical director had marked where the orchestra would begin and began following the music to the best of his ability—which was limited at that. On each page were the musical notes, the rests, the accidentals, the flats and sharps, the slurs, the ties, the phrase marks. It was the first time he had ever seen the manuscript of a symphony so it was all mind-boggling to him.

About two weeks prior to the concert, the music director arranged for Donny to come to the concert hall so that he could rehearse with the orchestra. Donny was extremely nervous when he stood on the podium. He was well aware that the members of the orchestra knew that he was a rank amateur who was going to conduct them. Despite that, they were kind to him when he dropped the baton onto the floor while fumbling with it—they didn't laugh.

He raised his baton and then when he brought it down with a quick down-stroke, the orchestra, began with the powerful beginning of the selection he had chosen. As he continued to move his baton in the air, this way and that, the orchestra followed him faithfully. And as a very special gesture of kindness, they didn't even snicker to themselves when they watched him as he performed not unlike a Whirling Dervish or while he spread his feet apart, he made pronounced stabbings of his left hand into the air. They were especially kind to him when his face contorted through the gambit of grimaces as another section of the orchestra took over the theme of the music while their own faces showed no sign of recognizing just how silly he looked.

On the night of the performance, he sat on a chair in the dressing room and with the earphones of his Walkman pressed close to his ears and his eyes closed; he began replaying the selected passages of the *First Movement* of the *Pathetique*, over and over again so as to not forget one note, one pause or miss the tempo.

After a while, Donny suddenly felt a hand on his shoulder and he looked up and saw the music director of the orchestra in front of him. He smiled at Donny and said, "It's time now." Donny looked up at him, not unlike a condemned man looking up at the warden who is about to lead him to the gallows.

As he walked along the short tunnel leading into the amphitheater, he heard the announcer say, "Ladies and Gentlemen. Our guest conductor for our orchestra's next performance will be Donny Davis who will lead our symphony orchestra as they perform for you, an excerpt from the *First Movement* of Tchaikovsky's *Sixth Symphony*, the *Pathetique*."

The audience's clapping hands reverberated through the tunnel as Donny approached the opening leading directly into the amphitheater. As he walked through the opening, he immediately thought of the Christians as they entered the arena to face the lions.

When the clapping of hands died out, all that could be heard was the whistling of the wind in the trees circling above the amphitheatre. As he walked towards the podium, the concert master, who is always the lead violinist, stood up and shook Donny's hand and said, "You will do just fine." Donny smiled in return and then stepped onto the podium and faced the orchestra. The concert master nodded his head to imply that they were ready. Donny raised his baton and a second later he brought it down forcefully. The orchestra then immediately responded with the powerful beginning of his selection. It was then that he began his own solo performance with his baton and his left hand accompanied by the orchestra.

As the members of the orchestra played the first part of the *Pathetique*, Donny waved his baton and he would on occasion point with his left hand to the section of the orchestra that was to play a prominent part. When he wanted a section of the piece to be quieter than the rest of the piece, he lowered his hand, palm down and when he wanted it to be louder, he raised his hand upwards, palm up.

He remembered from watching other conductors in the past, the music dictated the expressions on their faces so he let a part of the symphony dictate the expression on his own face as the orchestra played a sad part of the music. During that part of the symphony, his face had the look of anguish—the look of someone at the grave of a loved one.

The orchestra followed him into the final part of the piece. The music emanating from the instruments was as beautiful as he had ever heard. The members of the orchestra followed him without a missed note. The hundred members were playing the symphony just the way the composer wrote it. Donny's performance as a conductor was just as what was to be expected by the audience.

When the music subsided, hundreds of people in the audience stood up to show their appreciation of the performance they had just heard. Donny bowed to the audience and they in turn clapped enthusiastically. As he walked towards the tunnel, the concert master stood up and shook

Donny's hand while the other members of the orchestra applauded just as enthusiastically as did the audience. Donny was in absolute ecstasy.

The following night, he attended a party his friends had arranged for him. At least fifty of them attended the party and most of them had watched his performance the previous evening. At one moment during the party, he saw a face that looked familiar but he knew it wasn't one of his friends. Suddenly, his girl friend pulled the stranger towards him, saying, "Donny, This is Barry Davies. I think you two have met before."

Donny stared at the face and then the man said, "I was one of the violinists at the concert last evening." The violinist continued, "You did a very fine job on the podium, Maestro. The performance went off without a hitch."

Donny beamed when he realized that he was being referred to as Maestro.

While Donny was talking to another admirer, the violinist and Donny's girlfriend headed towards the table where the wine was being served. When they reached the table, she stopped and turned to the violinist and whispered in his ear. "Every one tells me that Donny was a great conductor. Please. Give me your honest opinion."

He drew her closer and whispered back, "Don't tell Donny or any of his friends what I am about to tell you. She promised to keep it secret. The violinist continued, "If we had followed his baton through the music, our performance would have been a disaster. Thank God our music director made us go over and over the music without anyone conducting us so that we would only have to look at our manuscripts and occasionally look at the concert master instead of our guest conductor for the beat in order to keep us playing in sync."

Near the end of the evening, Donny and his girlfriend were dancing the final slow number together; cheek-to-cheek. He moved his head closer to hers so that his lips were almost touching the ear lobe of her right ear. Then, while seeking confirmation of the accolades given to him, he asked her,

"Tell me, Honey. Am I a great conductor or what?" She began to smile and then she began to laugh silently to such an extent, that her body was shaking. She finally replied with a big smile, "My lips are sealed, Donny."

Of course, Donny never learned the truth. He would forever cherish the memory of the day that his greatest ambition was realized. One of the country's finest symphony orchestras played one of the nicest pieces of music ever heard, before an appreciative audience -and it was performed entirely under Donny Davis' baton -or so he believed.

LOVE OF HER LIVES
by Sharon Bernas

Prologue

Scotland, 1907

"YOU COULD HAVE BEEN killed, woman! What the devil were you thinking?" Colm shucked off his muddy boots and sent them tumbling across Bethany's polished pine floor.

Still wearing her cloak, Bethany stood dripping in the doorway. "What was I thinking? Did you not read Mr. Winterbottom's letter to the Dundee Advertiser?" Her legs clenched so tight, she was in danger of rupturing a good pair of stockings. Knowing damn well he'd read it, she reminded him nonetheless, "Winterbottom wrote: 'These women who fight for the vote are a blight on this great country of ours!' Those are fighting words, Colm. Make no mistake."

"So Winterbottom accuses you *gentle* women of violence and destruction, and you prove him right? Where's the logic in that, Bethany? Will you next be setting fire to our own church?"

She gritted her teeth together enough to feel her eyes bulge. She'd certainly not supported the suffragettes who'd set fire to Whitekirk, and he knew it.

He was still ranting. "How can you abide such desecration? You must know the government will not give in to violence. You are women. Fight your battle with words."

She couldn't believe her ears. Her own husband implying that being a woman was some sort of handicap. "How dare you accuse me of

violence? We were provoked!" She quickly eyed the hallway for something to throw. Damn him. That would only prove his point. Jerking the hood of her cloak up, she turned for the door.

Colm left his overcoat swinging on the coat rack, crossed the floor, and gripped her elbow. The usual warmth in his eyes was now as soothing as a belly ache. "You're not going back out in that weather. We both could use a hot bath."

She tugged her arm free. "Go find yourself a placid wife to warm your bath, Colm." Snapping the latch back, she ran out into the gloaming, knowing full well he'd follow her. If he had his way, he'd chain her to the kitchen table where she'd fit nicely under his thumb. The stupid ass.

"I'll not have you keeping company with Moira any longer," he barked from the door. "That one is nothing but trouble, Bethany."

"Oh!" She was too mad for words. Arrogant, barbaric throwback of a man! The wind slapped her face with a gust of rain as she hurried out the gate and across the cow trail. "And pissy weather too." Embedded in the earth ahead of her was the sickle-shaped stone, slick and glistening, that marked the bottom of the footpath up the Argyll Mountain. She skirted it and hit the trail. If she hurried, she might lose him. "Och," she scoffed. She'd have better luck escaping a depraved wolf.

Colm should know better than to blame Moira as if Bethany didn't have the mind to fight the cause on her own. The toe of her shoe caught in her gown. She stumbled, but caught her balance in time. One of their border collies, Dickens, beat the ground past her and kept on up the trail. Oh, to run like a dog.

It hadn't been Moira's idea to throw stones at the Dundee building; it had been Bethany's stroke of revenge. And a few broken windows were hardly violent. They had to do something after that newspaper printed Winterbottom's letter. So Bethany recruited Moira, and together they'd climbed onto the roof of an adjacent factory to launch their assault. She'd never intended to hurt anyone and had been truly horrified when her pebble had pinged off the head of the policeman. When the constable turned the fire hose on them, she and Moira had hidden behind a chimney refusing to come down. Well, what did they expect? Winterbottom had written: 'When women demand equality with men let us laugh at their madness! Let us inform them that equality is impossible—men are emotionally stronger and intellectually more capable.' Oh, her blood simmered at the arrogance.

As she climbed the mountain trail, the crack of their door slamming shut cut through the storm. She jumped just a little then carried on. Colm must have gotten his boots back on.

"Bethany, stop your running!" Her husband's voice boomed like thunder over the mountain.

So he thinks to chase me down again. The police had not been able to dislodge the two women from the rooftop, but Colm had. He'd climbed the fire escape and taken his wife down over his shoulder. Oh, the humiliation. The brute! She hoped she'd bruised him well.

He was afraid she'd get hurt. Bethany glanced over her shoulder to see him gaining on her. By the look of violence on his face right now, he was the only threat she need fear. Not that she'd give him the satisfaction of fearing him.

The rain had made the trail slick, and she knew she should move slowly, but she wanted to reach level ground before their next shouting match. The sounds of three-hundred bleating ewes just ahead meant she was close.

"I told the Chief Constable I'd keep you out of it, and I meant it." He was pressing on at alarming speed. She picked up her gown and started to run up the steepening trail.

"Damn it, Bethany, have a care. I'd no time to feed the sheep. For the love of God, lass, stop your running now!"

If he ceased his chasing, she'd have no need to run now would she? Reaching the plateau, she skidded to a stop and stood panting while her heart galloped in her chest. She was vaguely aware of the sheep turning their collective heads. Colm had stopped twenty feet down on the trail, his face burning with anger not exertion.

She faced him with hands planted on her hips. "I am not afraid of prison," she yelled through the wind.

"Well you damn well should be," he yelled back.

"I will gladly go to prison before I abandon the fight for women's enfranchisement." She took a second to gulp a deep breath. "If you think to force me to cease this cause," one more deep breath, "then you are no husband of mine."

"No husband? What sort of husband doesn't protect his wife? Do you wish to cut my balls off too, so you can be married to a eunuch?"

It was just like him to overlook her point. "This isn't about your balls, you bloody man!" The sound of bleating sheep grew closer. Glancing over her shoulder, she flinched to see them moving toward her at a quick advance. Dear God, they looked agitated. She took a step toward her insufferable husband.

"Bloody hell, woman, get down here now!" Colm roared.

And succumb to his command? Why couldn't she have married a more agreeable man like Moira had? She dug in her heels and spoke

through gritted teeth. "Stop using that tone with me. I am not your chattel to command as you wish."

A sheep's nose butted the back of her knee. Her leg gave way as a famished ewe knocked her in the hip. Dickens barked incessantly at her heels. Her arm reached, sought, grasped—nothing. Colm sprinted up the incline like a blur.

All the anger of her day fused with terror as she plunged over the cliff. Oddly, as she tumbled, she hoped to land on her padded behind. Foolish thought. She hit the ground with a sickening crack and ferocious pain. It all happened so abruptly.

Colm's cold cry cut across the mountains.

Sweet Colm. He needn't bother sounding so distressed. She wasn't hurt. She thought about that a moment. Why was she no longer in pain?

Oh! She didn't look good, not good at all. So much blood. From her head? Why could she see herself so clearly?

Colm was by her side, his shirt ripped from his body, now pressed against her head and quickly becoming saturated in her blood. Rain pelted down around them gathering into red rivulets that bled out from under her body.

No pain. No cold. No wet. The gruesome scene unfolded below her. Below her? She watched it all from the tree tops which made no sense at all. Unless...

Dear God. This was death.

RUKSANA'S STORY
by Mayank Bhatt

RUKSANA COULDN'T SLEEP. SHE sat by the kitchen window watching the road and waited for dawn, the time of the day, just before daybreak, when she offered her *namaaz*. But dawn lay far off, and she grew impatient. She got the *Janamaaz*, and spread it on the floor. She sat on it and began to read from the Qur'an. Ruksana had followed a daily ritual of praying at dawn since she was a child. Prayer was her moment to be with herself and with Allah – to be at peace. Ruksana never sought anything from Allah. But today she couldn't stop herself.

"Why are you doing this to me? Have I not suffered enough? Take me and stop my pain..."

Abdul had tried to sleep but couldn't. He came to the kitchen for a glass of water.

"Ruksana, Allah can't help you," Abdul said, filling a glass with tap water, gulping it down. "Rafiq was doing all this in the name of Allah. He is convinced Allah is with him." He sat beside her.

Ruksana kept reading from the holy book. Abdul had little patience with his wife's religiosity. His belief in the benign almighty had become tenuous after his mother Ameena's untimely death from tuberculosis when he was a small child. He was convinced that Allah only tested the good, and left the evil alone. His agnosticism didn't matter to Ruksana.

"Ask Ziram and Jameel if they can stay with us today," Ruksana said. She couldn't imagine spending the day with just Abdul at home.

"How's that possible? They can take leave from work only in an emergency."

"This is an emergency," Ruksana snapped.

Years of living together had not dampened their passion to argue, generally over trifles, and to nag each other. But even when he disagreed with Ruksana, Abdul always listened to her. He slowly got up from the kitchen floor, went upstairs, and softly knocked on the door of the master bedroom.

Ziram asked, "Yes, *Abba*?"

"Ziram, your mother wants you stay here today... I told her that it wouldn't be possible, but she's adamant."

"*Abba*, I'll stay. Jameel can't."

Abdul returned to Ruksana. Both kept quiet; after twenty-five years, they could understand each other perfectly without having to speak. Yet, when they choose to, they could as perfectly not comprehend what the other person was saying.

A couple of months ago they had celebrated their twenty-fifth wedding anniversary. Sitting beside Ruksana, who was trying hard to focus on the holy book, and wasn't quite succeeding, Abdul shuddered, thinking of the family outing to the Sarvana Bhawan in Mississauga. He realized that even then, Rafiq had been deeply involved with a group planning terrorist attacks across Toronto. Ziram had organized a surprise party and besides the family, had invited her in-laws Suheera and Tanveer, and their neighbours Kartar and Harminder. Abdul had made a joke about the quarrels he had with Ruksana. She, sitting besides him, savouring the special rice, *poriyal, appalam,* and pickle, had nodded and smiled.

In the kitchen, Abdul gently put his hand on Ruksana's shoulder. She put a finger on the page of the Qur'an where she had stopped and looked at him; her eyes had welled. He sighed: the family was unlikely to come out of this mess for a long time. He blamed himself for what Rafiq had done: he had neglected his children and his wife in Canada as he struggled to make ends meet. He wondered if that had changed him into an uncaring, selfish person. Ruksana became uncomfortable with Abdul's heavy breathing in the silence.

"*Saabji*, why did Rafiq have to do this now, just when we were all settling down?" Ruksana asked, merely wanting to break the silence, not really expecting a response.

"Our destiny is to suffer, I guess," Abdul sighed. He moved closer to her and gently pulled her towards him.

Ruksana put her head on his shoulder and, holding his arm said, "I suppose there are problems in everyone's lives, but ours change our lives. *Chalo*, come, you take rest now."

She got up, held Abdul's hand as he put the other hand on his

knee and slowly stood. She led him to their bedroom and made him sit. Abdul drank the water Ruksana gave him and then slid between the sheets. Ruksana switched off the table lamp and sat by until she could hear his rhythmic snoring.

✦ ✦ ✦

Finally, she was alone. It was near daybreak. Ruksana began to prepare for her prayers. She went to the bathroom and performed the *wazu,* reciting the words *Bismillahir-Rahmanir-Raheem.* She washed her hands up to the wrists, cleansed her mouth, rinsed her nostrils, washed her face, poured water over both her arms – right arm first and then the left arm – touched her forehead with her wet hand, cleaned her ears. Finally she poured water on her feet up to the ankles. She did all this three times. Then, she went to the kitchen and started her *namaaz.* After prayers, she busied herself with chores. Every day when she did that, her mind would drift into thinking about Dhinmant. But this morning she was preoccupied with what Rafiq would be going through at the police station. She was anxious to find out, but realized that it would be a while before they would be able to meet him. Yesterday evening, as the drama concerning Rafiq had begun to unfold, she had repeatedly asked herself, "How would Dhinmant have reacted?" She consoled herself by thinking that Dhinmant would have tried to see some justification in Rafiq's act of defiance.

Years of living with Abdul, especially since they came to Canada, had taught her a hard lesson of not talking about Dhinmant. She had stopped trying to explain her relationship with him, not because there was anything to hide, but because Abdul wasn't willing to listen. He had recreated a past that belonged to Dhinmant and Ruksana and felt strangely comforted in his belief that he was a martyr. Ruksana had learnt that it made life simpler to let Abdul feel this way.

Abdul's feelings for Dhinmant had changed as had his perspective about their past. Initially, Ruksana felt that Abdul was traumatized by his experiences in Bombay. Then, it dawned on her that more than trauma it was drama. Melodrama. He remained convinced that Dhinmant and Ruksana had been lovers. In Canada, Abdul tried to erase the painful memory by being sullen and not speaking of Bombay or Dhinmant. Ruksana had tried to talk to him, had even tried to engage him in gossip about their Teli Gali neighbours.

"Ruksana, live your life in the present," he would snap.

Yet, Ruksana knew that Abdul had not forgotten Dhinmant. He

remembered everything, especially the riots. Ruksana tried to keep Dhinmant out of her mind but it was impossible for her to forget someone who had given her a new life. Dhinmant remained deep within, guiding her while she spoke to him every day, seemingly lost in her thoughts. Dhinmant reacted emotionally to everything. Abdul's responses were always measured.

She couldn't forget her relationship with Dhinmant, because it had begun with a tragedy and it had ended with another.

✦ ✦ ✦

In 1992, the Hindu fundamentalists demolished a mosque in the temple town Ayodhya, the birthplace of Ram, the Hindu God: the epitome of all that is virtuous. They claimed that the mosque was built over a temple that was Ram's birthplace. Rioting engulfed India, including Bombay.

One evening, while Abdul and Dhinmant, who worked together in a trade union, were discussing the fallout of the rioting, they heard a mob nearing Teli Gali, the street on which Abdul lived with his family and Dhinmant had his union office. Dhinmant said Abdul should take his car and get Inspector Sandeep Waghmare to Teli Gali. Abdul thought it would be safer to take Ruksana and the children with him to the police station.

Ruksana remembered how Abdul had rushed her and the children in Dhinmant's car to the station. He left them there, and went home with Inspector Waghmare.

The police station was an ancient building near the Andheri railway station. Sandeep had asked her and the kids to sit in the visitors' room. The room had three wooden benches for people who came to file complaints. Large black and white photographs of Mahatma Gandhi, Jawaharlal Nehru, Sardar Vallabbhai Patel, Indira Gandhi, and a colour photograph of Ganapati, the elephant-headed Hindu God of knowledge, hung on the walls painted beige at the top and dark brown at the bottom, presumably to hide the stains from people spitting *paan*. A ceiling fan whirled dangerously; and a fan on the constable's desk made a lot of commotion but didn't circulate air.

The police had been on high alert after the outbreak of violence, which hadn't stopped since the demolition of the masjid six weeks ago. Even though it was close to midnight, there was a constant movement of cars and people, and the wireless radio crackled with each outbreak in some other part of the city. Ruksana knew some of the constables and almost all of the inspectors because she had met them during her work in the slums for Dhinmant's union. The constable on duty periodically

dozed off.

She remembered her silent scream, her palms clasping her mouth, when Abdul phoned that their home was burned down. He was calling from a public phone at Cooper Hospital, amid much noise. He told her that Dhinmant had been taken there. She had wanted to go to the hospital, but Abdul asked her to wait for him. He would fetch her and the kids later: right now the city was overrun by crazed mobs.

The wooden bench on which Ruksana sat with Ziram and Rafiq outside the station was near the main gate. The thick shrubbery outside attracted mosquitoes that, despite the fans, hovered inside. As she waited for Abdul to return, Ruksana swatted at the mosquitoes that wanted to feast on her children sleeping beside her. Several hours later, Abdul returned with Sandeep. Ruksana wanted to pray before going to the hospital. She spread a newspaper in a corner of the room and quickly offered the *namaaz*. Even that night she had not asked anything from Allah.

When the police van reached the main gate of Cooper Hospital, she saw workers from Dhinmant's union raising the slogan "Dhinmant Desai *Amar Rahe*!" Long Live Dhinmant Desai. She thought that the slogans were to support their leader, who had been so viciously attacked. When they reached the intensive care unit where Dhinmant was, a nurse told them, "*Neta mar gaya,*" the leader is dead. Ruksana screamed. What she had thought was a slogan for workers' solidarity was a slogan meant for the dead.

LIVING STILLBORN
by Jessica Borges

MRS. KUMAR JERKED AWAKE as screams ripped through the suffocating summer night. Taking a calming breath she lay down again. It was only Lalita, her maid, getting beaten up by her drunk husband, in the slum colony down the street.

"You make your bed, you lie in it," she sighed hefting her night-dress above her thighs. She wished she could close her window, blocking out the sobs and thuds. But at summer's peak, she welcomed the breeze that sometimes reached through her window like a stranger, caressing her sweating body.

"She'll come in late, blaming her injuries again," she thought, drifting off.

Mrs. Kumar was newspaper-fanning herself, gulping her second cup of *masala* tea, when Lalita slunk in. Her patched sari could not hide the bruises on her face. Mrs. Kumar frowned, flicking beads of sweat from her forehead. Even a cool bath before her *puja* could not dispel the cursed heat.

Eyes downcast, Lalita went to the overflowing sink. She would wash up, then sweep and swab the floors in all seven rooms... hand wash and hang the clothes for drying... water the houseplants...cart the garbage to the dump. While she was busy, cook roused-up the meal. Lalita then washed up again, and left for her own home chores. She was paid Rs. 600 (15 CAD) a month.

"You're late Lalita," Mrs. Kumar grumbled. "That's half a day's pay from your salary. I pay you so well and for what?"

Lalita tensed against the verbal battering, saying nothing.

"You know I have to dress for Mrs. Sharma's. I don't want to be late for the kitty party gossip, or they will start with me!" she stood, "And to add to it, I couldn't sleep last night!"

In her room, she surveyed her saris, eyeing the rose one. Such an innocent colour... her favourite. Mrs. Sharma's handsome husband would love it. She liked lingering after the party, just so she bumped into him returning from work.

Mr. Kumar was so boring! Thank God he earned so well, though it took him traveling for most of the month. She put on the diamonds he brought her from his business trip to Singapore. They went well with the sari, and the theme - 'Diwali' the festival of lights. These diamonds really lit her up.

Two hours later, Mrs. Kumar swept down the stairs to her car, a little pink handbag in her manicured claws.

"Driver! Mrs. Sharma's. Hurry. Drive like Mrs. Verma's driver does, so smoothly, one feels one is in an airplane's business class."

"Yes madam," he replied, thinking the closest he had ever got to an airplane was seeing one fly overhead. They rounded the corner and the slum colony. Mrs. Kumar held her scented handkerchief to her nose.

"Disgusting," she said. "Brings down the value of my house."

"But it was here before your villa came up, madam," said the driver.

"Yes, but that cheat of a builder promised he would get the local politician to tear it down.... "

As she ranted, she noticed Lalita sitting outside her hut. She was completing a design outlined on the road, from a plate of coloured powders. Half-naked kids sat around watching. Lalita looked happy.

"She's not too tired to make *rangolis* for Diwali, but comes in late to do my work! I'll show her," she thought, as her car raced by, engulfing the little group in black fumes.

"Now for a little yellow," said Lalita, carefully dribbling some powder into the white outline. She leaned forward to get to one of the corners and winced.

"Want some Iodex?" called her neighbour through a mouthful of *paan*. She was shelling peas at the door of her hut.

"I'm fine Shanti," called Lalita selecting some purple powder.

"Next time he beats you, I'm getting the police," said Shanti, tossing pea pods onto the garbage heap nearby. "It's one thing hitting you when you were just married, but now you are carrying his child."

"We all survive it Shanti. Our mothers, our grandmothers...

Maybe I'm paying for sins from my past life." Lalita stood up, dusting her hands. She gave the leftover powder to the children, who gleefully rushed away to make their own designs.

"If anyone has to repent for sins it's your jobless husband. Just drinks and gambles away your salary. And he thanks you with a punch in the face." Shanti angrily spat out a stream of *paan* juice, adding to the brown-red streaks crisscrossing the side of her hut.

"Let it go, Shanti. Diwali is coming. I saved up and bought earth lamps to light my doorstep. I have two for you too. Maybe Kumar madam will give me a Diwali bonus this year. I will save the money for my child... for school..." She stopped, afraid to put her dreams into words.

"Forget school. Just pray that God blesses you with a son... no dowry worries... a daughter-in-law to serve you..." Shanti went in to prepare dinner, leaving Lalita future gazing, one hand caressing her rounded belly.

The bitches fell silent as soon as she entered. Look at them, smiling like vultures... go on, gossip about me, thought Mrs. Kumar as she air-kissed her friends. Helping herself to a drink, she joined the group as smoothly as a knife slips into an unwary victim. The time passed in a binge of mithais, booze and cards. Feeling all eyes on her diamonds, she gloated inside.

She did not linger this time, because a 'friend' asked for a ride home, her driver having been suddenly ordered to a local pub to collect her son. 'Probably drunk or thrown out for improper behaviour,' thought Mrs. Kumar, as she graciously invited the friend into her car.

"So what were you all talking about before I joined the party," asked Mrs. Kumar honing straight to the point.

"Nothing much darling," said her friend.

"Come, come Hema, surely that buffalo Mrs. Khan had a lot to say about me."

Hema grinned at the venom. "Since you're asking, she couldn't stop talking about your sad life."

"What?" screeched Mrs. Kumar.

"She said, you have no child... your husband stays away giving the excuse of business... your in-laws hate you.... you don't want your parents..." she held back a smile as Mrs. Kumar turned an ugly angry hue.

"How dare she! A child? Who wants those ugly stretch marks?"

"Leave it be darling. She's just jealous. I heard her husband is sleeping with her maid. He does it with every maid they get. Mrs. Khan is now thinking of getting a dishwasher, a washing machine and a servant

boy to clean and cook."

But Mrs. Kumar was past listening. She settled into a gloom from which she barely rose to kiss her friend goodbye.

Entering her home ten minutes later, she sat in the dark. Her bones seemed heavy. Her heart seemed to be shrinking.

"She said you have no child." The words hit against her temples like hammers. No one would ever know how much those words hurt. Mrs. Kumar yearned for a child. A little one she could dress and pamper and flaunt to the world.

"I'm sorry Mrs. Kumar, the cysts are too severe. You will never have a child." The doctor had been apologetic. He was one of the best doctors in the city, maybe in the country.

After that, Mr. Kumar got extra busy at work, running away on business. Yes, there were the presents, and money for whatever she pleased. But what she 'pleased' was a child. She wanted her belly to grow and stretch. She wanted the dizziness of morning sickness. She wanted to howl in victory, as she pushed new life into the world. Her dark, dark world. She crept into bed when dawn broke into her thoughts with its prying fingers.

Lalita was agitated. She went about her work but her eyes kept darting to Mrs. Kumar.

'She is so sad today. Hope her parents are in good health. Maybe Mr. Kumar will be away longer? Poor lady, how lonely she is,' she thought. Then her heart raced again.Today she had to tell Mrs. Kumar her 'good' news. She was surprised she hadn't noticed her growing belly. Before leaving for the day, she stood with downcast eyes in front of Mrs. Kumar.

"Madam... I have something to tell you."

Mrs. Kumar lifted ravaged eyes to her face.

"I am going to be a mother. Just a few months to go now. Don't worry..." she rushed on, "I will only take two weeks off and come back to work. My neighbour Shanti said she would work in my place till I get back."

Mrs. Kumar only nodded. After a while Lalita left. The news filtered through her consciousness, cradling her bruised heart like a lover. It warmed and filled her with a soothing sweetness. In the warmth, hope began to take seed and grow.For the first time since she got back from the party, Mrs. Kumar smiled.

The last two months of Lalita's pregnancy passed by blissfully. Mrs. Kumar had changed overnight. She gave Lalita a Diwali bonus, along with some old saris, more beautiful than any she had ever owned. She was kind to her, taking care that Lalita did not strain too much.

"How many times have I told you Lalita, do not bend so much when you sweep. You could hurt the baby. Lalita before you leave, drink that glass of milk."

Lalita could not believe this was happening to her.

"It is like the news of the baby softened her heart Shanti. Today I drank milk in her house. Milk! My own parents didn't feed me milk!"

"Never trust the rich Lalita. Every paisa they give you, you'll pay back double."

"But she knows I have nothing to give Shanti."

"The poor don't pay with money, Lalita. We pay with our blood."

It happened one day while Lalita was squatting, washing clothes. She had been feeling pains all night, but she still went to work. A gasp escaped her lips now as the pains intensified. Then a muffled scream that brought Mrs. Kumar running.

"Lalita what is it?" she asked.

"Madam, I think the baby is coming," she bit back another scream.

"Let me help you up," said Mrs. Kumar.

"It's already coming..." panted Lalita.

"Call the doctor," Mrs. Kumar screamed to the cook, looking down at the straining Lalita.

Ten minutes later, the wails of the ambulance sounded in the distance. They were drowned by the lusty wails of the baby in Lalita's arms. The umbilical cord still attached the child to his mother. Lalita's exhausted face glowed.

Mrs. Kumar leaned close, "Give him to me Lalita."

"The baby is all bloody madam."

"No...give him to me as my child. I'll take care of him. He will eat the best food. Go to the best schools. Travel to foreign countries for holidays...."

Lalita looked up, understanding clouding her face.

"I will give you money Lalita. You'll never have to work again."

Lalita looked down at the baby in her arms. She held it close to her chest... then raised her arms obediently. Mrs. Kumar reached down.

The baby turned into his mother's body following the scent of milk. Lalita hugged the baby close. She looked up at her mistress.

"No madam. I cannot give you my daughter."

Mrs. Kumar's face, white with rage, her hands grasping at nothingness, panted, "You ungrateful bitch, do you know who I am? Do you know how much money I have? What do you have? A girl... What's a girl? "

What's a girl? Lakshmi, the goddess of wealth. Saraswati, the goddess of knowledge. Kali Mata, shakti, strength. Mother, the heart of the family. Wife, nurturer and soulmate. Woman. Gentleness. Laughter. Love. Beauty... There were so many replies Lalita could have given. But Lalita was busy; cooing to the baby, her eyes full of the future.

An excerpt from the novel
LEGACY
by Alison E. Bruce

AH, THE ROMANTIC LIFE of a private investigator, thought Joe Garrett, shuffling his feet to keep warm. His all time favourite movie line popped into his head and he smiled and said it aloud, albeit softly.

"I'm getting too old for this shit."

Fifty-three years, six months and – he did the math – eight days. He could pass for forty-something thanks to all the exercise and healthy diet that had been forced on him since his last heart episode. Even in his street clothes – designed for anonymity, not style – he didn't cut a bad figure.

"Vanity, thy name is Joseph Garrett."

Joe took a drag from his cigar and blew a smoke ring.

It wasn't a real cigar. He had given those up years ago after his first heart attack. Cigarettes had gone a decade or so earlier, when his daughter was old enough to question why he should say one thing and do another. Smoking, however, was a plausible excuse for otherwise furtive-looking souls to hang around doorways and cigars were easier to fake. This one was a particularly expensive fake since it also had a nano-phone linked to his BlueBerry, the law-enforcement-grade version of the popular consumer communication device. A relic from his past.

"Show time. Fifteen twenty-five hours, and the mark is moving."

The mark was fifty-something and looked older. His countenance was a map of worry lines across a pale face that was fixed in a frown. He was wearing one of those "enduring" overcoats and a matching hat, advertised as: "Guaranteed to protect your clothes from anything nature or environmental pollution throws at you." It made the short, stocky man

look like a walking tent.

Joe knew the man's routine, so he didn't need to follow closely. When the man turned the corner towards the municipal parking garage, Joe had to quicken his pace to keep up. He jogged across the avenue, then resumed to an idle pace once he was parallel with his mark again.

The man paused by a news box. Joe slowed and muttered to himself.

"Don't stop now. Don't look around."

A figure in generic baggy black sweats and an oversized hooded jacket stepped out from the shadow of an intersecting alley. The man Joe was tailing started walking again, hurrying across the garage exit and towards the pedestrian entrance.

Joe pulled an old-fashioned flip phone out of his pocket and answered it as if it had signalled. It looked like some vintage digital PCS with one of those poor quality cameras that inevitably led to jamming technology in order to protect people's privacy. Like the cigar, however, it was more than it seemed. The innocuous shell had a Nanotech audio-video recorder installed, which was now homing in on the person in black. Making a quick check to see if the road was clear, Joe started crossing, apparently headed towards the same garage.

At the very same moment, using a much cheaper piece of consumer communication technology, Mr Harrison F. Eldeeb was arguing with his wife about whose turn it was to pick up the kids from school. Unfortunately, he was behind the wheel of an early model hybrid utility vehicle, running late, and determined to get out of the downtown core before the buses arrived and rush hour started. He darted down the side street just as Joe Garrett was crossing it. The black clad figure sensed something and turned. Joe caught a glimpse of a ratty blonde goatee and furtive, watery-grey eyes.

"You?"

The HUV braked, skidded and stopped. Too late.

A wet branch slapped Kate Garrett in the face. It had sprung from the cluster of branches she was holding back as she searched the scrub growing along the fence line.

Ah, the romantic life of a police detective.

It was no longer raining, but that made little difference to Kate. The leaves showered her with cold drops that seeped through her disposable smock and wicked into her linen suit as she searched their branches. Mud oozed over shoe-covers which were not as weatherproof as advertised. Meanwhile, the instigators of this exercise were wrapped in blankets, waiting in the back of squad cars, one each for the three of them. She hoped they were currently in their own private hells, worrying

about what was going to happen next. She hoped the prospect chilled them as much as the grey November afternoon chilled her.

She doubted it.

They were probably pissed off that they were caught, that's all.

Kate spotted something in the lower branches – a small, clear craft jar with a cheerful red lid, the type used to store beads, sequins or other tiny items. Whoever was distributing the stolen medication had got hold of a case or more of these containers. They were turning up all over. This one had a couple of little blue pills left inside.

"Got it! Looks like one of the morphine derivatives."

After recording it's location, she backed out of the bushes, holding the container in her gloved hand, while the crime scene photographer logged the event as a digital video sequence. As soon as she could straighten up, she pulled a clear bag out of her pocket with her free hand.

"Don't seal it yet!"

Kate's senior partner, a handsome, dark woman, strode over, her black trench coat fanning out behind her. Mercy Rudra wasn't a tall woman, but her personality lent her height. She was a conservative dresser, favouring the neo-gothic look. The forensic technologist following her was tall but tried to appear shorter. He favoured the universal geek look. He took the container, carefully opened it and retrieved a sample.

"The hospital needs this," he mumbled.

Kate nodded. Then, as quickly as she could, she sealed up the bottle, marked the bag and passed it over to Mercy before giving into a staccato series of sneezes.

Mercy, as good as her name, directed her towards the unmarked hybrid wagon that was their assigned vehicle.

"Why don't you warm up the car and check on the status of the girl?"

Kate nodded. She dropped her sodden "clean gear" into the collection bag and stripped off her jacket before taking shelter, reasoning that her blouse would dry faster without it. Once the heater was going full blast, she also kicked off her shoes and warmed her feet. Thus, minutes later, it was in shirt sleeves and stocking feet that Kate numbly stepped out of the car and called out to get the attention of her partner and fellow police officers. It didn't matter that her voice was hoarse and barely audible. They could tell what she was saying from the look on her face.

"Fania Michaels' heart failed. She didn't make it."

When Kate was a little girl, her father took her to work. Back then, the detectives' room was a large open area filled with grey steel desks. Computer monitors and keyboards took up a large amount of the

available surface area. The rest was covered in stacks of paper, personal items and coffee cups. As Joe Garrett showed his daughter around, he painted another picture of a squad room, the one he visited as a child, for policing ran in the family. Desks were made of wood. No computers, at least, none generally available to the detectives. Officers entered their information in their Occurrence Books. Reports were produced on temperamental typewriters.

The Occurrence Book had been replaced by a personal electronic device that served as a multi-purpose information and communication tool that could do everything but make coffee. Work stations, with composite, oak-like desks, were equipped with flip up, flat-screen monitors, keyboards and docking ports so that detectives could plug in and upload, or download files and generate reports which were read on other screens. The desks were like hotel rooms. Officers moved in for the duration, spreading their personal property out – or not – according their personalities. With most policing happening out in the community, detectives carried their offices with them in a briefcase, a backpack or, in some cases, in their pockets. One thing that hadn't changed was the coffee cups. There were always coffee cups.

Kate found hers in the kitchenette and filled it with coffee from the thermal carafe. Warming her chilled hands on the hot ceramic, she staked out a desk and plugged in her BlueBerry. While it went through its automatic virus check and log-in, she headed towards the locker room and dry clothes.

In her father's day, the locker room looked and smelled like a locker room. The only seats were the benches bisecting the corridor between the rows of grey metal. You could hide in there. Little Kate had, and grown Kate would have liked to. Now the locker room was more like a communal living room complete with family photos and kids' art. There were comfortable chairs and a couch at one end, ironing board, hair dryers, and vanity mirrors at the other; and all around the walls were lockers, generously sized for multiple changes of clothes and full range of toiletries. Being a modern police officer meant always going out looking well kept and professional - even if you came back looking like something the cat dragged in.

It was nearing the shift change, so the room was buzzing with activity. Kate received a few offhand greetings, but most people were too wrapped up in what they were doing to pay her much attention. The one exception homed in on her like cat hearing a can opener.

"If you give it to me now, I can save the suit. The shoes are toast."

Kate grinned in spite of herself. She passed the water-stained navy wool jacket into the outstretched hands. They belonged to a pleasant looking man of uncertain years and somewhat academic demeanor. He reminded her of Mister Chips, without the cap, gown and English accent. He was one of a handful of people still in the department who had known her father since he was a police detective, before a gunshot wound and subsequent heart trouble forced him into medical retirement.

"Pants too. You can launder your own blouse, I imagine."

"You don't have to, Vince."

Detective Vincent Valerio bestowed a disarming grin. It transformed his face at once from mildly attractive to rather handsome.

"Everyone knows that rookies get all the worst jobs, but that suit did nothing to deserve to be so badly treated."

Kate let Vince have the suit. He had every right to feel proprietary; he had taken her out to buy it, as well as a few other essentials, when she was promoted. She stripped off the rest of her wet clothes and dumped them into the laundry bag she kept in her locker. She then picked out a sweater and linen pants, one of perhaps a half dozen combinations she could have pulled together from the clothes she kept at work.

Mercy was waiting by the desk, fiddling with her silver necklaces.

"Thorsen wants to see you," she said quietly.

"What did I do this time?"

Mercy gave a weak smile.

Thorsen opened his office door and ushered Kate in. This didn't bode well.

He was a giant of a man – a big, broad, Viking warrior, complete with long, red-blonde hair, full beard and the hint of an accent leftover from growing up in an ESL home. In comparison, Kate was a shrimp. She had made the minimum height requirements to join the police force, but just barely. She was sturdily built, strong and reasonably athletic, but Thorsen was a behemoth. Except right now he seemed to have deflated.

"What's wrong, Chief?"

"Sit, Kathleen."

Another bad sign when Thorsen used her full first name.

She sat. Then he sat. She waited while he gathered his thoughts.

"It's your father."

And then Kate knew. It wasn't just Thorsen that had shrunk. The whole world had suddenly grown smaller.

A LETTER TO ALEX
by Mary A. Bryant

Dear Alex,

THANK YOU. IT WAS exciting to read your letter today. I can just see you driving your big blue truck along the prairie roads, your arm at the open window and your old straw hat pushed back on your head. You slow down as you approach a small weedy field at the left. You stop and get out. You see the old school among the choke cherry bushes and the silver willows. You think of me who can no longer travel these roads, and you reach back into the truck for your camera.

Alex, your sharing of our beloved prairies is truly an act of friendship. I look long at the snaps you sent. I scan the blades of grass – and it seems I remember them! The picture of Cherryhill School – it chokes me – the memories flood my being. It is Friday night again, in the '30s and teenagers dance at Cherryhill on Friday nights.

On those winter nights young people accompanied by either a parent or both, came from the surrounding farms to visit and socialize. They drove horses either with buggies or, if there had been a good snowfall, sleighs and cutters. The horses were tied in the school barn until it filled then the late arrivals tied theirs to the wheels or fence. First arrivals hurried into the school, lit the gas lanterns and hung them from the ceiling hooks, then checked the furnace and, to clear the classroom floor, pushed the desks back to the walls.

We all knew everyone and this one-roomed building was our Mecca. The main attractions for us teen girls were the young French boys – how they could dance! (I had a favourite, the sixth son of a family

of twelve.) Some mothers brought sandwiches and cake. They put a large pail of water on top of the furnace for coffee, then sat near the door to visit while their babies slept on the desk-tops which had been pushed to the sides of the room. I know now, but didn't then, that they also kept close watch over us lively teenagers.

The old upright piano was soon surrounded by three or four locals with their instruments. "Kitty," a teacher from the next school south, sat on the piano bench pounding out the chords as a fiddle screeched. They were local farm boys who played – fiddles, banjos, ukuleles while the pianist chorded. And soon the rapid beats stirred us all. I remember the square dances – how wild, so much energy, and when the caller came to "swing your lady," I fairly flew into the air, being very light in those years. Our skirts flew about (luckily we girls wore slips)!

Between dances the men all clapped, took their ladies to one side of the room, thanked them and then returned across the floor to the other side. The instruments screeched and plunked as the musicians re-tuned them, before moving into a restful waltz. There were two-steps, one-steps, polkas, schottisches, circles, but about every fourth dance was a strenuous square when everyone except a few mothers joined in.

At the intermissions we girls pretended not to be slyly watching the other side of the room to see who was "eying" us for the next dance. There was one – a long, long fellow, very thin, with black hair – an old fellow, perhaps 25 (one girl, my friend Ellen, whispered, "He's like a crow on a telephone pole") and he always seemed to head my way. If I possibly could, I used to disappear into the ladies' cloakroom – especially if the next dance was a waltz. That fellow had a scary habit of holding the lady so closely and tightly she wondered if she could survive, especially since it was obvious that he had been working with horses all week!

Cherryhill school had a big wooden clock on the wall above the piano. As twelve o'clock drew near the fiddler played a slow waltz and, hopefully, your favourite partner got to you first. Together you danced a few steps until you saw an empty desk where you could sit for lunch. Meanwhile the women had dumped a pound of coffee into the hot pail of water. Someone walked around handing out big white cups from a wooden box. The coffee was doled out with a large soup ladle. Someone else came with a bowl of sugar in one hand and a jug of cream in the other. I never had coffee at home so this was a memorable lunch. Always there were big black rectangular pans of cake cut into 3" squares. There didn't seem to be a teenager watching her diet – what appetites! Actually there was one exception – one of the ladies known to us all, changed her baby's diaper as it lay on the desk, tossed the soggy cloth under the

desk, then, eager to help, passed her cake around. By then we had had enough!

Soon, while the piano led the way, the fiddle screeched as it was tuned and the desks were pushed back to the walls again, one of the men walked about with his hat asking for donations for the band – nickels and dimes – all gratefully divided. Another farmer followed, using his jack knife to shave a solid pound of paraffin wax to give the floor a renewed 'slide.'

Energy restored, the teenagers rebounded but not quite so audibly. By two o'clock, the slow "Home Sweet Home" prompted a scurry for one last few minutes of contact with one's favourite before the search for coats and good-byes, the horses were hitched, families boarded and the revellers went off in all directions.

Cherryhill was left quiet in darkness save for the colourful memories.

So, you see Alex, the gift of a 4x6 snap of "Cherryhill" has many memories under its faded paint and boarded windows. Thank you, my friend, for the 'throw back.' I hadn't thought of those Friday nights on the prairie for a long time.

I AM PROUD TO BE CANADIAN BECAUSE...
by Silene Bumbaca

I AM PROUD TO be Canadian because I am free. Free to say what I wish, and live where I please. I can practice my religion, and experience diverse cultures. I have great healthcare, and the opportunity to receive an excellent education. There are so many reasons why Canada is one of the best countries in the entire world.

One reason would definitely be that Canada is always peaceful. It is accepting of all cultures and religions, which makes Canada welcoming to all people. So many countries of the world live in violence and terror. Canada has equal rights and a democratic government, with plenty of land to accommodate its people. I know I am safe, protected and free.

Another reason why I love Canada is because it has many opportunities for its citizens. Since it is still developing quickly there are always jobs available. Canada's citizens love the Canadian workplace, and continue to live and work in this wonderful country.Not only is Canada free, but it is also beautiful in many ways. It is clean, and it has many great tourist attractions to offer. Places like; Niagara Falls, Rocky Mountains, the Great Lakes, Bay of Fundy, and big cities like; Toronto, Montreal and Vancouver. Although, Canada's climate can reach very cold temperatures, especially in the North. Fortunately for the most part natural disasters such as; floods, hurricanes, earthquakes and tornados are not very common. There are many countries which experience harsh weather conditions and natural disasters regularly. Canadians are lucky to be so safe.

I have visited many different places in the world, and they are

all beautiful in their own way. I absolutely love travelling the globe, and experiencing what the world has to offer. However, I'm always happy to return home. Although, sometimes I wish the weather was a little warmer, ultimately I would never choose to live anywhere else but our very own, Canada. It is free, it is beautiful.... It is HOME.

DISTANT

by Altug Cakmakci

BAD NEWS CATCHES YOU unexpectedly. I was looking at the panoramic view of Galata — the most attractive feature of my office on the forty-sixth floor of the skyscraper named after our family — and rehearsing my speech for the upcoming steering committee meeting, when my secretary's extension number appeared on my display. I answered the phone and without any resistance let her transfer the call from Sarigerme. We used the name of the small Mediterranean town where our company's founder was spending his retirement days to refer to him. He was Cevdet Basarir, a high school dropout, dedicated businessman, twenty-percent company share holder, and my father.

"Your father is not feeling well," said the soft voice on the other end of the line. She was a stranger, as usual. My father did not allow me or either of my twin sisters to interfere with his decisions. After giving control of the company to me, he chose where to live, which of his grandchildren would visit him each summer, and who would take care of him during his retirement. To be brutally honest, I didn't give a damn. I was grateful that I didn't have to discuss another pointless issue with him. Did I say discuss? For me, our debates were always more like a student trying to figure out what the teacher wanted to hear — hiding my own ideas, acting like a bloody mirror, flattering him, glorifying him, endorsing him. My father is arrogant, stubborn, and repulsive. I know these are not adjectives that a person should use to describe his father, but, I've already used them to his face — or similar words. I don't remember clearly. I was drunk, light-headed by the power of the booze, as I puked my thoughts out to him, my

intestines on the carpet right in front of him. What the hell. Even if I did say those things to his face, he probably wasn't paying attention. He was disregarding me as I was turning crimson in his study — his fortress, with its wall-to-wall shelves packed with hard-cover books of no importance to me.

"... asked if you would be able to visit him this weekend." I realized that I wasn't listening to the young voice, but was lost in my anger. It happens often to me; I think I inherited it from my father. My mother was the most attentive person I've ever known. She would remember every detail of every little incident that happened to her. Not like the way every other woman does — women have better emotional memory than men, I agree. Her memory was quite different. She was like a goddess controlling the small and limited universe around her — a goddess who knew everything and was capable of solving every problem.

"He says he feels a disturbing taste in his throat like the bitter taste of cheap olive oil."

"Bitter taste of cheap olive oil," I repeated. The pervert was turning into a poet as he was dying, preparing a Shakespearean end to his worthless soul.

"Those are his exact words," said the voice, stressing out the word *exact* to convince me.

"All right... Please tell him that I'll be there on Saturday. Probably late in the evening. I'll be driving."

She said something about a flight — his suggestion certainly. I didn't reply, but hung up the phone. On the drive, I would have enough time to go over the past and curse at every detail associated with him.

I was wrong. My restless mind left me loitering in the oppressive scenery, indulging in yesterday's disturbing thoughts, frustrating hatred, and my shyness of seeing him in a few hours. This went on until, approaching Adapazari, I saw the sign for Hikmet's roadside restaurant. Hikmet's place had been my mother's favourite. My mother would always ask my father to stop here whenever we travelled to the south coast — no matter what. He would obey happily. It could be early in the morning or late at night. One time, I remember eating meatballs for breakfast. It was fun though; everything was fun in those days.

I ordered meatballs with rice and yogurt. At that moment, my mother's face popped up in front of me, between the wooden chair facing the white-painted wooden table on the patio and the bus parked right in front of the restaurant. A young man was washing the windshield with a long brush, and the image of my mother's pretty face hovered on top of him. I shook my head. I didn't want to see her either. I could not forgive

her. She should not have died so young.

The fact is selfish people do not die young. My mother was anything but selfish; maybe she should have been. She should have been selfish for us, her children, for my father — well, at least for me. She should have lived a different life, not always thinking of others, but thinking of herself from time to time. No, I cannot forgive her.

Leaving Bozuyuk behind, the road makes a wide curve, and at the top of the hill the lowlands spread out in all directions toward Anatolia. From that point on, everything looks the same: calm, peaceful, and monotone. It is a different version of hell, meticulously decorated and endless. I caught myself reliving the day my father left the house after my mother's death. I passed another truck, and the man at the steering wheel honked his horn to salute me. This improper behaviour woke me from my thoughts. I admit that there was no good reason to think about that day. My twin sisters were already married, and my father decides to go, leaving the twelve-bedroom mansion to me and the servants. After the loss of his beloved wife, it was probably good for him to start a new life, move to a different place with no memories around, be alone to think things over, to recall the lovely past once again. Still, what I didn't like was his approach.

"I'm leaving the house to you," he had said right after the funeral. I remember our butler carrying the funeral flowers to the entrance of the house, converting the space to a small florist shop.

"Are you dying as well?" I had asked.

"Don't be smart. I'm just moving out. This will be good for all of us."

"You're moving out?"

"I thought it over, thoroughly. You need a house anyway. You can't afford one like this now-a-days."

"I don't need a new house. What will you do by yourself?"

"I can take care of myself. Don't think that I will need help from you or your sisters."

"But..."

"It's you that I'm concerned with. Can you handle everything yourself? Maybe it's time for you to find someone to take care of you."

I thought I would burst into flames. Words blazing out of my mouth, I would tell him he knew nothing about me, tell him that he was ignorant. But I said nothing.

Amid the high hills of the Toros Mountains are two restaurants famous for their trout cooked on clay tiles. Both restaurants hide in the shadows of the hills, providing a soothing retreat. I missed the first

one, reckless, thinking that I would not miss the second, in spite of the depressing memories. The second restaurant belongs to one of my father's friends, one of many he has along the road — almost anyone who can memorize my dad's precious name is a friend to him. I would not call these people friends myself. For me a friend is someone special, close, intimate.

Haluk, the restaurateur, gave me his best table, the one next to the ornamental pool where the trout and whitefish swim unaware of their future. I did not resist. I thought I could overcome the feelings of resentment or anything else the innocent table would remind me of. I was wrong again. Even the silky taste of trout couldn't block out the memories of my last conversation with my father in this restaurant, at this same table, the best in the house.

"I'm getting married," he had said, taking a sip from his *raki*.

"What?"

"I will introduce her to you tonight."

"It's been only..."

"She's an accountant — a very bright person — a straight A student at the college."

"Who gives a shit?"

"Watch your mouth. She won't be your mother, but she will be my wife quite soon. You have to learn how to behave. This is because you live alone by yourself, away from society, like a savage."

"I'm happy the way I am," I had said, shocked to find that it wasn't him, — but me — being interrogated.

"You'd do much better with a nice lady on your side. You know I only want what's good for you. All I think of is you," he had said smiling, taking a bite from the pool's laziest trout.

He has this constant desire to spread his wisdom around, no matter how reluctant the listeners seemed.

He married that straight A student a month later. A reception was held at his house at Sarigerme, giving me a chance to get drunk and humiliate myself in front of a small but quite wealthy crowd — all close friends of my father. He gave a short speech right after putting the ring on her finger. It was a well-crafted speech — cheerfully welcomed by the small crowd — a useless, selfish speech, which I tried to forget the moment I heard. It's ironic; I don't remember it right now - I never thought this day would come. But I do remember drinking a little more, maliciously criticizing the young bride to a few close fellows and, seeing my father walk into his study alone, going after him. I remember slamming the door, shouting to his face how arrogant, stubborn, and repulsive he was to

make that speech, and throwing up on his precious Iranian carpet.

At the seafood restaurant, I paid the bill, leaving a generous tip. As usual Haluk walked me to my car, asking his silly little questions: Was I satisfied with the meal? Was everything OK? Did I want anything more? He finished his farewell speech by asking me to give his regards to my old man. I wanted to tell Haluk that my old man was dying, but something stopped me. Maybe if I was able to remember my father's speech at the wedding, I would feel that power in me. I turned on the ignition and stepped on the gas.

He was dying. Was it true? The young voice told me that it was. What did she say again? He feels a disturbing taste in his throat like the bitter taste of cheap olive oil. I've heard that phrase before. Yes, I know I have. With a press of a button, I sprayed wiper fluid onto the windshield to clean it. The wipers stripped the dead bugs off the glass. The bitter taste of cheap olive oil. And just like that a bright light went off in my head. That phrase was from his speech — the speech he gave at the reception.

I felt nothing, looking at the lost horizon, my mouth open wide, driving. There were a few thoughts circulating in my mind: He was not dying. I had been tricked. I was going to yet another reception — one that I would never attend willingly. The wheels rolled on for another twenty minutes without disturbing me.

Just before taking the exit to Sarigerme, I stopped at a store to buy a gift for the new couple. The guy was selling handmade ceramic plates, marble sculptures, and animal figurines carved from wood. He was my father's friend. I did not remember his name.

THE RIVER GOD
by Jack Caulfield

A LONG TIME AGO, human beings thought the river that cut through their land was God. They knew this because they could not control it. The River God gave them life- but also death. He become the source of inspiration- but also the limit of their inspiration.

Then one day a man found a way to use the River God, to put its efforts toward something unintended. Travel came first, and then its force was put to moving gears on axles. Finally one man found a way to overcome the river's limitations completely, and built a bridge to travel over and beyond the River God.

That experience was more then just a first step for those people, it was a touchstone in understanding. When they looked upon that river again it was no longer a God but a tool; a force to be respected and understood- but not feared or worshipped. And as they now had the power to destroy that river they also had the power to save it, or help it flourish.

This once cosmic entity had now changed, though not literally - or through any power of its own. It was their perception and reaction that had altered. As the people expanded in numbers, diversity and depth, the image of the River-God remained faint and unyielding. There were moments when the overwhelming power the river once held resurfaced in the minds and hearts of later generations. When their surroundings felt uncontrollable, and they stood before grand new challenges, the people's humble meekness conjured up their old River God.

In times of great enlightenment we used to say 'just about time for another river-crossing' as our old God comes round into a complex pattern, and we admire our new tool of civilization.

SARA
by Shaheena Choudhury

IT WAS A COLD night and the bitter January wind blew across our faces as we rushed toward the emergency unit of the hospital. Sara was almost numb with fever. The doctor informed us that we had delayed giving her blood transfusion, and her hemoglobin had dropped down to a critical level. As Sara was being examined, my husband insisted on remaining by her side. One of the nurses showed me to our assigned room, where I would spend the night with Sara while she underwent the transfusion. The room was small and cold. Street lights filtered through the glass panes and cast strange shadows across the walls- everything seemed to be so distant, so alien. A waft of cold wind blew through the open window, sending a shiver down my spine. I quickly closed the window and arranged some of the things Sara would need for the night – water bottle, milk bottle and her night dress. It was getting late and Sara was still not being brought to the room from the ER. The stale smell of antiseptic and recycled air wafted down the hospital corridors making me nauseous. I sat on the cold sofa in the corner of the room looking repeatedly at my watch. Time seemed to stand still like someone had pressed the pause button on a remote control. My thoughts went two years back when we first took Sara for a physical examination.

I vividly recall that dreaded afternoon at the clinic, when my husband and I sat transfixed like two wax figures in a museum, as the doctor examined Sara's blood report.

"Our genes don't just determine the colour of our eyes, but can also decide what illness we'll suffer from," said the doctor.

"What are you getting at?" I asked, not sure if I wanted to hear

the answer.

"Your daughter is suffering from '*thalassemia major*'.

"Thalassemia! I've never heard of it."

"It's a blood disorder that reduces the production of hemoglobin," the doctor said. It is quite common in Southeast Asia including Bangladesh. It only gets detected when someone gets chronically ill with major thalassemia.

He further explained that the illness is caused by a mutation in a single gene. A person having thalassemia minor has one copy of the mutated gene, which is referred to as a 'carrier' or a 'tralt'. Carrlers are healthy but exhibit mild anaemia. Carrier parents have a 1 in 4 chance with each pregnancy, to have a child with thalassemia major.

I was dumbfounded and asked, "So you mean to say that our daughter falls under the unfortunate category of 25%?"

"Correct."

"Is there any medication that can help her"?

"No," he said flatly and explained. "She needs blood transfusions for the hemoglobin level to go up. If the condition is left untreated the anaemia will get worse, and your child will stop growing altogether. There might be other complications too."

"How often will she need transfusions?"

"I'm afraid, every two to four weeks."

"Oh, God!" I muttered under my breath.

We later on found out that even with transfusions, the life expectancy of a thalassemia patient varied between 20-30 years, depending on the compliance with medical treatment. Too traumatized to react, we didn't know what to expect next. The following days and months took a toll on the family, full of emotional swings of sadness, fear, and hopeful prayers. We were caught in a whirlwind, spinning from one lab to another, giving blood samples for 'hemoglobin electrophoresis' (a specific blood text), which confirmed our being the 'carriers'. That explained my frequent headaches and anemia. Since childhood, my hcmoglobin count has been low. The doctors always put me on iron supplements, which eventually proved useless, as being a 'carrier' they were never absorbed in my blood stream and the condition persisted. Unwittingly, we had passed on the 'recessive genes' to our daughter.

Sometimes a genetic illness shows up in a family with no previous record of the disorder. That was the case when Sara was born. She had inherited a condition which nobody in our families had ever heard of, let alone anybody suffer from it. When she was about five months, we realized something was wrong. She was pale and losing weight. You can

never be prepared for all the calamities that can befall you and change your life forever. When you know that there is a tendency for a certain genetic disorder to run in your family, there is usually something you can do to fight off the influence of your genes, but we were caught off guard.

To find a possible cure for my daughter became a mission of our life. Back in the mid eighties, we didn't have any advance medical facility in Bangladesh. We reached out to countless doctors in hopes of getting an accurate diagnosis. To prove our doctors wrong, we took our child to Thailand. In northern Thailand, around 30% to 40% of the population is affected by thalassemia; hence a lot of research is carried out on this particular field. Unfortunately, the diagnosis remained unchanged. We had no option but to give Sara the blood transfusions. While transfusion therapy was lifesaving, it carried a risk of transmitting viral and bacterial diseases. Transfusion also would lead to excess iron deposits in blood, which would eventually damage the liver, heart, and other parts of the body. To prevent damage, iron 'chelation' therapy was needed to remove excess iron from the body. The process worked best when given slowly under the skin, usually with a small portable pump overnight. The entire procedure was demanding and painful, and we were reluctant to put Sara through all that suffering.

The only speck of hope left was to do a bone marrow transplant. Sara's thalassaemic bone marrow was unable make a normal amount of red blood cells. If the malfunctioning bone marrow was replaced with normal bone marrow, she might lead a normal life. However, it was necessary to have a fully compatible donor with tissues that matched Sara's exactly so her body would not reject them. The most likely donors would be her siblings. As Sara was my only child, getting a fully compatible donor was one in a million! Yet, we continued to pursue the impossible.

I was pulled out of my reverie when I overheard someone say that a baby in the ER had suffered a heart attack and the doctors were trying to revive her. I ran towards the emergency room and saw through the glass door a doctor pumping her chest. My feet froze and my entire world came to a standstill when I saw Sara's fragile body. Before I even entered the room, everything was over. My husband stood there motionless, like a convict awaiting his death sentence. I screamed, "What's wrong"? He was holding Sara in his arms. "Is Sara gone?" I kept on screaming and repeating over and over again, "Sara is gone." My body shook in disbelief. *No, no, no.* I screamed and cried. How was it possible, she was here a minute ago, and how could she be gone? My Sara was two years and four months old when she passed away – twenty-two years back.

For the first time in my life I saw death from so close. It was so

cruel, and indifferent! I couldn't stop touching her. I couldn't keep my hands from her face, her tiny little nose, her long lashes sweeping down the cheeks, her firmly set lips, and her pale skin that was so cold! Even her long wavy hair was lifeless. I hoped that the warmth of my touch would make those beautiful eyes open. I held her close against me to feel, to share the last few moments before parting, but she was just not there. She had left without giving us another chance, without saying goodbye. The smell of death lingered on everywhere. The next few hours and days were a blur. I just went through the motions, the funeral, the burial and the final good bye. All I wanted to do was shut myself inside my room to get away from the nightmare.

We had gambled with Sara's life. In the hope of curing her ailment, we did not give her the blood transfusion, which would have diminished the success rate of bone marrow transplant. My husband and I agreed to take help of alternative medicine practitioner. We were falsely reassured by one of such consultants that her condition was curable.

"Don't worry, I've cured some patients with major thalassemia. Here are the files on my previous patients, you can go through them."

How unprofessional for a doctor to do such a thing! On the cover of one of the worn out brown files were red check marks indicative of positive outcome. Of course we didn't want to go through the personal documents of others. The consultant prescribed medication assuring us that it would increase Sara's haemoglobin level. We believed him or rather we wanted to believe him. Knowing all the consequences, it was our own imprudence and ignorance which led us to be deceived and beguiled by him. Finally, when we woke up from our trance and decided to give her the transfusion, it was too late! Who knows, even on Sara's file similar kind of red check marks are visible for others to see.

Coming to terms with losing Sara has been hard indeed. My life suddenly ground to a halt. When she was first diagnosed with the disorder, I quit my teaching job to give her my undivided attention, to spend my waking hours with her. Even when she slept, I stayed near her to see if she was breathing properly. Meal times were a chore for her, as she hardly had any appetite. It would take me three hours to feed her one meal. I never regretted a single moment I spent with her. She was a gift from God, and we were fortunate to have her with us, though for a very short while. I had been so much involved with her short life that all of a sudden my life seemed meaningless and devoid of purpose.

At times, when I look at Sara's picture, I miss her so much. I miss the future we might have had together – going to school, celebrating birthday parties, graduating from college, and who knows, even seeing

her get married someday would have been a wonderful experience! I miss the smile on her face – the smile she had to make us feel better, but her deep sad eyes would always give away the suppressed pain. The sickness impeded her growth, and she could barely stand on her feet due to weakness. With heavy heart and profound sadness I had watched Sara while she watched other small children walk and run around. Not being able to function like a normal child must have affected her, but she never spoke about it. She was a very observant child who was able to express herself clearly. It's painful to reflect upon the fact that I cherish so many of her memories, yet I don't recollect what she talked about. Recalling every detail is an emotional and mental trauma. Had I remembered every detail about her, it would've been difficult to carry on in life. It's the only rationale I have today to console myself with.

I know the day she left this world; it was her time to go. Why God decided this, is beyond human comprehension. I can try so much and be happy for her, knowing that she is in a better place, away from the pain that encompassed her little world. Sometimes I wonder, if timely blood transfusions might have saved her, she may have lived a little longer, but for how long, only time could tell. Despite everything, the dreadful feeling of guilt will always lurk behind us, like an evil shadow in a dark alley.

I've realized one thing for certain that human beings have infinite capacity for coping with tragedy. I found depths within myself I didn't realize I had. Anger was one of the most difficult emotions to keep under control when I saw Sara suffer. Watching my daughter's smiling face while she went through the agonizing journey of her short life, taught me to curb my anger. My eyes would well up in tears as I would inhale deeply in an attempt to overcome the newly inflicted wound — her death. When friends made disconcerting remarks like "you knew she would die," I felt like screaming back, "No, I didn't know." Instead, I would swallow hard and withhold my reaction to counter the remark. I learned to have patience — the hard way.

FORTUNES AND FORTITUDE
by Christina Clapperton

AS WITH ALL THE women he went out with from mydate.ca, Morton Kowarski met Melàni at the Chinese restaurant around the corner from his condominium on Fourth Street. This developed into a habit when he noticed that his neighbour Lucetta, whom he imagined he'd call Lucy if they dated, dining there alone. He also saw her at the dog park. Not being a dog owner himself, he wouldn't have found striking up a conversation with her there quite as natural as it was for the dog owners he saw chatting so easily with her. So he waited for someone at work to go on vacation so he could offer to pet sit.

Morton was going to choose a different restaurant when it occurred to him that bringing his dates to a place where he hoped to run into another woman could be considered ungracious. But by that time she stopped coming.

Melàni arrived, and he waved her over. *Melàni Pataya. Her name sounds like an exotic fruit salad, he thought.*

"You look just like you do in your photo," she said. The comment pleased Morton because he often found that people didn't look as good as in their carefully selected profile photos.

He cupped her hand in both of his. "I got a little peckish," he said when she looked at the fortune cookie wrapper, and he disposed of it between the salt and soy sauce. "They're only ten cents. You may have as many as you like."

"Thanks. I'll have one after dinner."

She has the honey-coated tone of a fortune teller. He hadn't read

his fortune yet, so he cleared his throat and read, "You have *razon*-sharp spiritual vision today," and he showed it to her.

The petite papaya laughs. "So their English isn't perfect," Morton said.

"Tell me something about yourself," she said, combing her ruby and sapphire-ringed fingers through hair only seen in ads for shampoo. "Your profile says you're divorced but it didn't say whether you had children or not."

"No, I don't like children. I wonder — Melàni, do you think maybe they spelled raisin incorrectly?"

"You mean the fruit?"

"Yes. It could be some kind of warning," Morton said, his eyes fixed on the three-inch piece of paper in his grip.

"I think they meant to say razor-sharp. Can we order now?"

"Maybe it's best if we go someplace else."

"You can't take those things so seriously." She nodded at the waiter.

"Actually, give us a moment please."

Melàni slapped the menu on the table, and he thought she mumbled something like, 'Oh God' under her breath.

"I'm sorry. I don't know why this is so important to me." He thought the misspelling could speak to the fortune's authenticity, but it could also mean what he initially feared. Sarcasm. His spiritual acuity was raisin-sharp. Shrivelled up like an old grape.

She was staring out the window now. He folded the fortune and tucked it in his breast pocket. "Sorry for being curt with you," he said when he thought she might be planning an early exit. "I meant to say that I don't think children would fit in well with my lifestyle. It's not that I don't like them; it's just that I don't think I'd like doing a lot of things that parents do."

"Well, that's an insightful answer. And it's the first honest thing you've said since I got here." Melàni picked up her menu again and gave the waiter a sheepish smile as though willing to shoulder some of the blame.

From that point on, Morton tried to say things she would find of merit but the fortune still pervaded his mind. *Should I buy another one to test the theory of it being simply a typo? No, I can't do that. What if conflicting profundities are destructive to the psyche?* The haunting thoughts distracted him for the rest of the evening despite how alluring he found her.

Morton knew he owed Melàni an apology. He just wondered if

he'd have to launch into it in the same breath as 'hello' or she might hang up first.

"I know who you are, Morton," she said when he repeated his name with his last. "I'm just surprised you called. You didn't seem very interested."

"If that's because of my silliness about the fortune cookie, I apologize. Things have been crazy at work. Our administrator quit without notice, and I have to set up all my own files and type my letters. You're probably thinking I sound spoiled, but the timelines we have to work with can't be managed with the extra work."

"Morton, if there's something that made you think I'm not a good match for you—"

"I'm sorry if that's the impression I gave you."

"Come on. Superstitions? You're an underwriter."

Morton had thought it was going to be a quick phone call; he'd apologize, and she'd say that it's fine but she has to go, wishing him good luck in his search. But, of course, this is what he had hoped for. "Well, I can see how my line of work could raise some questions about that. It's not all formulas, though. Deciding if someone is a good risk requires a certain degree of judgment and sometimes it comes down to a gut feeling. But you're not off base. I guess because I haven't had much luck with women lately I've lost confidence in my ability to tell whether one is right for me or not."

"So you were letting a cookie decide?"

"It seems that way. I thought it wouldn't work out so I sabotaged it. Like a self-fulfilling prophecy. But I do think you're great and I would like to get to know you better."

"So, how are you going to make it up to me?"

Morton couldn't believe his luck — first that she'd entertain the idea of seeing him again and now he sensed flirtation. "A nice dinner perhaps?"

"I was thinking more along the lines of an interview."

"Pardon?"

"You need an administrator, and I need a job."

"Hmm. Let me see what I can do."

The following week Melàni came in for an interview. Morton peeked over his cubicle at the sound of her laugh. She was talking with Morton's boss in the hall. All the men in the vicinity stopped and stared, elbowing anyone who hadn't seen her. An intern walking towards her bumped into a partition and knocked a plant onto an account exec's lap when she was on the phone with a client. She didn't miss a word of her

pitch as she shook soil out of her shoe.

Morton's boss had trouble connecting with Melàni's references but with their urgent need and Morton's good recommendation, he offered her the job. She seemed to be picking up on things fast and was asked to jump right in her second day. Morton kept his week free of meetings to answer her questions. When he didn't hear from her all morning, he walked over to her cubicle. She was head down, asleep, softly snoring.

"Melàni!"

"Oh, sorry, I must have nodded off."

"I don't think anyone noticed. I'm getting a coffee. Can I get you one?"

"I don't drink coffee."

"Tea then?" She just smiled. "Well, this could be a good time to start. How have you ever functioned at a job without caffeine?"

"I've never had a full-time job before."

"Why?"

"I used to dance."

"You were a professional dancer?"

"Not exactly. I didn't have the opportunity to train professionally when I was younger. But I practiced daily. The samba, belly dancing, ballet, modern. Almost every kind. I stopped around the time my mother passed away."

"I'm sorry."

"It was almost 15 years ago. Maybe I'll get back into it someday," she said, rubbing her eyes. "Anyway, with all the training I could only work part time and when I stopped I was so used to sleeping late and taking long baths twice a day. Part-time work seemed to suit me better." She smoothed her perfectly smooth, straight hair. "I guess I wouldn't mind a hot chocolate if there is any."

"Hmm? Oh, yes, there's some in the lunchroom. I'll be right back." He turned as if to leave then came back quickly, surprising her. "Don't fall asleep."

"I won't."

When he came back he asked her what she was doing Saturday.

"Saturday?" She looked over at the next cubicle.

"Just as friends," he said, sensing hesitance with continuing to date now that they worked together.

They made plans to meet at The Chocolate Shop Café Saturday at 11 in the morning. "They make a real hot chocolate. Not this packaged kind," he told her. "Okay, well, I'll get back to my desk. Stay awake," he

said, pointing a finger. She nodded.

Melàni stood in front of the café looking up, appearing half asleep again. Morton tapped on the window from inside. She laughed and walked in. "I was looking at the sign that says 'The Chocolate Shop.'"

"This is the café below it." Morton pulled out a chair for her.

"What's The Chocolate Shop then?"

"A dance studio." He grinned.

"What kind?"

"West Coast Swing. Ever try it?"

She eyed a gym bag on the chair next to him. "What are you planning?"

He winked as he went over to the barista. "Whipped cream?"

She narrowed her eyes at him. "Please."

When Morton came back with two steaming cups, Melàni told Morton the story of her mother. "She hadn't been doing well for a few years, and I noticed her age a lot the summer before she passed away. One night the phone rang when I was leaving to go dancing. I didn't answer it and forgot to take my cell phone to the studio." She scooped whipped cream onto her spoon then returned it to the glass cup, stirring it into the steaming liquid. "My mother was in critical condition for a few hours. By the time I got home and called my brother back she was dead." She swallowed hard. Morton took her hand; it was hot from her cup. "I didn't like myself for a long time."

Morton just stroked her hand as she told him how she gave up her childish dream, as she put it. He listened more intently than he'd listened to another person in a long time. Lucetta passed by the storefront in a short white down jacket, her poodle like a curious arrangement of cotton balls at her feet. The tableau normally would've garnered Morton's immediate attention, but he was so absorbed in her story that it went unnoticed. He even felt a prick in his chest as if a tiny knife was pointed there the whole time she spoke. He waited to make sure she got it all out. Then it seemed that she was trying to lighten the mood.

"I guess I have superstitions of my own," she said, taking her first sip of cocoa.

"You took what happened as a sign that you should give up dancing?"

"Yeah. And somehow dancing became a metaphor for living. Do you actually have something in there that will fit me?"

"I made a stop on the way over. Size small?"

"Why would you do this for me?"

"I want to see you dance," he said, raising an eyebrow. He stood

and offered his hand as if there were a dance floor behind him, but she didn't budge. "Okay, I've been a little neurotic lately."

"*Really?*"

"Meeting you has gotten me out of my head. Maybe I could use a little dance in my life too."

Melàni smiled and took his hand. "So what did you get me?"

"Oh, I went all out. I hope you like sequins and hot pants."

"Yeah right," she said, hooking his arm.

NOTES FOR A NOVEL
by L. J. Clark

THE SETTING IS A seaside town on the coast of Maine, bound in fog, the grey sea slapping coldly at the sand – the kind of place where in the sunshine, kids would paddle in the shallows or race shouting out to the waves, boogie-boards in hand. Toddlers would pile up sand into moats and castles, helped by their fathers. Kites would strain high above the beach, fluttering in the breeze. But none of these things happen; instead, it is foggy, the air clammy and cold. In the early morning drizzle, it is fine to buy a latte and go for a walk on the beach, leaving dents in the sand for the sea to fill in – but the mizzling rain continues all day and wears on the spirit. The extended family, gathered together for a long weekend, cannot frolic freely on the shore but are closed into their houses. They meet darkly in conspiring groups, gossiping and grousing. The many begin to splinter into the few, divided into mutinous duos and trios. The children are out of sorts, squabbling, and the adults are caught up in a more sinister game. That is how the family splits into warring groups, with teeth bared to expose the aggression underneath; it all begins with the weather. A rite of passage, perhaps, into the hard acceptance of adulthood, the leaving behind of childhood – days of careless happiness, which become a distant memory ebbing fast, sucked back out to sea with the driftwood on the tide.

There is a crisis brewing. The next scene could be set in the past, in an old-fashioned mansion with lace-doilies on the backs of the stuffed horse-hair sofas. A mantle-clock ticks ominously on the wall. In the circle of firelight, several black-clothed family members sit on stiff-backed chairs, leaning forward to hear the will as it is read aloud. They react in different ways. The voices rise in anger to shouts of accusation, chairs

scrape back, then silence. This scene would be a flashback, showing how feuds run deep in the blood, how the present builds on antipathies formed in the past. The fault lines and rifts of long ago have become entrenched. There is a history to it, a rhythm. It is archetypal, part of a recurring pattern, doomed to repetition. It is always so when there is a death in the family; the loss of the parents leads to a loss of control, a loss of civility; quarrels break out among the siblings as the family unit breaks down.

The characters would need to be developed, of course. The cast of characters – that's where the heart of the matter lies. Motivation must be clear; each individual has to act out his or her destiny. The eldest sister, chronically angry, rails against the world while nursing an eternal grievance; she distorts every action into an imagined injury against herself, to justify a never-slaked need for revenge. Her bitterness provides the underlying aggression that propels the action. Her sidekick, the second sister, has to be worn down into her supporting role. The wormwood and gall poured endlessly into her ears over the years act on disappointed hopes, a cheating husband, thwarted ambition – until eventually, she succumbs to the temptation of hatred as a focus for her frustration and an excuse for her failings. The brother, a weakling among these hard-edged women, flounders in the seething emotions they espouse. Essentially lazy, he just wants everyone to go away and stop needling him to action. Flaccid, blonde – once the golden boy but now in middle-age deflated, defeated, his energy depleted save for the tendency to carouse too freely; when in his cups, he sees the truth all too clearly. But at other times, his soul has shrunk into flashes of anger at the overwhelming claustrophobia; he simply wants to break free of the tangled skein of sibling rivalry. He will never rise to be a champion, nevermore risk his own peace to defend his little sister as he once did; it is easier to leave her exposed to the harpies.

And the youngest, the perfect victim: trusting, unsuspecting, she is startled and dismayed by the sudden exposure of the long years of secret hatred and plotting. Shy and overly sensitive, she feels each taunt and insult as torture; the anger and rejection bites into her soul. Cherished and protected by her parents, she is resented by her siblings who will make her pay for her favoured position. The parents die; protection is withdrawn. The bullying begins. What will happen next?

The action: will it be a murder when stirred resentment reaches the boiling-point, or something more subtle? Maybe something less dramatic: a coming-of-age story, in which the central character moves slowly towards awareness and acceptance of her loss. Burying her parents, she buries her concept of family along with them. The once-close unit is

now irretrievable and unimaginable, splintered into seething parts. She comes sadly into the full realization of adulthood, with all its diminishment. With the loss of love and certainty, waves of grief wash over her, eroding her blind trust, the naive belief in bonds of love that belong to the past. The memory of a sheltered childhood is a dream lost in the shadows, drowned in the rising tide of recrimination, as old rivalries fester. The once supportive family unit crumbles like a castle on the seashore in the face of the oncoming tide.

But where will redemption come from? What lessons are to be learned?

The conclusion will take longer to reach; the conflict is easy enough to develop: the broken dolls, the shattered illusions. But what comes after the denouement? Who will come to save? Who will ride in to the rescue on the tide?

We could go the route of the handsome stranger, blonde-haired, from an exotic land, Australia perhaps. Self-contained, muscular, a sunny disposition with a hint of depth – a warm smile, a strong shoulder; he could rescue the heroine with the promise of a sun-drenched land far away from the troubles of the present and the hauntings of the past.

A baby could come next: tiny hands curling around a finger, cradled lovingly at the breast, encircling warmth flooding the heart and soothing the pain, lulling the sorrow to sleep like the gentle lapping of waves on the shore. And slowly, like a wave forming far out to sea, rising and gathering force, comes the affirmation – a surge of strength arising in the will to try again, to build a better home, one that will stand firm against the tides on the sands of time, and carry the promise of love into the future.

And then, after a lapse of years, the closing scene: a sunny beach in southern Australia. The sea is warm; dolphins play in the surf off-shore. This scene reverts to the possibilities suppressed in the opening, to provide the perfect contrast. The sun is brighter on this side of the world. The Junior Lifesavers wear fluorescent wetsuits and splash on their surfboards. Teenagers throw frisbees and bury each other in the sand. A large family group gathers round a barbie, laughing and joking, sharing wine and food. The heroine is there, serene, with her children gathered round her. The boys kick footballs while the girls play music and dance in the sand. As the afternoon shadows lengthen, the sky glows crimson, yellow, and orange. A pod of whales could pass by in the distance, leaping high out of the sea to add to the wonder of it all.

If only it could be that simple. Will the ending satisfy and convince? Like a snake, the end circles round to the beginning; I think I've found the title: "If only" – and that's the end of the story. There is no more. I've worked it all out. Now I think I'm ready to begin again.

GHOST FROM THE PAST
by Dayle Cleveland

AS I STOOD AT the kitchen sink watching the sudsy water twirling around the drain, I had the intense feeling of being watched. Hesitating, I looked up and gasped at the sight of a face staring back at me in the window. It was a familiar face. The eyes and hair were dark; the mouth was plump with a slight hint of red. I looked closer and noticed sadness in the eyes that quickly turned to anger, a deep seeded anger that has been lurking in the background for a long time.

A chill ran from the top of my head right down to my toes. Of course, I was staring at myself. Not as I am now but from the past; a past that comes with a lot of pain and self-loathing.

There is a ghost that lingers in my head and it lies next to me as I try to sleep. It follows me into the shower; onto the train as I go to work. It sits with me as I watch TV and it interrupts me when I am listening to my iPod.

For years I have been fighting with this ghost. I scream at it, *"Leave me alone so I can get on with my life!"*

But it just stands there shaking its head "NO," whispering, "You know why."

I close my eyes and the mind begins to wander back in time. Bile rises in my throat and guilt accompanied by anger, hatred, and disgust overwhelms me. I was the lucky one, apparently, the one that got away.

Pictures flash before my eyes. It is the early 90's;...*FLASH...* I see the faces of two males... *FLASH...* it's the outline of a knife hidden by a piece of cloth; *FLASH...* one car... no two cars, same type but different colour at different times.

The flash I hate the most is one that reminds that I have come face to face with one of these males before, not once but at least twice. During one of these times, for a split second, a message came into my head that this was someone who was wanted, but I dismissed this thought as quickly as it came. I put it down to paranoia.

This is a male who in the end hurt many, many people and I felt somewhat responsible, still do I suppose.

Now my anger took on a whole new dimension, and I wanted to show *him* that I was not going to be intimidated by anything he or his friend did. This bitch was not going to play *their* game. This also seemed to keep their focus in my direction, which was part of *my* game. Whether this was out of obligation or personal guilt I'm not sure.

At about this part of the story, I know you are wondering why I did not call the police. Why indeed? Of the few personal experiences I have had with cops, none of them were positive. When I was 15 years old, I found myself the centre of someone else's attention. The neighbours called the cops. They eventually arrived only to say that nothing could be done unless there was some kind of personal injury.

Thanks, I will make note of that...make sure throat is slashed before calling, got it! On top of that, I was blamed, by others, for this guy coming around. So I learned a valuable lesson at an early age...do not involve anyone else; and rely on and trust yourself, only.

As the months went by, I discovered something about the mind... it has an amazing way of protecting itself. It goes somewhere else. There seems to be an "attic" in the brain; a quiet spot where logical thinking and the soft emotions can hide and not be disturbed, or found. This in turn leaves an opening for other ideas and thoughts to enter and take over. This is when I found myself going down a dark path that would only lead to a tragic ending for someone, and I was going to give it my best shot not to be "the one".

It got to the point that I *wanted* to do this. I wanted to get even and make these guys pay. I knew one male was strictly the driver; which meant I really had one male to deal with. I also was not going to let my size, or the fact that I was female, get in the way.

I started to "condition" myself. All I thought about was how I would get myself out of whatever situation they tried to put me into. *"What if I am grabbed this way, what do I do?" "What if I wind up in the car; do I make the car crash? If I was going, so were they!"* I thought of nothing else for weeks.

While in the midst of "conditioning" myself I hear an arrest was made. I didn't make the connection until later on, when I did, I felt lost. It

was as if I was left standing with something in my hand and had nowhere to put it. I should have been happy, jumping for joy that it was over. But I wasn't.

As crazy as this may sound, I felt the cops interfered as it meant this guy, or guys, would be going to jail instead of hell where they belonged. I was ready to give it my all. If I did not succeed at least I died trying. So how could they do this to me?

Also, once you go down that dark path, it is very difficult to return to a "normal" way of thinking, or feeling, right away. It reminds me of a song called *Long Road Out of Hell*. I was trying to find the exit, but at each turn, I found myself at a dead end.

For a long time after the arrest, I was overwhelmed with large bouts of both sadness and anger. What does this equal? The answer is guilt.

So much of it fills me for being alive; for not bearing a scratch compared to others; for not listening to my intuition at the beginning. If I had, maybe a few less would have endured the cruelty that was inflicted on them.

My eyes begin to focus back onto the window, and I shake my head to clear it of any remains of the former thoughts. That is when I noticed the ghost standing next to me. I turn, hold out my hand and feel the coldness surround it, followed by a squeeze. We stare at each other for a few minutes and it begins to speak.

"You say you want me to leave you alone, but I cannot do that. I am a part of you and always have been. Also, it's about accepting and learning from what happened. Let's take a look at the situation in a different light. You took some of the control away from them. You refused to run and hide; instead you to wanted to stand up to them. Right or wrong, it doesn't matter. You did what you could, at the time."

I ponder over this. As much as I agree and try to believe what was said, I still have trouble accepting it. Maybe in time I will, but how much longer will it take?

All of a sudden, I look over to find no one there. In a panicked fashion, I start calling out for the ghost, but nothing.

Ahhhhhh! I scream and bolt up from my pillow. Sweat is running down my face and my heart is racing. Nervously, I glance over at the clock; it's the same time... 2:55a.m. That damned dream!

An excerpt from the novel
DOWN THE STREET
by Cassandra Cronenberg Hunter

DOWN THE STREET ON the street these lyrics can't be beat. This is my head don't destroy it. I gotta place to be to be he said I gotta place to be he said. Bouncing along the street as he often did and always did before and forever this is the way he walks this is the way she walks he/she, he, she, he, she, this is where it is the never ending flow why does there have to be finality why does there have to be a finality can it not keep going can it not keep going. "This is she". This is a girl's life. The life of a girl not the life of this hustler this hustler who is on the street doing coke living to the beat coughing and cursing and hurting this is not his life this is hers this is her life now. Can this be it can this be the life she lives from then to now the street is hers she is a musician you can tell from the way she walks but not the irritating kind of woman who continues to sing all the time weather whether she is walking around or not she has the music in her head but she doesn't need to always show she is a singer and sing at every occasion but yes when she starts she can't stop she cannot stop she needs to find a guitar player but not to fall in love just to be able to still be married and to have this guitar this age she is now is this where the story begins or is she younger is she younger is this the way "what do you want?" "What do you want?" he said to me once and she crosses her hands in front of her and back out and juts her chin to him and he says I'll remember that for next time. A fight she wants to fight. No one had ever asked her that before or understood her actions like that or directed her like that before. What do you want what do you want, so quickly with his chin out with his British toughness and smoothness he

says I'll remember that for next time he says, she loves him then.

This is where she is now they are together and he is her producer. They have breakfast, they read the paper, is she "high or low", he gives her the thumbs up, they go on vacation together, they have a routine and they record her and he is behind the glass and she has to see him all the time totally dependent on what he thinks of her and he leaves her when she has to be alone. "I have to go." If he didn't she would never get off the couch as it is she can hardly get off. He knows her cycle where she is at ovulating or not he is controlling and sometimes she rebels. The Irish in her comes out and she breaks free and runs and runs free. When he runs free he used drugs and porn and prostitution when she runs free she is like a wild horse running free why can't he be? They do coke together some times but in a very polite fashion and grown up not like the bouncing at the reggae club this bouncing and bouncing doesn't work for her it's too speedy. This is another guy Tony let's say it's Tony and he is the coke and porn and speedy Brit they call him the brief kind of guy who comes into town when her and her producer are living their civilized music life with a bit of rock and roll he comes to visit them Tony and he causes trouble his fast ways are attractive to her scary and uncouth they stir up all of this she is ovulating and she ends up in bed with him one night after a few lines of lovely coke she wants him he reminds her of when they first met her and Jeremy when they first met and he was so beautiful and so strong and such a good driver and so on the edge of life and so raw and untouchable. Tony kind of reminds her of how Jeremy once was, way too into the London drug and music scene for her, coming from Toronto, it was a bit dark and fast and expensive but she liked that, that is what she liked. She wanted to be stabbed and put in jail too, it all seemed so romantic. Like her Yugoslavian lover who could not go home because of the war, that was when she travelled in Czechoslovakia as a teenager and searched about her Jewish identity and her father. That street life, the motorcycles, the coke, the music, the film, this was attractive to her of course.

Sitting at her vanity putting on her make up before the show, eye to eye, the line of mascara over the top eye lid, her silk blue dress half price with some bunching at the seams, with her fly London shoes half price and a half size too big, this was in the middle, to this, when she lived above the Italian restaurant on college street, her vanity but not the silk dress, this dress is now and Jeremy comes later when she is in her forties and doing large shows larger concerts. The seventies a girl, the eighties becoming a teenager and stepping out trying to learn guitar, trying, but it only happens for her later. Is this it? Her life didn't lend itself to that

of a painter. It made her feel like a junkie when she switched to oils and painted in the city. And she was always in school, always a student, that dream of a PhD has to go, that dream will go, can't focus on too many like Neil Young says, just get rid of the 31%, turn it into an incomplete and then carry on with this faith, with no money and put it into child care, this is what will happen. Does she have children now or later? As a married artist painter and musician and writer this is what she does, this is her, will she be a teacher too? Will she get her MA? Maybe not, it is too hard for her to do this now. Let that dream go and carry on with this one, thank you Jeremy for helping me this time, the people who help these are the ones to love and to help, these reciprocal relationships.

Now the lip liner, just a bit around the bottom and fill it in lightly so it will stay and bit of L'Oreal gloss, this is her now in front of the mirror seeing the lines by her eyes. She will be forty in three years. Her room is pale yellow the wood furniture is dark and a bit art deco as is she, the jazz singer. The full lips and dark eyes, her silk blue dress, her brown leather shoes with wood heels, she looks like she came out of the war, her thoughts drift to the war and Ester and Miles and the street on Crawford. Pilvishik Lithuania. She was an eccentric dresser and played piano for the National Ballet, he wrote for the Globe and Mail and collected stamps, the collection agency came and took all of their furniture away. Lie down with dogs and you get up with flees and they were an eccentric couple so her neighbours parents say now that she had moved south of Bloor with her husband, down where they would have been beaten up if they had lived down the street before. This is where it is, this is the place where they live. She is also like them, like her and now also like him, they are in her: Her jazz.

Jeremy said thank you or was that Tony when she dressed up for him when they went to see reggae as she had done many times before at Roots Bamboo in Negril Jamaica and at the Bamboo club in Toronto before it closed down on Queen Street, with her ex who just like him, like Jeremy except not addicted to coke of course, with blond hair and blue eyes just like her and his friend was her friend and they were the couple and now she is with the dark haired one and he the blue eyed one is the friend, opposites now and similar. The shark who cannot stop moving or else it will die, are all people with blue eyes like sharks I wonder, this is how it is, she is now a writer a musician and painter and likes to figure out the body and seeing into the future and where is it they go these will be her friends other people hurt her and they cannot be talked to anymore, it's only a friend if they don't hurt you, if they can't hurt you. It's fine if it keeps going in.

It is just that the father of her children, he was an owl and puffed out on occasion and she couldn't get to having sex with him again, she could never figure out how. Is that how she met Tony? She ended up in bed with him or was that Jeremy? That was how she ended up in bed with him but she had been with men like him before and was that Tony or Jeremy?

When he poured his rum into her glass she loved him of course she said "well I haven't been drinking that all night "and poured it back into his glass. Then softly she said "alright" and he poured it back into her glass and she drank it. She drank rum and cokes for years and years with her first love, the blond with blue eyes and they went to Jamaica together and camped on the beach. She lost her virginity to him but he also tormented her with his female friends. Although it's quite possible she could be tormented or would be tormented by any one of her lover's female friends.

She wants to smoke, always to smoke, always back to the cigarette, this will make it bad at the end it really will. She tries not to smoke as she has a drag and watches herself in the vanity mirror, must really try it would be nice to on occasion have one or two.

She doesn't want to depend on others, she cannot just bum from anyone, she needs her own but only for Saturdays, only for now not for later, what about her daughters and the love can't happen with smoke in the mouth and on the clothes, it's not good for them. But she has to be realistic. It is realistic. Just for today not for tomorrow or for when she is getting the kids or any of that it is not good for any of that, just keep going, only for going out if she goes out she can buy a pack otherwise she shouldn't do it, she shouldn't smoke at all, she can't sing and smoke anyway it's too painful. The energy comes out for painting, this is what she does with that and anger for painting and then for the exercise, it is important to exercise as well, this she can do sometimes and not others.

MOMENTS TO TREASURE
by Juliet Davy

I LEFT JAMAICA, MY motherland, on a quest to Canada. My humble intention is to enhance my life and to pursue the wealth of opportunities that Canada has to offer immigrants from all nations. I have been told all my life, that the grass is much greener abroad. Twelve months later, I delivered a 10lb bouncing baby boy that I named Michael.

Living in a strange and new country, food is an inspiration for me. I have been blessed to taste and experience a wide variety of food and dishes from all over the world. I must admit, food is one of my top three passions. I enjoy good soul food... Good soul food is cooked just right and with lots of love.

Cooking is an art. Planning and organizing is the key to preparing a good meal. Jamaicans are known for their exotic spices and cooking. Food is one of the legacies a mother like me can give to her son. This legacy passed down from generation to generation.

So many to choose from, but oxtail is the number one! Oxtail cooked with bake beans and basmati rice is Michael's favorite dish. Preparing this meal for him is very special to me. It creates the true bonding of mother and child.

Oxtail! I prepared it the night before. We Jamaicans wash all meat with lemon or vinegar, and then season it with different spices and herbs. I add onions, garlic, paprika, seasoned salt, cumin, thyme, scallion. Oxtail is placed in a container over night on the refrigerator. Baked beans. "Well! If baked beans is missing, it would be like a horse without carriage." He must have baked beans with his oxtail. The baked beans are added when oxtail is fully cooked.

It's 5:00a.m.; the alarm goes off, its music in the air; crawl out of bed, check the windows for the weather condition.... snow! Oh! I yearn for the sunshine.

It's 6:30a.m.; time to put the oxtail in the crock pot. Down below the earth, in the basement, is the laundry room. A plug posted over the green counter waiting for the crock pot to be plugged in. I take the crock pot from the old black shelf in the laundry room where it is stored and fill it up with the seasoned oxtail. Turn the button on high. It's time to leave for work.

It's a cold afternoon. I am coming home from work. Lots of snow on the ground. My thoughts are busy thinking of getting home on time to have supper ready. I open the door, and bolt down the basement. The aroma of all the different spices and herbs make me hungry and is so mouthwatering. Here comes our two cats, Jack and Jerry rubbing against my legs. They sleep all day. Jack is very special to me. He communicates with me just like a human being. He follows me everywhere around the house. He has a cute stare that is very difficult to ignore. Jerry is just cool. He is quite comfortable with himself. Just give him his food and he is fine. The cats are now rubbing on my feet and stretching. Jack is communicating now. I head for the crock pot. Can't wait to taste the oxtail. I hope it's ready to be eaten. I am sure the cats enjoy the smell of the oxtail too. Jack seems content. He has that oxtail look on his face.

Keys rattle in the door, loud bang, bags and shoes rolling down the stairs, crashing against the board wall.

"Mom! Mom! Is the oxtail ready? Um! Um! I could smell it from outside, smells good, Mom!"

Plates rattle, utensils' clang together, good energy, oxtail is ready. It's time to eat!

"Is the baked beans in, Mom? Can't wait to have oxtail with baked beans."

Rice is ready; the good old basmati rice served with garden salad. Um! Um! Ummmmm!

Keep going back for more and more and more.

"Thank you Mom! This is good! I love you Mom!"

Hugs! Um! Um! Ummmmmm!

This is the moment I treasure most. My friend keeps telling me to enjoy this moment, it will not last. He will change when he becomes a teenager.

Thank you Michael, for appreciating the time and love I spent in preparing your meal. Your actions and expression tell me that you are experiencing and feeling the love that is given to you in my cooking. You are very special and you will always be fed with oxtail.

JONESIN' FOR CREMA
by Susan Desveaux

SAMMI SAT AT A worn table at Café New Ronz checking e-mails from her boyfriend. Blah, blah, blah, we should see other people. I need to have more fun. You're not the same person. She held the BlackBerry over her coffee and contemplated dropping it into the steaming liquid. She set it on the table. Why waste a good latte.

The jerk was right, anyway. She had changed over the last six months. He was perfectly happy with his life and she was desperate to find the antidote to her creeping discontent. This café might hold all the answers. Was it possible to find her purpose in life in a coffee shop?

Café New Ronz was almost a dump. Years ago, it had been a saloon, and the owner had retained the massive wooden bar, brass fittings and nicotinic colouring of the walls. Music and smoke had soaked into the atmosphere of the place, and the posters of bands from years gone by. The juke box selections were all pre-1978.

The bar divided the room in half. In front, overlooking the street, were one-and-two person tables. In the back, roped off, were six- and eight-person tables and an enormous round table with 'Algonquin' painted onto the top. Sammi wondered if it referred to the beer or the park. Curiously, all of them had carved wooden centerpieces, and Sammi wondered about this too.

She picked up her BlackBerry and flipped to a bookmarked screen. *"Cure for Alzheimer's! New discovery to heal brain injuries! Finally, a cure for 'Stupid'!! What the Government doesn't want you to know!"* Yes, it was a conspiracy website and the bloggers were weird, but

Sammi had found an article that electrified her. The site owner claimed that Dr. J.G. Ryan had discovered a serum, code named "Crema," that made people smarter. The government was suppressing any information about this discovery. Bloggers claimed Ryan, in great danger, had gone into hiding. A relentless government agent, Greene, was on his trail. If you could find Ryan, wherever he was, you could be smarter.

She studied the man behind the bar. He was pushing 50, but he seemed perfectly at home slinging lattés. He could be Dr. Ryan, she couldn't tell from the grainy photo on the website. The photo of agent Greene, however, was a clear as a bell. She had followed the clues that had been posted over the months, and arrived at this café near the university where Ryan had done graduate work.

A striking old woman came down the stairs with a cream-coloured cockatiel on her arm. The bird hopped off her arm and onto a perch on the bar.

"JG," the old lady poured herself a coffee, "is this crap fresh?"

"You know it is, Jean," he replied. "You made it yourself 15 minutes ago."

"Was that me? Must be getting old," she joked as she turned to go to the back room. She noticed that the bird was watching Sammi. "Einstein?"

The bird launched from the perch, landed with a thump and slid across Sammi's table. She pulled back a little as he flapped his wings.

"Hi, dollface," the bird said. "Wanna fool around?"

Sammi laughed.

"Sorry about that," the woman said. "He's incorrigible. If he sees someone interesting, he just has to drop in."

"Do not," said the bird, and offered Sammi a claw. "Einstein." he said.

"Sammi." said Sammi, shaking the claw, marvelling at the bird's training.

"I'm Jean," the woman said. "May I join you?" They shook hands as Jean pulled up a chair. She was a magnificent woman who wore strength and peace like a warm cloak. Sammi looked into her eyes and wanted to be in the mindspace where Jean lived. Sammi was sure Jean never doubted her purpose in life.

"You OK, Sammi?" Jean asked gently.

"Yes, no," Sammi said, sipping the latté. "My boyfriend dumped me. I should care, but I don't. I want something more, something different, I just don't know what. He has no idea what I'm talking about." She shrugged. JG nodded to Jean.

"Our purpose in life is the ultimate search," Jean said. "My nephew needs me for something, but why don't you move into the back and we can continue this conversation later."

"OK."

Sammi followed Jean into the back room. She felt a small thrill as Jean unhooked the rope and showed her to the "Algonquin" table. Einstein flew over their heads and landed on the wooden centerpiece. "So that's what they're for." she mused, and then turned to Jean. "What's Algonquin?"

"In 1930's New York, a very famous group of writers met every day in the restaurant at the Algonquin Hotel," Jean said. "It was a daily meeting of the brightest and most talented minds of the era. We like to encourage talent, intelligence, searching."

Jean walked behind the bar, to help JG with the cappuccino machine.

"Well, I guess that's what I'm looking for," Sammi said absently.

"It's all here if you want it," a voice beside her said quietly.

"What?" said a startled Sammi, turning toward the voice.

"Brains," Einstein said. "I know you've been on the website, dollface. That's how you found us. I know what you want—answers to the big questions."

She looked into the cockatiel's shining eyes. There was something in there that contained so much more than she saw in most of the people she met every day.

"We're having a real conversation," she said.

"Duh," said Einstein.

"So it's all true," she said. "About the serum, I mean. The man behind the bar *is* Dr. Ryan."

"Could be," said Einstein. "All you have to do, is go up to JG and say 'I'd like a cappuccino...double double crema. He'll help you and then maybe, you can help us."

Einstein flew back to his perch on the bar and joined the conversation with Jean and JG. Sammi sat at the table for a few minutes and then, when the conversation ended, she walked up to the bar.

"I'd like a cappuccino please, Dr. Ryan, double double crema." She said the password with authority.

"Double double crema," he replied, met her eyes and nodded. "I'll bring it to your table. And I've never heard of Dr. Ryan."

He was at the table in seconds, with a big cup of cappuccino. She took a sip and stared into the crema. This was the moment.

"You know, it's not enough to be smart, Sammi," he said. "I

thought being smart was the answer to everything. That's why I developed Crema. But I found there are lots of brains in the world, but not much heart. Brains won't make you happy. Heart makes you happy. Helping people makes you happy, and that can manifest itself in ways you never imagined."

On the saucer sat a sugar cube stenciled with a blue parrot. Sammi picked up the cube, looked at it from every angle and then put it on her tongue. She took a sip of cappuccino and held it in her mouth as the sugar dissolved. She began to feel the rush immediately, the tingling in the back of her neck, the effervescence in her blood and the heat, as though a bright light had been shone on the top of her head. She trembled a little as a chill ran up and down her spine.

"You should go home now and rest. There are two more doses, to be had at weekly intervals." He put his hand on Sammi's shoulder. "Come back as often as you like, just for fun. You have a pass to the back room."

"Thank you," Sammi said. She gathered her things and left the café. Jean and JG followed her out with their eyes. They were a little concerned with Einstein's choice.

"You're sure she's the one," JG said. "A lot's riding on this."

"Trust me," replied Einstein, scratching his cheek with a toe. "Dollface will do just fine. She found us by following those obscure crumbs on the site and she's hungry for it. Once she's had the full dose, everything will be all right."

"Creating the website was a stroke of genius," Jean said. "Although doing all that blogging is a pain in the ass."

"Thank you," Einstein replied. "It was one of my better ideas. You won't need to blog much longer. We already have quite a following and the site visitors will take over the blogging eventually. We'll just need to pop in periodically, drop some clues so people can find us if they want to and stir the pot."

"And get ready to make another move. Our friends are sending up flares. Agent Greene is on his way," JG said with a sigh. "Too bad, I was enjoying this."

Two weeks later, Samantha was waiting as JG unlocked the café door. Inside it was warm and inviting, and she had spent every evening enjoying the company and the conversation.

"Samantha..." JG said with a grin. "The special, I presume?"

"Last time," she replied with a laugh. "Cappuccino, double double crema, please, Professor."

Samantha walked to the back room and sat at the Algonquin

table. Jean and Einstein had moved on, and she missed them. After placing her cup on the table, Samantha took the sugar cube. The effect of the serum was stronger than the previous two doses, or maybe she just opened up, mentally, emotionally and energetically. She drank the coffee and breathed rhythmically for a few minutes. Then everything settled down. She reached down into her bag, brought out a book and began to read.

There was a pause in the action at the bar and JG brought her another cappuccino.

"Bulgakov," he said, looking over her shoulder at the second hand copy of *The Master and Margherita*. "This is wonderful."

"Yes," Samantha replied, "but very complex. I'm not sure I'm getting all it has to offer, but I'm learning."

"I know you are," he said. "I'm really proud of your progress."

"Thanks," she smiled. "And I keep getting sidetracked with more spiritual reading. The energy work is particularly interesting. I may take a course."

"I told you brains weren't important without soul." JG grinned. "But now, I need your help. I have to leave soon."

A few days later, Agent Greene walked into the café, which was newly opened and empty. He walked over to the big bar and spoke to the young woman making cappuccino.

"I'm Special Agent Greene," he said, flashing his badge. "May I speak to the manager, please?"

"That's me," she said. He seemed puzzled.

"I'm looking for someone." He pushed a couple of photos of a younger Jean and JG across the bar.

"Aren't we all," she said.

"Have you seen these people?"

"Nope. What did they do?" She slid a cup of coffee across the bar to the agent.

"They're persons of interest in a case of mine." He ignored the coffee. "We have information that they were seen here."

"Don't know what to tell you," Samantha said.

"Where is Ryan, the owner?" he asked.

"The owner's name is Ronnie Dee," She grinned. "He's always travelling, leaves the grunt work to me." She wiped the bartop. "This is his baby."

"Nice place," Greene said grimly.

"It's a dump, but I like it," Samantha replied.

"Strange name, though."

"Ronnie had a coffee house in the sixties. This place is an homage to that one, the New Ron's, although the sign painter was spelling-challenged."

Greene nodded to himself, made a note in his BlackBerry, and sighed. He looked determined and frustrated.

"Thank you for your time." He left the bar abruptly.

Samantha shook her head. "New Ron's. Well, it's not a great story, but better than nothing."

She considered signing on to the website with her "Dollface" ID and updating Jean and JG about Greene's appearance. Then it hit her. "Oh, no." New Ronz. Neurons. Nerve cells. Brain cells.

"Einstein, you sonofabitch..."

RITUAL
by Heather Dick

BONG ! BONG ! BONG ! THE final echo resonates faintly then dies away. My eyes squeeze shut, my ears strain to hear every sound – the tick-tocking of Grandpa's Big Ben in the living room below me, and the whooshing of hot air suddenly exploding from the vents to warm the room. Then the deep rumbling of the furnace in the bowels of the basement, and the creaky moaning protests of the old plaster walls. Spirits, everywhere, envelope me. Huddled under the covers, my heart pounding, I gulp in air and wait; just a minute longer.

I cannot move, not until I am absolutely certain that everyone is asleep. So, I play a counting game in my head to pass the time. I count up to a hundred by two's and down by three's in a lulling, lilting, rhythm. When I come back down to one, I stop and listen again. This time only the whooshing air greets my ears. I let out my breath. Snap! Muffling the sound against my body, I flip on the pencil flashlight that I've been clutching in my fist under the duvet.

CREAK! FREEZE! Did someone turn a knob down the hall? Was that a door opening? I snap off my light, hold my breath, and wait, listening with the whole of my body, willing everyone to stay asleep. WHOOOOSH! MOOOOAAAAN! Silence. Relieved, I let out my breath, ease the tension in my shoulders and open my eyes. My room is shrouded in inky darkness but a soothing sliver of moonlight peeks out from under the edges of the window blind. Reassured, satisfied at last that I am alone, I inch back the duvet and click on my flashlight. Now our ritual, Grandma's and mine, begins.

Lovingly, I draw up my treasure from the warm depths of my bed

and rest it beside me. At first glance, it is nothing more than a battered, old shoe box pasted over with red paper that's curling up at the edges. Gold bells that once covered the cheery tissue have been caressed away over the years by sweaty palms and anxious fingers. The corners are battered and a crease runs the length of the lid. But to my eyes, and in my heart, this is a precious treasure, as beautiful as the day I made it.

I prop myself up with pillows, tenderly place the box on my lap and adjust the beam of the flashlight so that when I remove the lid it will illuminate the treasures inside. As I begin to swing up the lid, a flood of images and emotions sweeps over me. First, pride and joy as I paste on the last piece of delicate tissue followed by awe and then wonder at the way light dances across the glittery, golden bells. Suddenly my stomach lurches and a sick sense of despair hits me. I am eight again and standing in front of my mother who is seated at the kitchen table. Proudly, I offer her my box. She takes it, smiles dutifully at my childish gift and puts it heavily on the kitchen table before turning back to her cup of tea. Tears sting my adult eyes. Then, all at once, I sense Grandma's arms wrapping protectively around me. I shut my eyes and let her presence cradle me. As the tempest passes, her love, unconditional and unbending, fills every corner of my room. I draw her to me as I take in a long, deep breath.

Gingerly now, I raise the lid of the box. The beam of the flashlight, rock steady and strong, illuminates Grandma's treasures. Carefully, I lift out a delicate acorn ornament, Grandma's favourite. Paper thin, it is hand-painted in iridescent shades of lilac and jade. I hold it up by the red silk ribbon to let it spin in the light and splash rainbow reflections on the dusky walls and ceiling. Exquisite! The chubby glass Santa is hand-blown and almost weightless. In the shadows he looks dull but, when I hold him up, he comes alive. He winks at me and his cheeks glow rosy red. I laugh. He always makes me laugh. I will hang him where he'll catch the sunlight, for Grandma, and me too.

I decide to let the next treasure be a surprise. I close my eyes and reach into the box with my left hand. Not my right! Not my strong, sure hand, but my left, to upset my sense of equilibrium, to make me feel a little unsteady, a little vulnerable. With eyes closed, I reach into the box. My fingers glide over something downy soft and I draw out a tiny pink scarf, my first attempt at knitting! In a flash I'm nine again and sitting at the old wooden table in Grandma's kitchen. It's July, hot and muggy, and I'm pestering her as she knits Grandpa a new winter scarf.

"Come and sit here", she says drawing my chair close to hers. "Let me show you something magical." She puts short, fat needles in my hands then, fishes into her carpet bag and draws out a little ball of but-

tery soft, pink wool. Closing her big, strong hands over mine, she shows me how to cast on the first row of stitches. I'm awkward at first. I drop the needles. I drop the stitches. But every time, Grandma fixes it and encourages me to keep going. By tea time, I have knit a narrow, six-inch scarf that's just long enough for my Barbie. Grandma ties off the wool, weaves in the end with her big darning needle and pronounces my work 'beautiful.'

"You'll knit lovely things for your children someday," she declares. I roll my nine year-old eyes but I stick out my chest anyway.

So, all summer long that's how I learn to knit, sitting in the kitchen next to grandma, our heads bent over our needles, clicking, wrapping, pulling wool through and weaving magic with every stitch. I go on to more difficult patterns as the summer unwinds and I forget all about this scarf. But when we come back to Grandma's for Christmas that year, there it is, hanging from a red ribbon just below the star at the top of Grandma's tree.

"I love you, Grandma," I whisper now and put the scarf back in the box.

And so it goes for the next hour. Each ornament conjures up a memory, a dream, a hope, a laugh. Magic fills every corner of my room so that by the time Grandpa's clock bongs four, I am exhausted and joy filled. Unhurriedly, I ease out of bed to lovingly complete our ritual — Grandma's and mine. I suspend each ornament from a branch of the tiny potted fir tree that sits on the night stand. This is a living tree, my annual present to myself. There is no tinsel. There are no beads, no ribbons, no bright lights to mar the beauty of these precious treasures that Grandma saved for me.

When the last ornament has been hung, I close the box, tuck it safely away in the bottom drawer of my dresser, climb into bed and snap off the light. Our tree shimmers in the slivers of moonlight that escape the window blind and light up my room. I close my eyes, sigh and fall back asleep.

The day after New Year's, I will perform another annual ritual. But this time, I will be tucking each ornament safely away in my treasure box and then hiding it in my bottom drawer until next Christmas. And, in the spring, I will plant my little tree among the many others in the back yard, for Grandma and me.

CHAMPAGNE FOR A SPECIAL OCCASION
by Sally Dillon

SHE STOOD THERE IN her 5' 5", 130 pound frame staring out of the picturesque 50th floor office window, wearing her bright fuchsia silk suit with the short skirt above her knees. Underneath her jacket, she wore an off-white satin camisole with shoe string straps on her shoulders. Her long slim legs were acquired from long hours of rollerblading. She stood in her calibra leather high heels. Her honey blonde hair cut short in a stylish fashion. She had just put on some Crabtree Evelyn hand lotion (Summer Hill scent), which she had taken from her office desk drawer. Gloss coloured lipstick matched her suit. One would say she was very attractive at forty-two.

It was 5:00pm. on a warm Friday afternoon in June of 1981. All of the staff had left for the long week-end. The children under her care (all fourteen of them) along with their counsellors had been sent off to camp the day before, for ten days. She imagined the echo of the children's voices as they boarded the large greyhound bus headed for camp Point Pelee, Ontario.

"Goodbye Miss Crawford, see you in ten days," they had shouted. She felt relieved to see them go because she could spend Friday at her office doing her administrative work.

Her office was very quiet now; only the ticking of the clock on her desk could be heard. Her mind seemed to be in deep thought as she gazed out of her office window, high above the street level, at the sail boats on Lake Ontario.

She was happy in her job and now with a whole week to herself

with no immediate plans. It was June 23rd — a special day in her past. Twenty years ago she had married; fifteen years ago her mother buried; eleven years ago divorced; four years ago she graduated cum laude from college. What would happen in her life today? In the quietness she asked her higher power to grant her one wish that may be added to her present happiness. Her higher power never said "NO" to her, not once — "ONLY WAIT."

It was getting late. It was time for a celebration – but no one to celebrate with. Suddenly she thought of the bottle of champagne that she had kept in the refrigerator at the private kitchen attached to her office. It had been placed there only to be used on a very special occasion.

Startled by the ringing of her telephone, she picked up the receiver. The voice of the security guard downstairs advised her there was a gentleman to see her, asking for her by her middle name - MARCELLA. She thought to herself, 'this is part of my wish; there is only one person who knows me by my middle name, and who would dare to call me by this name.'

She gave permission. Within a few moments she heard a gentle knock on her locked office door. She looked through the peep hole of the door and there he was. She recognized the Irish eyes immediately.

She opened the door and instantly recognized the smile that was embedded in her mind. Was her secret wish actually happening? She invited him to enter and locked the door behind her. It had been twenty years since she had seen him.

"Marcella, is this really you? How beautiful you still are after all of these years."

She knew he would use this name.

"Security downstairs told me that you were in your office, so I just took my chance and came up. I hope you don't mind. My name is Bill Zirell. You wrote to me some time ago to let me know about your graduation from College in the Social Work field. I still have the letter. May I sit down?"

"Of course."

"I read in the newspaper about your arranging for fourteen children to go to summer camp. I found your office address from the newspaper staff."

She had met him when she was twenty. They were employed at Eaton's Department Store. She was a sales clerk and he worked in the adjoining department part time while attending Dental College a few blocks away from Eaton's. They often met on their coffee breaks. She admired everything about him, and fell in love with him, instantly.

Though he was attracted to her too, he could not afford to take her out on an expensive date on his small salary. He asked her to go to a restaurant with him and then for a drive in his blue 1958 Ford convertible. She happily accepted.

The day arrived for her special date with Bill. She had purchased a special mauve silk dress with a full skirt and starched net crinoline underneath. Her slim waist was expressed in the tightness of the dress from the waist up and over her breasts. She felt like a princess. Her honey blonde hair was longer then, and her fluffy curls swayed in the soft breeze as the open top car moved along the highway on a hot June evening.

After a delicious dinner at a modest restaurant, they drove to Scarborough Bluffs. She remembered the beautiful view she saw of the City from the top of those cliffs. After Bill parked the car he looked at her like a prince and suddenly their lips met in a warm kiss. She had never been kissed like that before, but she had often dreamed of this moment. She imagined that he was her Prince and that she was his Princess. It was June 23rd 1961.

Unfortunately fate did not allow this relationship to develop in the way each of them had expected it would. She was now twenty-one. ready for marriage and children. Bill had three more years to go before graduating from Dental College and was not prepared for marriage at that time.

She met another man who offered her marriage, financial security, a home, and children. She graciously accepted, but after having attained all of the above she found that she had made a mistake. After eleven years in a frustrating marriage of which two precious children emerged, she divorced her spouse and decided to live her life as a single parent. Now her children were grown up and living abroad. She remained single but she had never forgotten Bill.

Then today, suddenly, he just stood in her office before her. He looked like he had just stepped out of a modern male magazine, with his tanned face and hands, beige suit, and starched white shirt. He wore a Tiffany diamond tie clip on his soft brown tie with cufflinks to match standing out smartly on his shirt sleeve cuffs.

"Bill, of course, I did write you a note. I found your name in the Ontario Dental College Registry. I just felt compelled to write to you. When I have a strong feeling about something I just know I must do it. I felt, at that particular time in your life that you needed prayer and your name kept coming up in my mind. I hope you didn't mind receiving my letter."

The cleavage between her two small breasts was quite visible to his eyes as she leaned over to sit down in the chair beside him.

"Of course I didn't mind you writing to me. Though, I must admit, I was very surprised to hear from you after so many years. Yes, I did need prayer at that time. My Mom had just passed away and your letter was very comforting to me. Somehow I had forgotten how to pray. I felt God was speaking to me through your note. I came to see you today because I wanted to thank you personally. Perhaps you might call it fate."

Bill then told her that he had never married but spent most of his working hours in his dental practice and writing articles in various dental journals about his recent research in that particular field. He said that he had dated various women but just could not find one that would fit his desires as I had, when I was in his life.

"This calls for a special celebration," she said as she walked toward the small kitchen near her office desk.

"Would you like to assist me Bill?" she asked.

He arose and she handed him a nickel plated cork screw. She took the bottle of champagne out of the refrigerator and handed it to him to open. He poured the sparkling bubbly into each of the two glasses sitting on a tray she had set out on the counter. He was very careful not to spill any of it by professionally twirling the bottle after each glass had been three-quarter full. She carried the silver tray containing the two glasses of champagne and he carried the bottle outside to the small balcony where they were set on a small patio table. They raised their respective glasses and offered a toast to their friendship and future happiness whatever it may be. She smiled happily as she sipped her drink.

"You might say this is champagne for a special occasion," she said.

He heartily agreed.

They looked into each other's eyes. He very gently took her glass from her and set it down on the patio table, then placed his glass beside it. He then pulled her to him and kissed her ever so gently on the lips. The warm feelings brought on by that kiss were recalled by each of them as they remembered a warm summer evening in a blue convertible at Scarborough Bluffs many years ago when the sun set and the sky lit up in a beautiful array of colour.

After they had released each other he said, "Would you like to go for a ride in my car? Its' just such a lovely evening and I would love your company. Perhaps we could have dinner together."

"That sounds wonderful," she said.

She freshened up in her private bathroom just off of her office.

They drove to Scarborough Bluffs directly to the spot where they had parked so many years ago when they were both twenty one. He stopped the car and looked at her. She was surprised that he had remembered this particular spot. The sun was sinking slowly in the west and looked very beautiful showing an array of exotic colours on this cool summer evening. She immediately thought of the verse she had read on a plaque in the Christian Book Store:

> If you love something, set it free,
> If it comes back, it is yours,
> If it does not, it never was.

At last her final wish had been granted. Bill had set her free and now she had returned to him just as he had always dreamed she would.

"You never left my heart or my dreams," he said. "I often thought of you."

Likewise, the memory of Bill had never left her heart.

Perhaps now it was the time for them to open a new chapter in each of their lives. They had parted and gone their separate ways, but their feelings for each other had not disappeared. They were put in escrow for another place — another time. NOW WAS THAT TIME.

They went to dinner at a downtown hotel where they danced on a balcony under the stars to music they knew many years ago.

INCORRIGIBLE
by Michael Robert Dyet

HUCK STOPPED TO REST halfway on his trek back from the barn to let the pain in his leg subside. The pain came in waves, of late, each one seeming to crest higher than the one before. He squinted to look up at the sun. Coming on to two o'clock, he judged.

Sure as God made little green apples he had forgotten something. There was a buzz in his memory that would not let up. Truth be told, he couldn't remember why he had gone to the barn in the first place, he reluctantly admitted to himself. So it wasn't likely he could put his finger on what he had left behind.

"What the hell?"

There was something inside the hollow fence post he was leaning on. He reached inside and pulled it out.

"My fence pliers?... Right, that's where I kept them back when I was still working the farm. The boys thought it was flat out stupid. But I always knew where to find them."

He resumed the journey back to the house. The door to the shed was open. How many times had he told Vera to keep it shut to keep the coons out? Or was it Vera who kept telling him? Same difference either way, he decided.

Huck lit a cigar as he settled behind the wooden desk that balanced precariously on three legs. The pain flared again as he sank into his chair. Out of the corner of his eye he saw the mouse peer tentatively around a box. It surveyed the scene and seemed to take the measure of him. Satisfied that all was well, it skittered across the floor to the crackers

in their usual spot.

"Huckleberry, I've told you a thousand times, you shouldn't feed the mice."

Vera's voice startled him but resonated in his ears like a finely tuned bow string.

"I swear you make less noise than a feather in a wind storm. After 60 years you'd think I'd hear you coming."

"Don't go changing the subject on me. I'm wise to your wily ways."

"Ever seen one in the house? No, because they know this is where the food is. There's a method in my madness. And for the love of Lucifer, for 60 years you've called me Huck. Now out of the blessed blue I'm Huckleberry?"

"Time was you'd be tickled pink if I called you that."

"Well, no more. I'm Huck and leave it at that."

"You'll always be Huckleberry to me."

"Have it your way. I'm not of a mind to argue," he relented, resisting the fond smile that tugged at the corners of his mouth.

"Are you of a mind to clean up this shed? Every newspaper that came into this place in the last ten years is still here. What will people think?"

Huck scanned the confines of the shed. Small motors of every size, shape and make rested on stacks of yellowing newspapers. A path, barely wide enough to navigate, wound from the shed door to the desk which was littered with spare parts.

"You think I don't know what people say? Crazy, old motor man. Couple bricks short of a load. I don't give a good goddamn. Nobody but you ever understood me, Vera. I expect that's not likely to change."

"Huckleberry, what am I going to do with you? I won't be around forever, you know."

Huck's brow furrowed. His bad left eye, on the side where the cow kicked him many years back, drooped half shut.

"You're always talking that way. But you're too stubborn by half to give up the ghost."

The sound of a pick-up truck, navigating the potholes that punctuated the long, gravel lane in from the road, blew in through the hole in the window.

"There's a customer for you. Let them haggle for once. They won't buy unless you do."

"My price is my price. They buy or they don't. It's all the same to me."

"Incorrigible. You're perfectly incorrigible."

The shed door opened with a screech like a startled cat.

"Good afternoon. Mr. Fryman?"

A barely perceptible nod was the only reply.

"Mr. Fryman, I'm Jack Willis – the new Chief of the Volunteer Fire Department. Can I call you Huck?"

"No."

Unprepared for such a dubious welcome, the fire chief paused to reconsider his tack.

Mr. Fryman, I think you know why I'm here. You've had warnings before and a citation if I'm not mistaken. You've got to clean up this shed. All these old motors lying around... I could smell the gas before I opened the door. This place is a fire trap."

"It's my place. I keep it how I want. It's no business of yours."

"It *is* my business. It's my responsibility to ensure your safety."

Huck's eyes narrowed. The legs of his chair creaked as he leaned harder into them.

"Get out of my place, you piss ass."

"Mr. Fryman, I can come back with the police if you don't cooperate."

Huck reached for the shotgun he kept under the desk. He leveled it at the intruder and closed his bad eye to sight down the barrel.

"Get the hell out of my place before I blow a hole in your holier-than-thou ass."

The fire chief backpedaled down the narrow aisle.

"Jesus Mary, they told me you were odd. But this is way past eccentric."

"Don't come back. Next time I'll shoot you on sight."

Huck watched through the hole in the window as the fire chief's pick-up went bouncing up the lane. He ground his cigar butt into the dirt floor with the heel of his good leg and lit a new one.

Jack Willis? He turned the name over in his mind groping for a connection. Had to be Buck Willis' boy, he decided. Was old Buck still around? Most likely not with his bad heart. No one that he grew up with was still above ground.

"Buck'll be rolling over in his grave with you pointing that old relic at his son."

"I'll be rolling over in *my* grave if you don't stop sneaking up on me. Lord woman, make some noise already – especially when I'm holding a shotgun."

"Is the confounded thing even loaded?"

"Damn right it's loaded. And I'll point it anyone I damn well please."

"And when they come for you with a posse?"

"Let 'em come. Piss asses every one of them. Not a full set of balls between 'em."

"You promised me, Huckleberry. A year ago to this very day, you promised me you'd stay out of trouble."

"I don't go looking for it. But if it finds me, that's no fault of mine."

"Trouble finds people who want to be found. You promised me, Huckleberry."

"Alright, alright. Enough said. Let me be for a bit. I still have work to do."

Huck picked up the motor on the desk and began to disassemble it. His gnarled fingers fumbled over the small parts, searching for a dexterity which time had stolen from them. Contentment softened his perpetual scowl.

An hour and a half passed in this fashion. From time to time, he rummaged for spare parts on the desk, or in wooden crates on a shelf behind him. An uncharacteristic patience guided his movements, as if the ramshackle shed was a sanctuary where time held no sway.

At length another vehicle sounded in the lane kicking up a dust cloud behind it. Huck frowned at the interruption. He stood to peer out the window. A jolt of pain ricocheted up his leg which gave way under him. He toppled into the chair with a mumbled curse.

"It's Kevin, Huckleberry. Now you be nice. He's the only one of our three that still comes to visit."

"In that damn Japanese car. Why he can't buy what's made here I don't know."

"Kevin says they're built right here in Canada now."

"Still foreign to me."

"Be nice. Send him in to see me before he goes."

The door to the shed creaked open. Huck crossed his arms and hunkered down in his chair.

"I swear, every time I come here this damn aisle gets narrower. Do you ever sell any of these, dad?"

"You looking to buy?"

Another wave of pain shot up Huck's leg all the way from the ankle to the hip this time. He closed his eyes to fight it off.

"That leg gets worse every time I see you. I don't suppose you'd let me take you to the doctor?"

"I've made it through 80 years without seeing a doctor. I'm not about to start now."

"You're 85, dad. You don't even know how old you are."

"You come all the way out here to tell me my memory is bad? I could have saved you the trouble."

"Jack Willis called me. He said you pointed a shotgun at him. You can't do stuff like that, dad."

"Why the hell not? It's my place."

"You just can't. There are laws and they apply to you just like everyone else." Kevin's eyes swept the shed again. "This has to end, dad. Enough is enough."

"My place. My rules."

"No, I'm not taking that crap anymore. I have your power of attorney, dad. Don't make me use it."

"Power what?"

"Power of attorney. It means I can make your decisions for you."

"The hell you can."

"What do I have to do to get through to you? You can't be on your own anymore."

Huck took another long puff on his cigar and fixed his stare on the wall behind Kevin.

"For Christ's sake, dad, put that cigar out. One spark and this whole place will go up."

"Ain't happened yet. I expect no one will much care if it does."

"You're not leaving me any choice. I'll do what I have to do. I'm the only one of your sons who still cares enough to do it."

Huck shifted his gaze to the ceiling. Kevin shook his head and started for the door.

"Go in and see your mother before you go. She'll blame me if you don't."

Kevin stopped in his tracks. Sadness ebbed from his eyes as he turned to face Huck again.

"Mom's gone, dad. She died a year ago. You know that. You didn't say a word for a month after the funeral. She's gone, dad."

Consternation leaked from Huck's eyes and spread across his grizzled face. Snatches of memory flashed like heat lightening; a hospital room in sickly white; a rattling breath, another, and then silence; a church half full of grim-faced mourners.

Huck willed his memory's eye to close. He picked up the motor on the desk in front of him and hurled it in Kevin's general direction.

"Goddamn it, dad!" Kevin ducked away from the missile. "You're

incorrigible. There's no talking to you anymore. Say goodbye to this place. The next time I come it'll be to take you to a nursing home where you belong."

Kevin stalked through the shed door leaving Huck in a vacuum of silence. Huck waited for Vera's voice to fill it. The silence grew thunderous as he waited and waited for the only thing he had left in this world.

"Huckleberry, my sweet, incorrigible Huckleberry. Come be with me."

A weight fell from Huck's shoulders as his heart rose to the long awaited invitation. He pulled the whiskey bottle down from the shelf behind him, took a long swig, then another and several more until the bottle was dry.

He waited patiently for the fog to descend to blur his senses and dull the pain. When his eyes were heavy and he could not hold them open any longer, he picked up the cigar butt from the table and flipped it onto the newspaper pile beside him.

A thin wisp of smoke rose from the newspapers and spiraled gracefully toward heaven. Huck's eyes closed as the peace of love everlasting lulled him to sleep.

THE ENCOUNTER
by Fran Edelstein

SHE STUDIED THE RECLINING form before her and worried about her surging restlessness, rousing her to soar one moment, leaving her to weep the next. For what purpose had He selected her above all His other handiwork on this sixth day? As the wind clothed her with its caress, she gloried in His creation of her, but questioned what use she would be to Him....

Unaware of His scrutiny, she was startled by the stern quality of His voice.

"Why are you questioning; why are you not content to simply have faith?"

How could she explain herself?

"I cannot bask solely in Your accomplishments. You have made me a free creature. I must find my own purpose." A cool wind bent the surrounding grasses as she attempted to sort out her puzzlement. "What is the reason for me?"

"Look into My eyes," He commanded, "and see in their depth, images of eras to come. This present will form a future that will either extol or ravage its past."

"Then I should find my place in it," she said, not entirely convinced that she wished to be involved. Her wisdom warned her that it was He who created, but she who must foresee.

In a nearby glade some crickets mocked her with their importance. Stubbornly, though with fear, she awaited His answer as she traced a finger along a caterpillar's thick fuzz and watched it wind its way around her wrist. He rose and stroked a growing smile.

"I see I'm going to have trouble with you."

"If I am here to make a difference, trouble might be part of it."

He waved away her sententiousness in favor of His next decision. Warning others that it was solely for her use, He offered her a box of color and a brush. "Paint," He commanded, not unkindly.

She accepted the gift that came to her directly from Him with instructions to add the crowning glory to the savage beauty of the planet.

So when churning seas, in their state of uncertainty, broke over rocky shores, she capped them with silver. Calm waters reflected the heavens, and horizons floated in pastels. With her brush she added gold to the sunrise, dabbed it with lavender and took away the grey. As the earth warmed beneath her feet, she anointed the flowers blooming brilliantly at her touch. Groves of trees became filaments of green. Purple and bronze spilled down the mountainsides. All life responded to the sweep of her brush.

"You have done well," He praised. "My world, and your artistry, form a magnificent blend."

"As vistas widen, all is lovely to behold, but they do not have the depth I crave," she struggled. "An artist must do more than beautify what exists: she must create new dimension, depth and truth to allow more and more revelations. Because there is no past, this moment will need to launch all meaning to be found," she breathed. "And we've got to get it right, for this cannot be all there is...."

He thought his work was finished. He looked forward to his rest. And now she'd given Him more to ponder. Sensing His agitation, all the wary wildlife, alert to the slightest signs of discord, scurried, slithered, dove, ran or flew from the clearing. "Oh, go paint another mountain!" He rumbled across the plains and marshlands.

Her anger rose. Lightning flashed against a darkening sky; huge pellets of rain lashed at the earth, unleashed by a crashing volley of thunder.

Having said that, she settled down. A frog jumped. She comforted it. "You, too, have woes, though you're such a little creature. You, also, are confronted with how to meet them." It's eyes rolled in huge sockets. It responded with a throaty croak. "But what a noise you make!" . *Sound.* Resonance. The caw of the crow, rumble of the dinosaur, cattle lowing, elephants trumpeting... such stirring cadences of Life! She hated to ask another question, but were they meant to respond to one another or only to her will?

He called upon an eagle. With a spread of its wings and a screech,

it soared, then swooped off. "Right," she acknowledged. "Art and beauty can indeed exist on their own. On the other hand, if they are to be seen, heard, appreciated or directed, art requires others."

And so, the two Partners in Creation joined hands. In their dance, they outpaced the wind, sailed over swamps, deserts and wilderness, where hundreds of species awaited them, barking, mewing, cackling, roaring, each with its own fugue.

A moose bellowed; a bear growled and a pack of wolves cautioned with their howling. The laughter of hyenas allowed a moment for the coo of a dove. As they swung to higher ground, the hoot of an owl and the rasp of a hawk accompanied them. Communicating with all creatures, listening as well as responding, she gifted them with emotion, taught them how to vary their tones to accommodate it, and how to project their individuality with pride.

"Sounds," she explained in her rapture. "Now that they contain emotion, are not just noise, but strains that communicate levels of distress or delight, displeasure or satisfaction, hostility or welcome... made dramatic by intensity, such as the rumble of a herd, the wail of a sandstorm or the crash of thunder. Everything that moves with its own purpose, or in response to that of another, tells a story with its sound. I shall gather these and give to this planet my miracle to the ear. Communication."

When she finally set down beside Him, having created a myriad of frequencies, she had a plan. She would change the climate in the creation of seasons, with heat and sun, snow and ice, and commission the groundhog to lend merriment with its predictions.

She reached the edge of a lake, and with eager fingers felt beneath twigs, leaves and branches. An iguana jumped. She grasped at it, and with a whisper in its ear, carried it to the greenest marshland. It raised its voice, striking its sound into one glorious "Thank you!"

"Where I place each form of Life must be compatible with its nesting place and where it must thrive in order to endure," she explained.

By now, He was frankly impressed. "Such places must then be protected by a higher, more intelligent form of Life."

There was something new in the way He looked at her, which convinced her that together they would be able to enhance this planet, a round planet with no starting place, no finish line, no favored spot. They chose to call it Earth.

A thousand flamingos glided to the ground; their flapping providing huge applause.

"We will call this 'The Beginning'," He proclaimed in a resounding voice. "Earth will take this moment to infinity. Sound, place, color, life...

You will bring them together as though they are your children, and you their mother. No attempt by man will ever duplicate what you do, though it may come close."

"Children? Man?" The words had no meaning for her.

"Man and woman... male and female. The highest of my creations. At this moment, they *are*. And their children *will be*." In tribute, He gazed upon the Earth and lifted his mighty voice. "You shall be known as Nature, the Mother of it all!"

He was her challenge, and He would be her refuge. She loved His approval, feared His anger, yet knew she could never survive His indifference. His commands inspired her vitals – her imagination, courage, and skills. She sighed, content with what her eyes saw and what her ears heard.

The day slipped calmly toward dusk. As she dangled her fingers in the cool waters of a pool, a fish looped with waves that slapped at her wrist. She studied her reflections... so many of them, frowning, pouting, staring, narrowing and widening. Images drooped, slanted or blinked, and in them she looked not at all like herself. Laughter rippled from her belly. When the waves smoothed out, she tried to bring the images back. But the waters had stilled.

She thought about that.

Beside her a rodent twisted its nose with curiosity and a young deer drank thirstily. Enticed by what was going on, squirrels, chipmunks, ground hogs and skunks scurried to the water's edge. Disturbing countless worms and insects, she lifted a rock and tossed it into a clump of lily pads to stir the placid surface of the pond. "See? You have a dozen shapes!" she exclaimed to the animals. "Now you must use such reflections to make-believe!"

"Why would you suggest that?" He asked, disturbed once again by her restlessness.

"Pretending brings laughter and change of spirit," Nature answered. " For example, if sadness invades, it shouldn't be wrong to pretend happiness... to change a mood."

Sensing an unusual storm, a snail, wishing it were somewhere else, retreated into its protective shell. This time, it was the Maker's thunder that ran among the foothills. "For the sake of You and Me, this Earth, and all the Heavens I have created, we are approaching a day of rest, and I am decidedly in need of it!"

It was then that Mother Nature anticipated that her sex would be unable to rest for any lengthy time. Female would ceaselessly be forming ideas, reacting and soliloquizing, often for lengthy durations. Decisions would, in many ways be instinctual and based on several senses; differ-

ent from the concentrated toil of male.

She offered no comment.

So He lengthened His protest. "I have attempted to create an honest world. How might it be protected from the deceit that accompanies 'pretend'?"

Mother Nature considered this, but only for a moment.

"It will not be," she announced. " Even the jaguar acts out its own sly drama for survival. Attempts to manipulate will be found in human nature as well - as part of the drama of living." She brightened. "All life must trust *Your* role and *Yours alone*, to judge truth for itself; for what is true for the hawk is not so for the chicken. Apart from deceit, it shouldn't be difficult to detect the kind of pretense enjoyed for its own entertaining sake."

Entertaining? He supposed that he could live with that, and might concede after some deliberation, the importance of an aspect of life He hadn't considered. Moments earlier He had writhed with wrath; but her reasoning had changed that. "I will permit this... thing called 'pretend', but only if others can be made aware of it."

She begged Him to reconsider. "What of the element of surprise?"

"I expect we will need to deal with that on a few levels," He mumbled. "Right now, in order to identify this mimicry, we must give it a name." He surveyed the arena surrounded by forest, the boughs overhead and the animals at their feet awaiting the verdict that would very much influence the existence of every form of life.

"A type of Art, I suppose." He stroked his chin. "The *Performing* Arts," He declared with satisfaction.

As if to prove her talent, Mother Nature embarked on a campaign using her animals as willing actors. One moment she wore a crown of moss and a gown of flowers to waltz with the birds and insects on her own flight of fancy. The next moment she swung from a tree, surprising the chimpanzees with sounds for them to assume, which they did with their natural talent for mimicry. With poise, she danced in a field of corn to entice small animals to scurry about and trouble one another.

She toyed with moods and identities as she pleased.

"All you do is play-act," He remonstrated as the first stars began to show themselves and finally there would come time to rest.

"Steps in making changes, meeting challenges, forming dreams and having them come true, will require effort. Play-acting will involve wishing and finding a way... for no wish will be an impossibility; once captured, it will likely be attained." Mother Nature examined the stars. "Star-

dom. A good word for those so enjoying the process, enabling the use of art, music, language and imagination. It is the very heart of *my* occupation; it's what *I* need to be happy."

"All things considered, your work has many times made this day, uh... interesting," He had to admit.

"Then please use of it what You will... to lend this planet honest versatility," she urged, "so that my function does not provide only for indolent past-times."

He nodded His agreement while extracting her promise, "Do not ever cease what you are doing. And now, let us welcome Man and Woman, whom I have created in Our image. The world cannot exist, function nor endure without their higher capabilities."

"I truly believe," she crooned. "for that higher intelligence, contrasts and levels will present themselves, to provide one's gauge for making decisions based upon wisdom or foolishness, with the ability to detect both and choose either one."

From His lips she heard, "I love you." Simply stated... yet surprisingly profound.

This time, she no longer wished to soar. The desire to touch Him, if only with her fingertips, was stronger.

"What mood is this?" she trembled.

"That which will make the Earth expand; a joyful exchange between beings that must be honored and nourished by giving it away. It will simply be called, Love. And while Love exists it shall be the crowning of all My intentions and manifestations. All will reach for it. It will signify the meaning of Life."

She looked puzzled but trusting. "You will see," He promised.

She did. And she was replete with joy.

"But Earth will not be a place to languish," He decreed. "Reward will be found in achievement. Let them leave who will not *work*!"

Earth had to be the perfect planet... with Man, Woman and Love... art, music, emotions, and all living things... working.

"Earth-shattering!" He said.

"With everything beautiful and everything possible!" After some hesitation, Mother Nature altered her statement. "*But not everything easy.*"

"Poets will inscribe their anthems to all of this," They chanted together. "Let's commit!"

And that's how Life began and The Arts were born,
On the day that God embraced Mother Nature.

GROWING MENACE
by Jude Paul Fernandes

THE MOVING VAN SCREECHED to a precipitous halt outside an old bungalow with a little balcao. Its signage said, "Margao Movers and Packers" with the line drawing of two hefty men with muscular forearms, carrying what appeared to be a cupboard. At the back of the truck, piled up to the very roof was an assortment of merchandise, artifacts, furniture and a variety of plants of different hues, shapes and sizes. There were so many plants that any passer-by would have mistaken it for the opening of a new nursery in Borda, the little village in Salcette.

A white-haired elderly lady, spectacles perched precariously on her nose, peered out of a window fringed with lace and brocade curtains and motioned to the workmen to carry everything indoors. Ironically, the workmen were the very antithesis of the picture on the van. They were thin and scrawny. But that belied their cardboard Tarzan appearances for in no time at all they were able to haul every piece of furniture, and every plant from the van, into the house. And, they also put everything in place. The grand table next to the piano, the century-old carved cupboard next to the antique Grandfather clock.

The ornate picture of the Holy Family, Jesus, Mary and St. Joseph, placed near the wooden altar in the living room; and the plants, her dear plants, all forty of them, were given a warm welcome in the spacious backyard.

As soon as the workmen left, the petite lady sat on her favourite leather armchair and languidly sipped a cup of freshly brewed tea that had the aroma of roses. Her only son, in his late thirties, had recently

left Goa to live in Toronto, leaving her his furniture and the plants to look after.

She treated the plants like her very own children. On some days, she would even talk to them as though they could listen and reciprocate. Her neighbours called her "Pixen, silly old woman," behind her back, but, the plants bloomed, swayed, and flourished. Not a leaf was brown, and not a single one ever died under her care; except for the Chinese bamboo shoots that sulked and felt jealous when she paid more attention to the Aloe Vera and eventually decided to give up on life.

As she buried the plant outside, her neighbour Mr. D'mello laughed out loud. Not that she minded, for, if Mrs. Aplonia D'souza loved anything to a fault, it was her plants. She treated them with a sentiment that most people would have reserved for their dearly beloved. Somehow, the plants seemed to understand her affection, and on touch, they nuzzled her. Even dying creepers and foliage would spring back to life under her green fingers.

Dusk was beginning to fall, and from where she sat, she noticed something lying on the verandah. She stood up with difficulty, ignoring the shooting pain on her lower limbs from the arthritis, limped towards the object and recoiled with horror at the sight of a torn pigs ear... the blood still fresh on the pinkish edges.

Unobserved, peeping from behind his drapes, her neighbour from next door, Manuel D'mello, gave a malicious chuckle of delight. On his kitchen table lay the fresh carcass of a pig, the laceration around its throat slowly beginning to congeal, the fresh basin of blood alongside its corpse to be used for the Sorpatel, to intensify the flavor of the curry.

Mrs. D'souza was busy for the next few days. She requested her Parish priest to lend her the services of the church gardener, a wizened man to help her loosen the mud; and barely two weeks later, the transformation was complete.

The lady surveyed her masterwork with satisfaction; an adder's fern nestled against the chrysanthemum, the asphodel surrounded the cactus, a young fir tree leaned against a sturdy twig, keeping it propped up until its roots grew big and supportive. All the plants swayed in the light summer breeze... burning bush, holly fern, and hart's tongue. Mrs. D'souza' heart gladdened on seeing them rustling and swaying in the wind. She sat at her piano and began to play a lovely Goan mando and to sing "Tambdey Rosa..."

The next day, at the break of dawn, she stood on the fringe of her garden, shocked and hurt at the damage. Her cherished plants lay still, torn apart, mangled, uprooted from the soil she had planted them

a couple of weeks ago. Tears trickled down the creases in her face, and then on to her ponderous breasts. She tried to bend low to pick up the shredded stems, as if to piece them together and create an off-shoot. To graft a tree that could perhaps take new root. Sadly, they were past repair.

These dastardly acts continued day after day. She would either find the plants stamped upon or worse, stolen. Some malevolent person out there was spitefully enjoying her sorrow at the bereavement of her prized plants. Her only strong support came from her next door neighbour, the portly Mr. Manuel D'mello, who would invariably land up at her doorstep to offer false sympathy.

"Oh, you poor thing," he gushed, small beady eyes glinting unkindly, large nostrils quivering in delight and no sooner did she turn around to make him a cup of tea, he scratched the veneer of her table with the sharp edge of his door key.

Mr. D'mello, filled with angst and a deep resentment against humanity, for absolutely no reason at all, had made his main aim in life to be uncouth and unkind to anybody he met. Age, instead of mellowing him, had made him arrogant, sly, and conniving. To your friendly neighbourhood psychiatrist, he was dangerously tethering between sanity and insanity. Had the doctor delved into his past, he would have also found out that Manuel's mother had several nervous breakdowns in her life, for apparently no reason at all. Had the kind doctor hypnotized Manuel, back into his childhood, he would've found out that Manuel had drowned the family cat, Kitty, in the twenty foot deep well at the back of their home, after setting her tail on fire, causing his mother to have her third nervous breakdown.

But to our kind and generous Aplonia, he appeared to be anything but that. He is gentle and lonely, is what she thought as she watched him slurp the tea with an excruciating noise, which, fortunately she was nearly stone deaf to hear. While leaving, Mr. D'mello remarked, *"Maybe you need to get yourself a bulldog"* and laughed unkindly at her alarmed expression, as he knew that she feared dogs.

The next day as Mrs. D'souza stepped out to gather some cilantro to garnish her Masala omlette, she was horrified to see her beloved fir tree missing. Later while reciting her morning prayers, she invoked God to save her nascent tree from being destroyed. Then lips pursed firmly, refusing to let herself cry, she set out to buy the day's groceries. She looked forward to buying some large crabs to make some coconut curry and treat herself to fried mackerels plumped up with *raichaddo masala*, tied up with a string and shallow fried.

As always, the market place was hot and humid and reeked with the annoying stench of rotting fish heads that the fisherman's wives, who sold the fish, carelessly threw aside into the gutter clogged with plastic. She opened her purse and took out her embroidered kerchief to mop her brow. She sprayed a liberal amount of the Charlie fragrance, that her cousin Philomena had brought her from the Middle-East, into the air and she bravely ventured into the place. The fish sellers spotted her and implored loudly,

"Bai, Ing Yo Go, Bai!!! Baieee!!! Madam come here."

As she made her way towards her regular fisher-woman, the only one whom she could haggle with, she noticed the gametophytes-like plant that a native woman was trying to sell. The dark-skinned, almost charcoal coloured woman looked like an outsider and Mrs. D'souza's gaze once again fell on the thickset blackish-green plant. About four feet tall, it had a huge pink flower at the top, and viewed from the side, it resembled the reddish-pink gums of a toothless geriatric.

Mesmerized by the beauty of the exotic plant, she moved closer and touched its silky petals. It was uncanny, but at that moment the plant almost moved and if it were a kitten it would've purred, as if it had found favour with her delicate touch. And at that moment, time stood still as a bond developed between mother and nature, blood and chlorophyll.

While her favourite fishmonger called to her loudly over the din of the market, Mrs. D'souza was way too busy admiring the plant; for her it was love at first sight. She bargained furiously for the next few minutes with the native woman. Finally, they arrived at an agreeable price: two hundred and fifty rupees.

The native woman carried her prized possession and placed it on the seat of a rickshaw. Aplonia looked lovingly at the new acquisition, the huge leaf of the plant resting against her hand, like it held hers, as the three-wheeled rickshaw sputtered to life. It may have been a bumpy ride home, but the lovers didn't notice a thing.

On arrival, she planted it in exactly the same spot of her dear departed fir tree. The roots of the unknown species of plant welcomed the chocolate colour, mildly stinking soil; like it was meant to be in that spot forever. Entranced by her new acquisition, Mrs. D'souza stood there transfixed, admiring its unique beauty. Unknown to her, a set of hooded eyes peered from the slits of a curtain.

She found it difficult to sleep that night. Afraid that her new plant would be stolen, or worse still, destroyed, she kept awake for almost half the night. But as the moon crept into the silver trellis of the clouds, at 3:00a.m. to be exact, she drifted into sleep. In minutes, she was snoring,

her dentures lightly clattering against her jaws.

Stealthy footfalls broke the still of the night, followed by the muffled sounds of a man's scream of fear and terror. As if to silence the human anguish, a squish-squash monotonous drone could be heard, such as that of a gluttonous python, who chancing upon a meal after months of starvation, was pulverizing it to death.

The first beams of glorious sun fell upon Mrs. D'souza's face, waking her up. Her plant's safety was the first thing that dawned on her mind and she rushed to the window as fast as her age would permit. Straining her bleary eyes to peer out against the blinding rays of the sun, she spotted it, resplendent in the brilliance of the morning light. She unlocked her back door and walked towards the plant.

Peering at it from close quarters, she noticed that the flower was now red and the plant seemed more corpulent than ever... and hey, what were those purple things lying face down in the mud?

On closer inspection, she realized they were Mr. D'mello's bedroom slippers. How dare he throw slippers at her plant, how dare he! Now irritated, she decided she would openly show her displeasure the next time he came over to visit her. As she walked back indoors, her favourite plant could no longer contain itself and burped loudly in quick succession.

GETTING HOME TO MY GUY
by Frances Frommer

I WAS FRANTIC TO get home to Toronto, seething with impatience to speed along the QEW Highway and zoom up Yonge Street to my apartment. A snowstorm was predicted for early in the evening. I hoped to be home before it started. My neighbor, Nelly, was waiting to give me her keys and instructions for taking care of her apartment, before taking the train to Montreal. My friend, Linda, was arriving later in the evening from Victoria. Most important was the fact that my guy was waiting for me.

I remembered when we first met. It was love at first sight. When I looked into his green eyes that sparkled like emeralds, I was hooked. My guy is an attentive listener, loves to cuddle and is always there for me.

I had missed him as I spent the last three days at a conference on "Coping with Change in the Workplace" at Hamilton Public Library. I worked there and was sent to acquire techniques to help the library staff to deal with new computer systems. When the last meeting ended, I stumbled from the windowless room. The final session on relaxation techniques had lasted for three hours. I felt rather tense during the last hour. When I got out of my chair, my legs felt like Jell-O and my back was vibrating like a toothache. I was planning to return to my room at the Sheraton Hamilton Hotel, have a steaming hot shower, order a club sandwich and coffee and then jump into my car and drive home as quickly as possible.

However, when I stepped into the lobby of the library, I was startled by a view of enormous snowflakes and sparkling ice pellets pounding against the glass of the doors and windows facing York Boulevard. The howling wind sounded like white noise, simultaneously sinister and serene. The street looked both menacing and exquisitely beautiful. Cars

were sliding to the right and left as snow trucks were weaving around them to deposit salt on the roads. The sidewalks were covered with a blanket of pure white snow. Crowds of people huddled by the door, buttoning coats, winding scarves around their necks, and pulling on hats. Suddenly, there was an announcement over the loudspeaker, telling everyone that the library would be closing in fifteen minutes due to inclement weather.

I strolled through Jackson Square Mall to the Sheraton Hotel. When I arrived, there was a long line of grouchy people at the front desk inquiring about reservations for the night. The television in the lobby was turned to the weather channel. The reporter announced that a winter storm warning was in effect for the Niagara Region and the Greater Toronto Area. I took the elevator to the second floor and sank into the only vacant chair in the corner at the Tonic Lounge. Finally, the waitress came over.

"Sorry for the delay, but we're terribly busy due to the storm. What can I get for you?" she asked.

"Please, fix the weather," I requested. "Also, a strong cup of coffee would hit the spot. Any news about the weather?"

She said, "I can get you the coffee. I'm sorry that I can't meet your first request. I've heard that the storm is getting worse. All flights are cancelled out of Mount Hope. I recommend that you just relax and enjoy your stay here in Hamilton."

"My guy is expecting me at home," I told her.

"Lucky you. But he'd better be patient," she replied. "You can't rush about in this weather."

I sipped my coffee and wondered about my options. Should I leave my car and take a plane, if the airport was open? Could I depart immediately and drive right through, beat the worst of the snow, trusting that the salt trucks would be out in full force? Might I leave my car and hop on the express GO bus to Toronto? Would it be best to get the bus to Burlington, if it was running, and then catch the reliable GO train to Union Station? Was I stranded here overnight?

I paid for the coffee and left the waitress a tip of two dollars. She looked so weary as she constantly shuffled from table to table to meet customer demands. I went back to my hotel room, full of anxiety. I did one of the exercises on relaxation from the conference. I took 12 deep breaths and visualized myself in my living room, cuddling with my guy, surrounded by my pink satin cushions on my mauve velvet couch. I had missed snuggling with him in bed before falling asleep. Just thinking of his brilliant green eyes made me smile. I felt a bit more relaxed after this exercise and able to face the situation—me against the elements and my

burning desire to get home to my guy.

As an organized person who always likes to be in control, I decided to drive right through from Hamilton to Toronto. I knew that I could always stop in Oakville and get on the GO train to Union Station and then take the subway to Yonge and Eglinton if the roads were too treacherous.

However, when I went to check out, the clerk said, "I hope you know that there are warnings to stay off the roads unless it is an emergency."

I replied, "I'm an excellent driver and will just take it slow and easy." I was about to pay my bill when the reporter on channel 11 announced that the exit from York Boulevard to Highway 403 was closed, except for ambulances and buses.

I felt a loss of control in face of the violence of the elements—the howling wind, the noisy ice pellets and the enormous falling snowflakes. I was still determined to get home as soon as possible. After I returned to my room, I ordered coffee and carrot cake for comfort and strength. My diet could wait for another day; sugar was essential to lift my spirit. I started to telephone the GO station. After busy signals for fifteen minutes, a recorded message came on stating that there would be no bus or train service until tomorrow morning. I had to accept that I would be in Hamilton for the night. I admitted defeat. I immediately telephoned Nelly.

"Hello Nelly," I said. "I won't be home until to-morrow morning. How is the weather in Toronto?"

"Hi, Sandy. It's snowing buckets here. But, I'll still be leaving by train for Montreal. I can leave my keys and instructions for taking care of my apartment with the superintendent. Linda sent a telegram that she won't be arriving until to-morrow night."

"Good luck and have a safe trip. How is my guy?" I asked.

Nelly replied, "I just finished watering your plants and took in your mail. Your guy is just fine. He's sleeping now. Would you like me to wake him?"

"Oh no, don't disturb him."

Nelly added, "He's eating well and loved the chicken that you left for him."

"Thanks for checking up on him. You are a great neighbor."

I decided to take a brief stroll around Jackson Square before settling in for the night, glad to be inside a mall. It was tempting to have a donut at Tim Horton's, but I could not face the crowds. I browsed in Cole's Bookstore and bought a book by Woody Allen—*Without Feathers*, and a *Toronto Star* newspaper.

After I returned to my hotel room, I relaxed in a hot lavender-scented bubble bath. I called room service and ordered stir-fry chicken, hot rolls, chocolate cake and chamomile tea. I need extra food when I am under stress—especially bread and sweets. Following my meal, I read my Woody Allen book and had many laughs. Then, I fell into a deep sleep amidst four pillows, soft as a baby's cheek. I dreamed of sunshine, clear roads and my guy. I saw my arms around him as I expressed my deep gratitude for our loving bond.

When my wake-up call came at 11 a.m., I whooped with joy when the golden rays from the sun burst through the windows as I opened the drapes. King Street looked clear and traffic was moving well. I felt in control of my life again. I ordered a continental breakfast of coffee and croissants. I ate quickly, packed in ten minutes, checked out and was on my way within the hour.

I had to drive carefully and remained in the slow lane as a few flurries were still coating the highway in spots, like a light icing on a cake. I was returning home with a reverence for winter's power to stop all outdoor activities like walking or driving to the grocery store. I do not ski or skate and so do not welcome snow. Spewing salt from passing trucks gave me some peace of mind and I felt glad for human help in dealing with nature during this winter weather. Police cars appeared regularly. I stayed within the speed limit.

I chanted my winter mantra as I drove. *Dear God, please get me home safely to my guy*. I turned the radio to 91.1, Toronto's great jazz station, and was delighted that they were playing selections as a tribute to Chet Baker, one of my favorite musicians.

It took me three hours to get home. It was usually a trip of forty five minutes. I parked my car in the underground parking of my apartment building, grabbed my suitcase and ran to the elevator. I arrived at my floor, unlocked the door of my unit, and dropped my coat and purse on the floor in the hall. I felt exhausted from the stress of my trip, yet exhilarated to be back in my home. Nelly had left a huge bouquet of pink carnations on the kitchen table with a sign that said, "WELCOME HOME."

I shouted, "Home at last. Where are you, darling Tiger?"

Then, my guy appeared, walking slowly from the bedroom, slightly dopey from a nap. We gazed into each other's eyes. Each of us had a long drink of water, giving and receiving love with our eyes. When Tiger jumped onto my lap and began to purr, I knew that I had reached my desired destination. I stroked his silky fur and the stress of the last 24 hours evaporated. My guy and I relaxed on the couch for a long time.

GEM

by Marilyn Garshowitz

Gem sighed.

ONCE AGAIN THE WOMAN found herself bent and rolled up into herself — if not physically this time, certainly on mental, emotional, and spiritual levels. It was such a long and, for the most part, lonely journey. The event that had left her struggling with post-traumatic stress disorder had occurred so long ago. In all fairness it was many events and individuals that had left her devastated and beyond vulnerable. Truly her condition was compounded. Her mind, tortured and abused, had become somewhat dysfunctional. Her recovery was incredibly slow. And yet her battered soul contained an even greater essence than the brokenness. Gem really was precious strength as her name so implied. She had on several occasions been referred to as being sweet and strong. Such a combination! She was considered a survivor but in her books that was not a sufficient goal. Her natural disposition was vivacity and thus she should thrive; less was... well... less than alive.

She was far from thriving — indeed, she was barely surviving. Although, many probably did not realize how badly off her situation was. Gem often did such a good job at "faking it till you make it" and she worked hard.

Of course there were all these strengths and talents she possessed... and then there were her looks. It was not as if she was the most gorgeous. She certainly did not look like a model but she did have some nice qualities. Her eyes and smile were mentioned as being particularly

special and her legs were known to have stopped traffic. Yes, she did attract some attention.

It had not been uncommon for her to be stopped by passer-bys with such comments as "you have what it takes," "you're going to be rich" and "you look like Princess Diana." This latter comment voiced by many and reinforced by pictures of the two, showed the uncanny likeness.

Though her years were getting on, she did look at least ten years younger than the 46 years that was her true age. But it was true her youthfulness was seeping out of her. She really would need to do something to restore some of the lost exuberance. Losing twenty five pounds would likely help as well. It sure wouldn't hurt. Though she knew the solution would be somewhere beyond the physical realm.

Her greatest strengths went far beyond her looks though, and she still attracted some very strong and impressive individuals. There really was that certain 'je ne sais quoi' quality to her. Her intelligence and determination and passion were listed high among her attributes. But as her physical shape had altered over the years, this special quality of hers was fading too.

There was enormous frustration with her situation. It may have something to do with having so much potential and being so far away from actualizing it. The more the discrepancy between her actual position and where she might be, the greater the frustration. It was such a long tiresome road with little immediate gratification and she was weary.

Again she had found herself immersed in self-doubt about what was set before her to do. Her challenges were, seemingly, unrealistic expectations. Who was she to think she could champion such a cause? How could she do what was set before her to do? How could she do it NOW???

If she could not have achieved it when she was younger and void of the aches and pains, and more energetic, how would she possibly be able to do it now? Now that she had no money behind her...and that had been the case for such a long time. She had run out of her savings long ago and over-extended herself on credit cards and lines of credit. This was the way society had gone but intrinsically it was not her way. She was a saver by nature. Prior to the events she had been quite adept at handling her finances exceptionally well and had taken great efforts to make for a good life, but how illusive it all was for her! The loss of good life was made even more agonizing by having no loving partner and children. She had very little.

There was no house. No cottage or condo either. There was no shiny brand new car. There was neither a second-hand car nor even a

beat-up one. She really had to put some effort into not looking shabby and sometimes, unfortunately, she just missed the mark. Truly she knew how close she was to being homeless... again. If it hadn't been for her father coming back into her life and helping her out... he was buying her time. But she was running out of that.

Her father wasn't the richest of men who would be able to maintain his assistance with rent, bills and food indefinitely. He was helping out until she could make a living again. It had been a very long time since Gem could work and make any significant amount of money.

Recovering from the post-traumatic stress disorder was arduous and had made it impossible to work at times. It was certainly difficult to find a safe working environment for her to work a traditional job and, besides, most employers had biases against people like Gem. Furthermore it was more than plausible that she had been blacklisted.

Everything had always been done with struggle on some level, having left home years before in her early teens. She continued with studies giving great credit to education. She did so much right; how could her life be so wrong?

Such debt...how would she be able to repay?...how would she be able to make her life liveable?...how would she be able to do all that had to be done? How could she rebuild her life?

Focusing on these aspects...it all was much too overwhelming. Gem closed her eyes. A long drawn-out breath of air escaped her. She whispered "Help me, please."

And for a brief instant...Was that loud booming sound coming from the sky?... was that a flash of lightening illuminating the darkness?

She had written a book to save herself, and society, by educating others on the problem of bullying and misuse of power. It had devastated her life and threatened the well being of all mankind. There was something for her in finding her voice but more in her being heard. She needed to continue enlightening others about her past difficulties to prevent anyone else from experiencing similar problems. It would make her negative positive. She had so much to give. She knew there were steps to take to resolve the systemic problem of bullying.

The journey she was on, was her mission and it was very important. It was not finished. It was time to expand the work she did. It was time to make her business work. The help would be there. Take the steps.

Be brave!

A gay perspective from the top of the world
TOPPING MOUNT KILIMANJARO
by Jefferson Guzman

SIX MONTHS AGO, MY partner John announced that he and our friends, Elaine and her partner Barbara, wanted to go to Africa and climb Kilimanjaro. It was then that the importance of couples taking separate vacations from time to time became very clear.

I'm not a sporty fag. Camping on the side of a mountain for a week is not my idea of a vacation. But the man I love was heading off on an adventure, one from which he might not return. I was scared of going, but I was more afraid of letting the opportunity pass me by.

Kilimanjaro is the highest mountain in Africa and although you don't need specialized training or equipment to hike to the top at nineteen thousand, three hundred forty feet, less than seventy-five percent of those who attempt this feat, make it all the way. In fact, the mountain claims an average of thirty lives per year. So why exactly was I about to embark on such a challenging and dangerous trek? What else makes us act like fools? Love!

There was one element of this adventure that was right up my alley — shopping for a trekking wardrobe. As I crossed each item off my three-page list of clothing and gear, it became apparent that the only training I was going to cram into my busy schedule was climbing up the stairs to the second floor at Mountain Equipment Co-op.

We flew over Uhuru Peak en route to the beginning of our mountaineering adventure. At a cruising altitude of thirty thousand feet, we were closer to the summit than we would be when we touched down. We landed in Tanzania and made our way to the Marangu Hotel, the home

base for the company organizing our climb. I laid out my gear and matching mountain ensembles on the bed as instructed. Everything was inspected to ensure we had all we needed. We were briefed on the journey that would start the following morning.

It was a bumpy four-hour drive to Naremoru gate where we started the climb at an altitude of five thousand nine hundred feet. Our team of fourteen porters made quick work of unloading the truck. Our head guide, Valerian, led the way into the forest. Elaine, Barbara, and John had no problem keeping up with Valerian's brisk pace. I trailed behind and our two assistant guides, Michael and Gaspar, kept me company.

"Is John your father?" Michael asked. John is twenty years older than I am, so I've tackled this embarrassing question before. But this time I hesitated to tell the truth.

In 2004, Zanzibar increased penalties for gay sex acts. Zanzibar, a group of islands off the coast, is part of Tanzania but partially self-governing. At first the government was considering instituting penalties of up to twenty-five years for sex acts between men and seven years for sex acts between women. Our decision not to visit Zanzibar's beaches had been easy.

Since Zanzibar's economy relies heavily on tourism, activists called for a travel boycott in hopes that the government would reconsider adopting the penalties. The bill ultimately passed with adopted penalties set at five years for sex acts between individuals of the same sex - male or female — and seven years for same-sex couples living as spouses or celebrating a wedding ceremony. Still, many gay travel websites continue to advertise trips to Zanzibar.

In mainland Tanzania, the debate on same-sex marriage is now underway. Currently the sentence is fourteen years for sex acts between men. (The law makes no reference to women.) Same-sex couples risk attracting negative attention if they engage in public displays of affection.

"We're friends," I answered.

Like John and I, Elaine and Barbara also grappled with how to handle questions regarding their relationship. Lying didn't sit well with any of us, but in the end we all agreed that before coming out there had to be certainty that it was safe to do so.

An hour into our trek it began to rain. It was the dry season, and we were on what is thought of as the dry side of the mountain. But on Kilimanjaro, you must be prepared for all weather. After a four-hour, eight-kilometre hike, we arrived at our first camp at nine thousand feet.

In addition to food, water, and tents, the porters carried our duf-

fels; a maximum combined load of twenty-five kilos each. Despite being heavily weighed down, they beat us to camp and had everything set up for our arrival, as they would continue to do each day. In need of dry clothes, we were shown to our tents and given our duffels. Cisco, the camp cook, had supper waiting.

We had immense respect for how hard the porters worked, and constantly expressed our gratitude. We were glad we had selected a company that abided by the working conditions set by the Kilimanjaro Porters Assistant Project and paid above the minimum rates set by the Kilimanjaro National Park.

The rain let up in the night. After breakfast, we followed the path through alpine moorland, past scrawny trees reminiscent of Dr. Seuss illustrations. It was hot and my head pounded with each step. What happened to "pole, pole" — meaning slowly, slowly — which I'd heard so much about? In our briefing we were told it was crucial to hike slowly in order that our bodies acclimatize to the altitude. Drinking four litres of water each day would also help avoid the headaches and nausea known as mountain sickness. After a seven-hour hike we reached Kikelewa Cave at twelve thousand, one hundred feet. Having hiked fifteen kilometres, I collapsed into my tent, sweaty, dirty, and exhausted. We wouldn't be able to shower for another four days. Sex was officially removed from the agenda.

At night, the temperature dropped dramatically. I shivered in my sleeping bag. I felt certain I wasn't going to make it all the way to the top, and I'd made this clear before we started. John, Elaine, and Barbara have each run numerous marathons. I have no athletic accomplishments. I'd been trailing behind all day.

Day three, we climbed a steep ridge to Mawenzi tarn, at fourteen thousand, two hundred feet. By late afternoon on day four, we had crossed the high-altitude desert of the Saddle to Kibo Hut at fifteen thousand, four hundred feet. The mountain loomed over us. At midnight, we would begin the final six-hour climb to the summit. At night, the terrain - which is mostly loose gravel, called scree - freezes, making it easier to climb. Plus, starting at midnight puts you at the top in time for sunrise.

As I tried to sleep, I felt like my head was going to explode. The nausea was extremely intense. Altitude kills; we were told to be vigilant of the warning signs. Cerebral edema: build-up of fluid around the brain; symptoms include severe headache, loss of balance, fits of anger. Pulmonary edema: build-up of fluid in the lungs; symptom is a liquid wheezing sound. Both kill within hours. The only cure is immediate descent. What would happen if I went any higher? Would I forgive myself

if I didn't try?

After three hours sleep, my headache subsided. I dressed for severe cold, estimated at 20 below zero. Note to self: never again go camping in winter conditions. I turned on my headlamp. I had saved my iPod for this part of the climb, having been warned it would be the hardest. I listened to Radiohead's then new album *In Rainbows*. The music energized me.

We followed the mass exodus out of camp and merged into a single-file line. The climb was physically and mentally taxing. The thin air made it difficult to breathe, and move. Every three to ten steps we rested briefly.

There could have been a hundred people in the line, yet there was a feeling of solitude. Looking up, it was hard to differentiate between climbers' headlamps, and stars. The processional was spiritual, peaceful, beautiful. I gave myself over to the rhythm of the shuffle.

Three hours later we arrived at Hans Meyer Cave at seventeen thousand feet. Barbara didn't look well. Hypoglycemia, and hypothermia, made it impossible for her to continue. She urged us on and hugged us goodbye. Gaspar accompanied her down.

We pushed ahead as others turned back; some were carried. With no end in sight, it was time to admit that I too needed to turn back. I paused and looked down at my boots in the snow, searching for the words to explain to John that I couldn't go on. I looked up and found myself face to face with a woman I did not know. She smiled reassuringly and said, "You're three minutes away from the top."

"Three minutes!" I thought, "I can do another three minutes!" With a renewed sense of determination I forged ahead.

It was still dark when John took my picture next to the welcome sign at Gilman's Point. We had made it to the crater's snow-capped rim. If we turned back now, we would receive a certificate documenting our accomplishment. But, if we continued another ninety minutes, we would reach the highest point on the rim, Uhuru Peak, and our certificate would have a gold band.

The sun was rising. My headache was back with a vengeance. It took everything I had just to get here. I couldn't imagine another hour and a half. Michael saw me struggling and took my backpack. "You will make it," he said, "even if you go slowly, slowly."

Those ninety minutes were the most challenging of my life. It wasn't until I could see the sign for Uhuru Peak in the distance that I knew I would make it. When I arrived I started to cry. John held me and whispered, "I knew you could make it."

At nineteen thousand, three hundred, forty,feet, we were above the clouds. The sunrise revealed immense glaciers. Valerian announced we only had fifteen minutes to enjoy the view, as it was dangerous to remain at this altitude for long.

Our decent was a relief, but also daunting. Valerian moved quickly to gain momentum, then dug his heels into the melted scree and slid down fifteen metres. It was faster going down but not easier. Elaine and John quickly mastered the technique, but I could not find the balance needed to surf the scree.

Michael and Valerian each grabbed hold of one of my arms. For three hours they pulled me along as we surfed the scree at an overwhelming speed. By noon we reunited with Barbara, and by evening had arrived at Horombo Hut. We had hiked a total of fourteen hours; six kilometres up, twenty one kilometres down.

The next morning I could barely move. A final six-hour, twenty-seven kilometre hike stood between me and a shower, and real bed. As we concluded our adventure, Elaine and John agreed it was the hardest physical challenge they had ever undertaken, harder than any marathon.

After returning home to Toronto, I edited together video clips I took on the climb, setting them to the song I'd listened to during that final push to the top: Radiohead's *Reckoner*. I was reminded of the beauty that surrounded us on Kilimanjaro, the amazement of walking through diverse climate and vegetation zones, the exhilaration of standing above the clouds.

I was thankful I had stopped to marvel at all this, to take pictures and video, even though it often meant trailing behind the group. As I watched the final cut I found myself thinking, "I will climb that mountain again... but first, I have a marathon to run."

Maybe I am a sporty fag after all.

An excerpt from the novel
CORBETT'S DAUGHTER
by John R. Hewson

IN CRISP WHITE SHIRT, brown silk tie, and immaculate beige suit, Blent—Zachariah Blent, Manager—closed his office door and gestured Daniel Corbett to a chair.

"You play real good, Corbett. Upbeat and sophisticated. Just what I'm lookin' for." He flashed a momentary smile.

"You're hired."

"Thank you, sir."

Blent shot his cuffs, fingered both cufflinks, then settled his beefy frame behind his desk. April sunshine trickled through his midlife perm, bleached almost white, above his dark-tanned face.

"You work Wednesday through Sunday. Noon to three, five to eleven. Except for Sunday—the brunch—when you crack the keyboard at ten." A smirk tugged at the corners of his mouth. "Long hours, but you're used to it."

Had bloody Preswyk talked to him, spilled the beans?

"Sir?"

"Come on, Doc. I know all about you."

It had to have come from Preswyk. Wasn't a parole officer supposed to help? Did he *want* him to fail? Two-faced bugger. Corbett held gaze, said nothing.

Blent gave a have-it-your-way shake of his head. He shifted in his chair, had a discussion with himself, took a breath.

"I run a high-class restaurant, Corbett. No punks. Toronto's carriage trade. Our patrons spend big, tip well." He flicked the corner of a

trayful of invoices. "But business is falling off. Tough economy. When they spend, they want more for their buck." He pointed a finger. "That's why I'm hiring you."

Blent's bear-like paw triggered a rush of images, of flailing fists, blood-spewing nostrils—in the heaved-cement schoolyard. In the orphanage basement. In the penitentiary's laundry room. Corbett fought the clamour in his head. "Music? Yes, music. Music. That should help."

"There's a bit more to it, Corbett."

He should wash dishes between sets?

"I'm afraid I don't understand."

Blent grinned now, a twinkle landed in his eye. "You're a good-lookin' guy, Corbett—when we get you into some decent clothes." He paused, like a teacher trying to pace his lesson. "Nowadays, it's the ladies that decide where they're gonna eat." He paused again. "And whether they're married or single, they're rich, Corbett, and they're bored." He tapped his temple. "Get what I'm sayin'?"

Good-lookin' guy... ladies rich and bored... "You want me to have a 'presence,' right?"

"Couldn't've put it better myself." Blent examined Corbett's eyes, back and forth, right and left. "Yup, bit of the devil in those baby-blues. The lovable rogue—just what the ladies like." He chuckled. "So, Corbett, when you're workin' the keys, you catch milady's eye. You smile, all discreet-like, then you nod like you and her was talkin', startin' to glow. You swing into somethin' suggestive, like... *Come Fly with Me*, say, and after a few notes, if you're doin' your job right, she smiles back, maybe even blushes. Sure, she shakes her head—cause you're forbidden fruit—but she likes it. She feels alive. And next week she's here again—with a flock of girlfriends. And their wallets."

Corbett didn't know how to feel about this. Amusing, sure, flattering, but crass, and a little demeaning. Eye candy. Like being pimped. What choice did he have? Ex-cons didn't top an employer's shopping list.

"I understand."

Blent studied him for a moment.

"Why the glum face? A little eye-sex with smart, rich cougars ain't exactly a death sentence." His chair creaked as he leaned closer. "I'm givin' you a break, Corbett. I expect you to come through." With a thumb and forefinger he pushed his mouth into a happy-smile. "Get with the game, Corbett. Crank a grin, pretend life don't suck, and make us both some money. You read me?"

"Loud and clear, sir."

"Good." Blent's gaze slipped a little lower.

To Corbett's moustache. To the mask he'd grown in time for parole, for his coming out. A new Corbett, on the outside. Trying to hide the Corbett on the inside, the one who's clean-shaven face, in photos and then in courtroom sketches, had fouled a million breakfast tables. "Should I shave it off?"

"No way. It's retro-chic. Sean Connery, Tom Sellick. The lovable rogue." He looked, peered closer. "The ladies'll like the bit of grey at your temples, Corbett, but not in the moustache. *That* you're gonna dye. Nothin' goofy. Medium brown. All the drugstores sell it."

What choice did he have?

"Yes, sir."

"Good." Blent eyed him up and down. "Now for the clothes." He scanned him again. "Week-days, I want you to wear a neat suit, white shirt with French cuffs, four-in-hand necktie, and maybe a fedora like Sinatra—yeah—dark grey, and wear it at an angle. All jaunty-like—a let's-do-Rio look." Blent nodded to himself as if conjuring and approving the image. "On Sundays you wear a tuxedo—you're James Bond, straight from the casino in Monaco. You're cool and fun, more than a pretty-boy—so we downplay the tux—just a regular white shirt. French cuffs, though. And a black bow tie — medium width. Hand-tied, not one of those damn clip-ons. You do know how, right? To tie 'em?"

The Annual Hospital Ball, the January Jive for Justice, the Swinging for the Cure. Back in the early years, when Melissa still loved him.

"Yes, sir."

"And you don't wear the fedora with the tux."

"No, sir."

"Stop with the yes-sir/no-sir, Corbett. You're a *rogue* now, got it? And rogues don't kiss ass."

"Right... Boss."

"Much better."

"When do you want me to start?"

"Soon as you've got the clothes." Blent's face softened. "I suppose your lawyers fleeced you, right? Cleaned you out. You need an advance? For the duds?"

"I'm sorry to say I do... On that subject, I don't believe we've discussed... you know... "

"Your pay?" Blent held a conference somewhere under his perm. "You start at seven hunnert-five a week—fifteen bucks an hour. Business picks up, you're careful not to piss the ladies' limp-dicks, then I'll up it to twenty." He pulled a pen and chequebook from inside his jacket, scrib-

bled, and slid a cheque across the desk. "Two thousand. Interest-free. I'll hold back forty a week." He frowned his way through the calculations. "Fifty weeks, two weeks unpaid holiday—one year from the day you start you're all paid up." He looked down at his own lapels then at Corbett. "Don't scrimp on the quality, hear? Ladies can spot a crap-rag from the other side of the room. They hate cheap. Turns 'em right off." He waited for Corbett's nod of agreement. "Good." He scrawled something on a notepad. "My own tailor, Corbett. Pick two suits and a tuxedo. And socks, ties, shirts, cufflinks—everything. Tell him I sent you, that you're workin' for me." He slid the paper across the desk. "Don't forget the fedora—a good one—nothin' under one-fifty, hear?"

Corbett held back his groan. He'd be living on Kraft Dinner—with a sprig of broccoli at Christmas. "For sure."

Blent nodded, wove his hands together over his midriff and examined a corner of the ceiling. "So, Doc, about your... little run-in." He leaned forward, eye-to-eye. "You had a kid, I hear."

Corbett felt the tightening in his throat. Becky would turn fourteen on Friday. He'd last seen her when she was three, at four-thirty in the morning, when he'd hugged her close while her Pooh-bear nightlight smiled warm in the corner... You smell good, Daddy. And your cheek's all smooth like Mummy's. Can I go with you some time to Wi—Wimpug? ... Winnipeg, Sunshine. Winn—i—peg. But I have an even better idea. ...What, Daddy? ...Why don't you, Mummy and I go to Disneyland next summer? ...On a airplane? ...A great big one, Sunshine. ...You mean it, Daddy? To Dizzyland? For real? ...For real, Pumpkin. Now give me a great big hug-and-kiss and go back to sleep until Mummy says it's time to get up, and then say Hi-Daddy-out-in-Winnipeg and I'll say Hi-Sunshine-back-in-Toronto, okay? Now let's have that hug ...

Every night when the door of his cell clicked shut, ten years of lockdowns, he'd remembered the softness of her cheek, its warmth, the fresh-laundry smell of her long blonde curls, and he'd buried his face his flimsy pillow and said I-love-you-Sunshine. Would she believe that? Did she have a new dad to love her? Did she ever think of her old one? Could she imagine how much he loved her, how much he missed her, still, every day, after all these years? Did she know he had to wait through seven more before he could even write, via the courts, and pray she'd answer? Would she even care?

Corbett managed a breath. "That's a rather painful subject for me, Mr. Blent. I'd rather not go into it, if you don't mind."

"As you wish." Blent looked away as if embarrassed by, and for, the quaver in Corbett's voice. "Tell the tailor you need everything for

Thursday morning."

Thursday. And the next day, April twenty-third, while he churned out ditties and smiled at strangers, Becky would blow out candles and hug some lucky man, the man she called Dad. "Thursday. Yes."

Blent checked with his Rolex, stood, and extended his hand. "You gotta be a showman now, Doc. Not like surgery, where they're asleep." He laid his other paw on Corbett's shoulder. "You'll do fine. Just shut off the noise in your head and move on." He turned away. "See you Thursday."

Corbett tucked the tailor's address and the cheque into his jacket. "Sure thing," he said to Blent's back.

No one looked up as he left.

STORY TIME
by Steven Jacklin

UNDER A WINTRY MOON I shovelled the driveway. Crunching in arctic boots, I'd been at it for an hour, digging out, piling snow deep as January.

I leaned on the shovel puffing and blowing, but the night air, keen as crystal, was pure elixir at ten-below zero.

Refreshed, I surveyed the progress of my labour. Almost done. Just one spot left, down by the road where the snowplow had left a Himalayan mountain range blocking the driveway. With the shovel over my shoulder, I marched towards it. But then, behind me, I heard a voice from the porch.

"Neville," said Janet. "You almost done?"

"I've still got the snowplough bit."

"Well, you'll have to do it later. Leigh and the boys are waiting."

I checked my watch - 8:30. I could picture them now, Leigh in her bed, Ben and Scott in their bunks - restless, expectant.

I slammed the shovel into the summit of Everest. Nothing delayed story time.

Inside, in the hall, I shed my coat, scarf, and gloves. Only my boots caused trouble. The right one, mainly, icy-tight. Wincing, I wiggled it off.

"Problem?" asked Janet, holding a cup of cocoa.

"My blister's burst."

"Hurry, Daddy," Leigh said from the bedroom.

"In a minute," I said.

"Here," Janet said, handing me the cocoa. And while I sat on the stairs drinking it, she stuck a Band-Aid on my heel.

"We started a new story last night," I said. "It's a good one. It's about a band of ... well, they're called Dwarfgiants. They go on adventures."

"What kind of adventures?" Janet said. "Not dangerous ones?"

"No. Not *too* dangerous."

"Now don't you be scaring Leigh. She's only six."

"Don't worry, it takes more than a Gorax to scare *our* girl."

"Gorax?"

"It's just a creature."

I gave her my empty cup and limped upstairs.

"Just a short one tonight, Neville," she said. "It's getting late. Lights out in ten."

I turned and nodded. But I didn't mean it. *Ten minutes? Yeah, right.*

I shut the bedroom door behind me.

What Janet *didn't* know was that the lights were already out. Only the moon, filtering through the gauze curtains, softened the darkness, a sort of curdling twilight - the moment before the arrival of Dracula - filled with the promise of shadows and blood.

But the Count was old hat. Now we were into something new. The Dwarfgiants and the mystical island of Kamistra where danger grew like Dragasps, Goraxes, Raslatombs, and the Lost Souls of the Moon. I couldn't wait to start.

In the middle of the bedroom, I lay on my back. When I *read* stories I sat in the rocking chair in the corner, with the lamp on. But since we put carpet down, I made stories up on the floor, in the dark.

"Are we ready?" I said.

"*I* am," said Ben from the top bunk.

"Me too," said Scott from the bottom.

The bed to my right stayed quiet.

"Leigh?" I said. "You ready?"

"Daddy," she said, "is the Gorax a boy, or a girl?"

"It's a *boy*," said Ben from the top bunk. "All Goraxes are boys."

"*No*," said Scott. "Not *all*."

"*Some* have to be girls," I said. "But there's a good chance this one's a boy. It burps and it's got warts.

"And what else has it got?" Ben said cheekily.

"A dinky," said Leigh.

All three laughed.

"All right," I said. "That's enough. Now look, we don't have much time, so let's get started. Where did we get to?"

Ben said, "The Dwarfgiants had stopped to rest at the edge of the Dark Wood."

"It was gloomy," Scott said. "So they lit fire torches."

"Then they saw the Gorax," Leigh said.

"That's right," I said. "Up the trail, about fifty paces - the hulking, demon-eyed beast stood deathly still."

"What was it going to do?" said Leigh.

"Charge," said Scott.

"Eat," said Ben.

Call it parental instinct but I suddenly sensed in Leigh - in her voice - a level of trepidation. She sounded - if not quite fearful - at least a touch queasy. This was in contrast to the previous night when we'd come up with the idea of the Dwarfgiants - a human-like species whose supernatural powers enabled them to extricate themselves from the stickiest jams by changing up, or down, in size. Last night she'd been excited about everything - the quest, the battles, the serpent. She'd even matched her brothers' flair for the picturesque when she'd pegged the Gorax as an ooey-gooey poo-poo head.

Still, it was one thing to call the Gorax names, quite another to actually face one, head-on. To hear it growl, feel its power, smell its breath. To behold, in all its abomination, the frothing flesh-eater - its swivelling head, its bloodstained teeth - albeit within the cozy confines of the bedroom.

I guessed that bravado was behind Leigh's initial enthusiasm. If so, it was really too bad. With the Gorax drooling, hungry for the kill, there could be no turning back.

"Daddy," she said, "how big is the Gorax?"

This was good. She was still in the game.

"Oh, about four times bigger than a wild boar," I said. "But more ferocious - *way more*. It's got two faces - one with eyes at the back of its head - the other with teeth like daggers, at the front. If ever the Dwarfgiants needed to squeeze out of a jam it was now. But how?"

"Change up," Scott said. "Change to giants."

"But they can't," I said. "Once Dwarfgiants have used their special power, it takes them three days to recharge. Only two days have passed since they last changed up, battling viper snakes in the Kindoo Wetlands."

"The Dwarfgiants could spread out," said Ben from the top bunk. "Surround the Gorax and attack it with their fire torches."

"Not a bad idea," I said. "But Roberto, the Dwarfgiant leader, knew they were in trouble. Even four against one, they'd be no match for the Gorax. If they attacked, they'd get picked off. If they ran for it, the beast would chase them down. What do *you* think, Scott?"

"Grrraaah!" He growled like a mad dog. "The Gorax's head turned around its neck. Its long black tongue wiped the blood off its teeth."

"Where did the blood come from?" asked Ben.

"Probably a duck," said Scott.

"A duck?"

It was Leigh's turn, but I had to jump in: "The Gorax's head swivelled again. With eyes burning like fire it charged like a bull, running backwards down the trail. 'Brace yourselves,' said Roberto. 'Here it comes!' Huddled on a rock the Dwarfgiants pointed their fire torches at the onrushing predator. But there was no stopping it. At twenty paces the Gorax launched itself, hurtling through the air like a bloated slingshot. The sight of the beast brought panic. 'Scatter!' screamed Roberto."

"Daddy," said Leigh, "I don't like the Gorax."

"Not now, Leigh," I said. "It's crunch time."

"What's crunch time?"

"It's... it's when things get tricky."

"But I'm scared."

"I'm sorry, Leigh but..." There was a knock on the door. *Janet.*

"Neville," she said. "What's going on? Is the light out yet?"

"Yes," I said. "It's out."

"Then say goodnight to the children."

"Yes, alright. Just give me *one* minute."

The room fell silent. I lay on the carpet hardly able to breathe. I hadn't heard Janet leave. *She was still at the door.*

"Who's been eating *my* porridge?" I said, gruff as Father Bear.

"Goldilocks," whispered Leigh.

"Who's been eating *my* porridge?" I said, soft as Mother Bear.

"Goldilocks," she said again.

"And who's eaten *my* porridge?" I said, squealing like Baby Bear.

"Goldilocks," said Leigh. "I like Goldilocks."

"Me too," I said, yawning.

I heard a shuffle. Janet's footsteps creaked down the stairs.

From the bunk another yawn - this time from Ben. Or was it Scott? No matter, again the room fell quiet. Only distant sounds - the last of the dishes put away, the television switched on. *Knots Landing.*

It was safe to continue.

"Right, then, kids," I said. "Sorry about that. It's just that sometimes your mom thinks you need more sleep. So, where were we?"

Silence.

"Ben?"

"Scott?"

"Leigh?"

Well, wasn't that just great? All three dead to the world. Oh, well, I'd just have to finish the story myself. "Now, where was I? Ah, yes, the Gorax. Like a plague from the bible, the black-tongued flesh-eater hurtled towards the Dwarfgiants. With no answers and even less hope they abandoned the rock they'd been standing on, scrambled for whatever cover they could find. But the beast, unable to alter its course, hit the rock teeth-first, crashing in a squeal of blood and spit. Furious, the beast staggered to its feet, fixed its eyes on Roberto. Just ten paces away, the Gorax who stood twice his size, roared, smelling the blood of its first victim."

Wait - footsteps on the stairs.

Janet. She was back.

Through the gauze curtains, a cloud blotted out the moon. Darkness descended. Holding my breath, I peered in the direction of the door, thought I saw the skim of light under it fade. I waited to hear her voice. Probably not good news for me, but it could mean everything to the Dwarfgiants. If Janet insisted I come out of the bedroom the story would be on hold and the Dwarfgiants would get the extra day they needed to recharge. In which case, tomorrow night would be the Gorax's turn to tremble.

I lifted my head and listened. But no voice came from the other side of the door. Just a... just a bump, a dull thud on the landing. Not like someone falling, but a thud just the same. What was happening out there? I strained to hear. Nothing now, except the muted voices on the television...and the sound of the doorknob. A jiggle. Who was there? Was the doorknob turning? It couldn't be Janet. She'd *never* leave *Knots Landing.*

A cool breeze blew in from the window. The gauze curtains lifted high. Without a prayer, I shivered in the dark.

An excerpt from the memoir
"Breaking Through The Bull. How God Works"
THE DEATH MEDITATION
by Manny Johal

SHE SAT THERE SMILING. I couldn't read her eyes. I was not sure if it would be the mother I knew and loved or that distorted version of her acting possessed, suffering from delirium. Noticing the stool glistening on the floor, answered that question. The hospital stay saved her life but, also stole her mind.

If God does exist, he would definitely not be able to ignore the pleas from the waiting rooms outside Intensive Care Unit. The sheer volume and intensity of cries for help is overwhelming to watch and feel. The pain in their eyes crosses all cultures and religious barriers. As I spent five months in the hospital at my mothers bedside , one thing was clear- God was clearly on many minds of those who passed through the waiting room doors. Regardless of whether they were Indians, Chinese, or European faces, it didn't matter. The great equalizer of death and despair filled those eyes.

People lean on each other when death is nearby. Strangers offer sympathetic glances and smiles of support. My sister, the atheist, had a conversation with a woman of faith whose mother was also in a critical condition. The stranger said that she did not know how anyone could get through this, without having faith in God for support.

"If you can't believe in God, then what do you believe in?" she asked. My sister looked down. Everything I believe in, is lying on that hospital bed in that room," she said solemnly. The first day we found ourselves at the hospital is still freshly etched in my mind.

"Your mom's condition could have been avoided with a sim-

ple vaccine," the words from the good doctor haunt me to this day.

My heart sank and I felt ill. My attention quickly turned to my sixty year old mother lying in the ICU, motionless - a feeding tube and intubation keeping her alive. The doctor gave her a five per cent chance of survival. The pneumonia went septic.

I can still see my mom dancing Bhangra with her two year old grandson, my son. Two days ago, we all danced and laughed watching Arjun`s antics. My mother's face was alive with laughter, her eyes sparkling. Everyone who knows mom, loves her. She was always the good natured aunt, the one who never had a harsh word for anyone. The one whose doors were always open, and her table laden with food for all of us – sons, daughters, nieces, nephews, grandchildren. My fondest memory of her was listening to her recite the Gurbani (Sikh prayer) while puttering around the kitchen doing her household tasks. She was not religious but she was spiritual. She never imposed religion on us but did tell us stories of her mother and how dedicated she was to her morning prayers. My grandmother spent most of her day working while repeating the Naam (meditation technique) Vaheyguru Satnam continuously. My mother always advised me that if I ever ran into any difficulty, or had any fear in my heart, to repeat the Naam.

A few days in, as my mother lay on that bed with no change in her condition, I remember my eldest sister crying and hugging mom, trying to pour love into her some way, so she could open her eyes once more. I sat on the bed with my Nitnem (daily prayer scriptures) in my hand. I did the only thing that I knew how to do. I recited the poetry of the Nitnem, reading the English translation through tear filled eyes. Desperation and grief clouded my eyes, but I focused on the words; it was all I could do to keep it together.

The next few months were a trial of endurance for our family. We supported my mother on a journey through hell. I would reach the hospital before dawn; a peaceful time. The inky blackness of the night sky gives way to a deep blue as the sun's rays emerge and energizes the earth. This is why this time of the day is considered sacred by the Sikhs. The hospital became my church, my temple. I climbed the stairs to reach mom bedside to worship every morning.

The poetry I read was inspirational. It gave me comfort, and strength, and allowed me to pass that on to others. With my Nitnem in hand, I would walk down the hall to the ICU filled with sadness, but also with hope.

There were days I gave up. I was home in bed when I received a call at two in the morning, on the third day mom was in the ICU. I didn't

want to answer the phone but I did. My brother was on the line.

"The doc says it looks bad and she probably won't make it through the night."

Nothing could prepare me for that call. While I knew this was a possibility, I was stunned. . I hung up the phone and stared blankly at the ceiling, wasting precious seconds. My wife turned to me to ask how my mom was doing.

I responded with, "That's it, they are done. They think she won't make it through the night." I turned my back to her to retreat. She grabbed me by the arm and forced me out of bed.

"Come on, let's go," she said. She got down on her knees in the middle of our living room and pulled me to the floor. "Just pray to God like you never prayed before. Just ask. Ask God to make her okay. There is nothing else."

I grudgingly went along. We both knelt down on our knees on the living room floor. I don't remember ever praying that hard. I have never prayed for anything except to have God in my life and keep my mind focused on him, the infinite spirit.

I found it difficult to plead for my mom's life, but I did. Bawling like a child, I pulled myself together and drove to the hospital still praying. I wouldn't wish those moments, those feelings on anyone.

I walked into the ICU suite expecting the worst, only to find smiles on my family's faces. Somehow, in those moments, she pulled through. Doctors were shocked. Nurses shook their heads in disbelief. Anyone in that room could only call it a miracle. Later they told me that upon hearing that this was the end, my father started reciting his usual prayer. As he recited, my mother's oxygen saturation levels started rising. "Don't stop. Don't stop what you're doing," the nurses ordered. My father continued. My mother stabilized.

Over the following months we watched our mother recover only to fall ill to various hospital infections. It was a living hell for her - we were the witnesses. All the family members responded differently in this crisis and engaged spirituality to varying degrees. My eldest sisters mothering nature smothered her sick mom with love. My atheist sister struggled with what she saw and experienced, with nowhere else to turn but to faith and God. My superstitious father had a new appreciation for his wife who he now cherishes. I, unintentionally, became a spiritual support and guide for my family. She ended up recovering completely and all we were left with were the lessons from that nightmare.

By turning to prayer for strength and support for myself a ripple effect occurred that served me as well as others during our darkest

hour. Maybe that is how God works in the end. If he doesn't heal, per-haps our faith in him gives us the support we need to face mortality and endure suffering.

In Sikh philosophy, death, pain and suffering are considered a gift, as they direct us as a catalyst to a higher state of consciousness. Sanitizing death behind the doors of nursing homes and hospitals may disconnect communities from an opportunity to probe deeper into life's mystery. Without grief, pain, despair, illness, death, maybe we would not need faith or God.

Dukh daru sukh rog bhaia ja sukh tam na hoi - Pain becomes the remedy while joy becomes the disease, when there are worldly pleasures then man loves not God. (GGS)

SO THIS IS CHRISTMAS
by Fatmatta Kanu

I HAD HAD VERY little sleep the day before I left Sierra Leone and during the two days of travel to Canada. I felt anxious about travelling and also had to deal with the discomfort of having a chest full of breast milk. The unknown of Paris was very intimidating. However, thanks to the stranger who came to my aid, my stopover in Paris went rather smoothly.

My exhaustion was compounded by the fact that Sheka had scheduled a social activity for us to attend on the very evening I arrived. I was ready to drop any minute. The positive aspect of our evening out was that I was able to get some medication from a doctor at the professor's house to dry up my milk before heading back to our apartment. I took the medicine immediately and went to bed right away. I was too tired not to sleep. I woke up the next day feeling rested. Sheka and I had breakfast. I took the medication again. I was feeling better. The breast milk would dry up in a few days.

It was Christmas Day. I expected celebrations. I expected to see people out and about. Although Sheka had been in Canada for only three months, I expected him to have visitors and for us, in turn, to visit his friends.

Christmas Day was my first morning and first full day in Canada. I looked around the small attic flat that was my new home. It had one bed-room, one sitting room, and one bathroom. In one corner of the sitting room there was a fridge, a cupboard, and zinc counter top. Here, Sheka had a kettle and a burner. It was where we could prepare snacks. But we could not cook upstairs, Sheka told me. We were to share the main

kitchen and other facilities with the old couple that owned the house.

Since it was Christmas Day, my landlady would not have the time to give me a tour of the areas of the house downstairs where there were appliances I could use. I had to wait till the holidays were over to get a "guided" tour. I waited a while for Sheka to tell me what the program was for the day. He was quite busy rearranging the furniture in the bedroom to make space for my few belongings. I, on the other hand, did not want to be caught off guard when his friends came by to celebrate Christmas. We could not shop on a public holiday. I looked in the fridge and the cupboard to get whatever I could find to prepare something to serve to our guests. I found a head of lettuce, tomatoes, baked beans, eggs, onions and bread. I had enough to prepare a plate of salad. I decided to make some egg sandwiches. We would make do with the soft drinks we had in the apartment. I could have made a non-alcoholic drink called ginger beer, but Sheka had no ginger. In any case I did not have any type of appliance I could use to grind the ginger to prepare the drink.

I started work in the little corner. Sheka came up to me about half an hour later.

"Are you preparing lunch?" he asked.

"I suppose we can have some of the sandwiches for lunch," I answered. "The rest of the sandwiches and the salad I have made, are for our guests."

There was a blank look on Sheka's face.

"Guests?"

"Yes, guests," I answered. "Are you telling me that no one will visit you today and we will not go out?"

Sheka took my hand and walked me to the sitting area. He asked me to sit down. He sat beside me.

"I will answer the second part of your question first. We will be going out later in the day. Karl will pick us up to go to his house. Until then we will stay here."

"Aren't there any celebrations in Edmonton for Christmas?" I asked.

"According to the explanations I have heard from my friends and colleagues, Christmas is a family affair in this part of the world. People stay indoors, have their Christmas dinner and exchange presents. People travel to family homes. In many cases, families travel to the grandparents' homes. Those who go to family homes in the same town or within a reasonable distance go back to their individual homes late on Christmas night. Those who have travelled from farther away leave the next day to resume regular activities."

"Oh!" was all I could say in utter disbelief.

"But there will be some activity later, as I said. Like us, people from the Caribbean are used to having outdoors celebrations for Christmas. Here, they are unable to do so. In order to get into their version of the Christmas spirit, they each take turns organizing an evening party every year. This year, the Gordons will host the party. That is better than not having a celebration at all."

"I see," I answered absentmindedly.

I pulled a chair towards the window, sat on it and stared outside, paying very close attention to what was going on. But except for a few vehicles that drove past, there was hardly any human activity. I saw white mounds of snow on either side of the road and the pathways of the houses. The white fluffy snowflakes were falling. The night before, I had been too cold and too busy wrapping myself up to ward off the cold, to observe my surroundings and take everything in. I sat on that chair by the window absorbing the scenery in amazement.

"It is Christmas Day," I said to myself. "I have not heard church bells ringing."

At home, church bells ring on Christmas Day. Thousands of people dress in their best to attend church.

In Sierra Leone, that was how Christmas morning started. Later in the day, the streets would be filled with people walking or driving to various destinations to visit families and friends taking gifts and food with them. Later in the afternoon, Christians, and non-Christians, would have masquerades all over the city with extensive dancing to celebrate. In the evening, up to the early hours of the next day, dance halls were packed with people attending ballroom dances organized for the day. Here, I was sitting alone on a chair by the window and nothing much was happening. It was past midday.

"So this is Christmas in this part of the world," I said to myself.

It was on that day that I finally understood the meaning of some of the Christmas carols we sang at school. The first one that came to mind was:

> *I'm dreaming of a white Christmas*
> *Just like the ones I used to know.*
> *Where the treetops glisten,*
> *and children listen*
> *To hear sleigh bells in the snow.*
> *... With every Christmas card I write*
> *May your days be merry and bright*
> *And may all your Christmas' be white.*

Ah, I get it now, I said to myself. The white snow covers everything outdoors. That is why Christmas is white. But this has not been my experience of Christmas. My Christmas' were never white until this Christmas. As for the rest of the song, I do not hear any type of bell ringing. I do not know what a sleigh is. I am certainly not having a merry and bright Christmas!

Even though I am Muslim, at home, I would usually take the time to send Christmas cards out to my Christian friends but had been unable to do so that particular year as I had been too busy making arrangements to travel to Canada.

Another carol that came to mind was:

> *In the bleak midwinter,*
> *frosty wind made moan,*
> *Earth stood hard as iron,*
> *water like a stone*

It certainly is cold, this Christmas Day. I can attest to that from last night. Today when we go out I may experience the hardness of the earth and the frozen water. Not that I am looking forward to it. But if that is the reality, there is nothing I can do about it.

I found myself crying bitterly. It was Sheka's first Christmas, too. There was nothing much he could do other than to console me. He held my hand and moved me away from the window. The pain of realizing that my world had now changed irrevocably subsided after a while. I went back to the kitchenette corner to finish a small late lunch out of the food I had found in the fridge and cupboard earlier. We ate around two o'clock in the afternoon. We spent the rest of the afternoon quietly at home.

Around five o'clock, Sheka reminded me that we were to get ready to go to the Gordons. Karl pulled into our driveway about an hour later to pick us up for the party at his home. The brightly lit streets with Christmas decorations were new to me. Both Sheka and Karl promised to take me to different parts of the city the next day to see more decorations. The Gordons' party made my first Christmas Day. I was introduced to more people. There was plenty of food. We danced the night away. Karl took us home close to three o'clock in the morning.

We slept in on Boxing Day morning to make up for the lost hours of sleep the previous night. I was not expecting much to happen by way of entertainment on Boxing Day.

This is not Sierra Leone. This Boxing Day, the sounds of drums will be missing. I will not experience the gaiety and the sweet laughter

of people enjoying the holidays. I have no idea whether there are sports activities today, as is the case in Sierra Leone and I have no intention of asking questions in that regard. We were expecting Karl and Edward to visit that evening. That was something to look forward to.

Both men arrived as promised, around five o'clock that afternoon. For my Boxing Day treat, Karl, Edward, and Sheka, took me out on a short tour of the main street to view the Christmas lights. The sight was spectacular and breathtaking. We did not have the tradition of Christmas street lighting in Sierra Leone. At the time, I did not know that this type of the scenery would become a regular feature of my Christmas for many, many more years to come.

An excerpt from the memoir
FINDING MATTHEW
by Donna Kirk

"Finding Matthew" is the story of a first-born son who suffered severe oxygen loss at birth in 1970. His parents, Donna and Ed were told that if Matthew survived he would be a vegetable with a heartbeat and should be institutionalized. This story is the second chapter of the book. Donna and Ed are seeing Matthew for the second time since his birth the previous week.

1970

WHILE WE DROVE TO Sick Kids, I tried to remember what Matthew looked like. The pictures in my mind blurred and danced.

"Do you think he's still in an incubator?"

"We'll soon find out." Ed said. Even though my husband seemed to be concentrating on driving, he was flushed and sweating on a very cold day in February.

"We saw him for only a few moments, nearly a week ago." Talking stopped me from worrying. "I hope he's breathing better."

Finally, the hospital building loomed in front of us and Ed parked the car. Dizziness overcame me as we walked towards the entrance.

"I'm going to faint." I clung to him. "I feel so weak."

"You sit here," he said, ushering me inside to a chair near the information desk. "I'll find out where Matthew is."

Enquiring about our son's location, searching for the appropriate elevators, and riding to Ward 7G, happened in slow motion. We were all thumbs donning the sterile gowns, booties, and caps, required to enter

that ward. Finally, we opened the door to a large antiseptic white room filled with more babies than I'd ever seen. The tiniest ones lay in huge incubators, hooked up to a maze of hissing, throbbing machines.

"You can stop crying now, Matthew. Your parents are here," said someone behind us. We spun around to see a nurse who introduced herself as Miss Violet Gayle.

"Here he is, Mom and Dad," she said, gesturing towards a tiny, wailing infant lying in one of the steel cribs. No equipment was attached to him.

Could this be the same plump, rosy baby we saw in the incubator a week ago? He occupied so little space in the huge cot. But I recognized the beautiful blond hair and tightly closed fists. His nostrils were such little pinpricks I wondered how any oxygen got through. We stared into his bed, afraid to touch him.

By then, Ed and I were crying. "He's been waiting for you," said Miss Gayle. "Don't worry. He'll be all right now that you're here." She handed us a box of tissues. "I'm 65 years old and retired, but I work here part time because I love babies." She was tall, brisk and British. Her gray hair and friendly manner gave her a grandmotherly appearance, just the person to be caring for sick infants.

Although we couldn't appreciate Miss Gayle's cheerful way, we had no choice but to follow her instructions. I was escorted to an over-sized white rocking chair with plump cushions. Matthew, yelling and flailing, was plucked from the safety of his crib and placed in my arms. Even though I was afraid of him and terrified to be his mother, I felt compelled to hold him.

"Just hold me tight," said Miss Gayle, speaking for Matthew. "We need to get to know each other." Ed stood beside us, looking relieved that she hadn't handed the baby to him.

"Your turn next, Dad," she said, with a wink in my direction.

"He has so much beautiful hair," I managed, through tears.

"He's just perfect, Mommy," said Ed, on one knee in front of us, as he held Matthew's little hand. At this first touch, I knew we were committed for life.

"He's out of the incubator and breathes normally now," I said, looking up at Miss Gayle. "Isn't that a step in the right direction?"

"He's stopped that horrible jerky gasping," Ed said. "And he sure can yell."

"Matthew weighs six pounds," said Miss Gayle. "He's gained weight in the last few days." Our son had lost a pound since his birth a week ago.

I can't remember if Matt cried throughout our first visit, but we did. Ed and I took turns holding him. Frequently Miss Gayle or one of the other nurses offered cheerful comments and words of encouragement, none of which we recalled later.

As I held Matthew, a nurse wheeled a machine over to the rocking chair. A long wand with a rubber hose was attached to the side. We watched her snap open a small plastic device from a sterile pack and attach it to the wand. Then she flipped a switch and the machine made a loud sucking noise.

"Matthew, look this way, sweetheart," she said, turning his head in her direction. "You need to get rid of that saliva in the back of your throat. His swallowing reflex is not fully developed," she said in answer to my surprised expression. The wand was inserted into the back of Matt's mouth and the machine gurgled as mucous was drawn into the tube.

Shock rippled through my body. Our baby couldn't swallow his own saliva. We also learned that he was fed by a process called gavage, a tube inserted through the nostrils into the stomach. Sucking and swallowing, those two basic instincts were things Matthew couldn't do. We watched his feeding process which was over as quickly as it took the liquid to disappear down the tube and into his stomach. He could not be held during the procedure, receiving none of the touching and stimulation so vital to a new- born infant. The nurse just poured the liquid in as he lay in his crib.

This process kept our son alive but how could a baby ever thrive without being picked up and cuddled? These little ones on 7G needed to be touched and stimulated, but with their busy caseload, the nurses didn't have time.

"I have to be here every day, Ed," I said, no longer tired and weak. "Matthew needs to be held and he won't get any special attention on this busy ward."

Ed nodded. "I'll come in after work so I can see him too, and give you a break."

We were determined to give our son every chance, regardless of how difficult this new schedule would be for us.

Before leaving the hospital that first day, I uncovered Matthew. His shirt and diaper were enormous on him. Once free of the swaddling blanket, he moved his arms and legs, particularly his left arm and leg. His right side seemed slightly slower and less active. I reached down to him, prying open one of his hands. The gentle pressure from his little fingers reassured me. On our way out of 7G, we cornered the head nurse.

"Do you think that Matthew has improved since he's been

here?"

"Matthew is receiving the best of care, Mrs. Kirk," she said, her eyes avoiding mine.

"Will his swallowing get better?" I persisted.

"Only time will tell how much improvement he makes," she said. "My suggestion is that you see Dr. Bentley, the head of pediatrics, tomorrow morning to discuss your son's condition. I can make that appointment now, if you like." We waited in the hall while she scheduled a time for us.

As we walked to the car, Ed said, "Do you think she was keeping information from us?"

"What could be worse than we've already heard? At least he's doing much better than last week. I'm so tired," I said, stifling a yawn. "Let's just go home and get some sleep." I didn't want to think about what could be coming next.

"I can't believe we left Oakville hospital only a few hours ago," he said on the drive home. "I'm glad we came right down to Sick Kids. I couldn't have gone another day without seeing him."

"He looks so small and delicate," I said, wondering how I would ever cope with such a fragile baby.

"Small but feisty," Ed replied. "That's my son."

Matthew was discharged to his parent's home after a two month stay at Sick Kids Hospital. He had learned how to swallow and suck and could hold his head up.

THE MERMAID
by Enxhi Kondi

SHE EMERGED FROM THE water, slowly and elegantly. There was a rock near the shore, near enough for a young man to walk through shallow water to it. She grasped the rock and pulled herself up, her bare chest grazing it gently. She brought the top half of her tail up, as well, and turned to sit on the flattest edge of the rock. Her sleek, wet, blond hair flowed silkily down her back as she slapped the end of her blue, scaly tail in and out of the water.

A young man, on the shore, was lying on the sandy beach when a glint in the distance caught his eye. The mermaid tilted her tail so the sun would glint off her scales. The man sat up and gasped, for there he saw his first mermaid. She caught him looking and slightly turned her head in his direction.

"Come," she said in a dreamy, high-pitched, lovely voice sounding like velvet silk. The boy got up and smiled as he splashed into the water. The mermaid's voice infiltrated his small mind as he came closer. She whispered words of love in the wind, and the words circled through his mind, reeling him in closer and closer. The mermaid ran her fingers down her body, slowly, intoxicating the young man coming toward her.

"Come," she squealed again. Her perfect red lips curved upwards in a smile, so amazing, that even the sun couldn't match its brightness. She turned her body towards the man and watched his gaze move from her eyes, to her lips, then to her bare chest. The man reached the rock and told her he had come to her, just as she had requested. He sat on the rock beside her. She put her lips to his ear and whispered, "I can show you love and many things." The man reached a hand out to touch her

cheek but she quickly moved away.

She dove into the water; the way a dolphin does, and resurfaced to look at the man.

"Come,"she squealed again. The man jumped into the water and floated beside her. She giggled and swam farther away. The man swam after her, caught in a hypnotic daze until he was too far from shore to swim back. He called out for the mermaid with no success.

The waters were calm and silent around him. He looked at the sky but it, too, was unwilling to acknowledge him. Suddenly, the water began to ripple and tremble. The man looked around in fear, trying desperately to stay afloat. Heads of flowing silky hair surfaced from the water. They were all around him, circling him. They rose higher out of the water until their bare breasts were visible. Their scaly, shiny tails splashed at the water. The mermaids were laughing and cackling with joy. "Man, man," they squealed excitedly to each other. "He's human," one cackled. "He's warm," another said excitedly.

One of them placed a hand on the man's shoulder and when he turned around he saw the mermaid from the rock. She circled her arms around his neck. The man stood frozen, unsure of what was happening. From a distance, everything would have looked like a tableau; frozen like a picture. But the man's face was changing; the skin was getting darker and darker. The mermaid entwined her fingers so tightly around his throat that the man couldn't breathe. He shut his eyes. The mermaid smiled and released his body. "Let's eat now, sisters, before his blood grows cold," the mermaid proclaimed. The mermaids around her made noises of agreement before moving in on their prey. As the man's limbs were torn off, blood seeped into the water, reddening the sea.

The mermaids squealed in delight as they rushed to drink up the bloodied water. Meanwhile, the mermaid that had hypnotized the man took the man's bodiless head and swam away from her sisters.

She reached the underwater site of a sunken pirate ship and swam through one of the round windows that led into a cabin room that had been occupied by a married couple before it drowned. A trophy case was displayed along one wall and lined up on that case were a countless number of heads.

The married couple's heads were up there among those of the men and women... The mermaid opened the case and cleared a space between a head with multiple piercing and a head with no nose.

She put the young man's head in that cleared space and gazed adoringly at her collection. Then she swam back the way she had come,in search of another trophy.

STUBBLE JUMPER
by Mary Ellen Koroscil

SHE SLID INTO HER wildest mini dress with the hot pink geometrics running diagonally down the side. She cocked her head and turned at odd angles as she gazed at herself in the mirror. Her friend Linda, exclaimed, "That's some crazy outfit."

"Do you think I'll get noticed by those account execs.?" Sue said demurely.

"Are you fishing for approval? My gawd! Every eyeball in the place will zoom in on you."

Linda surveyed her friend's short mini that caressed her slim, but curvy body in all the right places. She walked over and reached into the closet, rummaging through a dozen or so pairs of shoes, and finally producing a pair of black patent platform heels.

"Try these they will complete your look."

Sue grabbed the platform shoes and put them on.

"Thanks, I'd forgotten about this pair. These were a real "find" in Germany, just before my money ran out and I had to return to Canada. You look pretty jazzy yourself, but then you always do," she said teasingly and smiled at her new friend as she picked up clunky rhinestone earrings that were on her dresser and clipped them to her naked lobes to give her outfit a touch of glamour.

Feeling very chic, the girls went clonking on down the two flights of stairs from Sue's attic retreat on Charles Street. It was an old, rather run-down house and she occupied the top attic suite, (the penthouse, she called it) but it was cheap and a hot house when the temperature soared. This was an era long before air conditioning. She loved the tiny

roof deck, but there was a glitch. There wasn't a door to the deck. To gain access to this rooftop paradise one had to crawl out the window to set foot on the flat area of asphalt shingles. In the dark of night when she couldn't sleep or to escape the heat, Sue pushed her folding lawn chair through the window opening and sat out beneath the stars just looking at the skinny Toronto sky scrapers. The scenery was a far cry from what she was accustomed to.

The girls arrived by subway at the hotel. Everyone was hell bent for leather rushing into the posh "Canadian" Ballroom. Her friend Linda took off in a different direction, seeking her agency table and Sue searched for her staff at McCain and Burnbach. Looking very spiffy, the masses of ad types were all a-flutter. This was the biggest night of the year. Clear across Canada, for the advertising industry, it was the awards night.

She tried to pick up on snatches of conversation; which agencies worked on the plumb accounts and who was merging with whom... She hovered near some guys discussing the merger of their agency, with Dork and Duck Inc., at least that's what it sounded like to her, but what did she know? Being the rookie at the agency she was just learning the ropes. Being hired as a copywriter at a big agency was a thrill beyond belief and this invitation to the awards ceremony had shocked her out of her socks.

She smiled and nodded at the staff who she barely knew and pulled up a chair beside Hans, the Art Director, who had brought his wife along. This appeared to be the safest spot around the table. Hans was always friendly towards her. She loved going into the art department with all of Han's paints and brushes lined up along one wall as he worked on the ad signage using some Letterset. The place smelled a bit like varnish as, the paints, glues, and chemicals were constantly in use; but it was a homey smell. Sue also loved to look at his illustrations for the clients story boards - such a talented artist!

She would be working with him on a cosmetic account next week, as she had almost completed her training program. Thankfully, she was getting accustomed to her fancy new red typewriter that possessed so many new, confusing features. In another week she also had to learn how to use the telex machine, that constantly tap, tapped, tapped all day long in a corner of the Creative department.

The seat beside her was vacant and she wondered who would sit there. The ceremony began with the first award being presented to Doyle & Alexander for the most innovative ad campaign for 1969, for the series of Volkswagen ads. Sue loved the Beatle print and billboard ads, they

were such fun. As everyone applauded, a guy named Chad introduced himself and sat down next to her. He looked a few years older than she, but kind of cute. She secretly wondered if he had an oil derrick permanently stuck on the crown of his head as his hair was falling in oily strands over his forehead and around his ears and over his shirt collar. The long hair and an unkempt look were still big in '69.

"I'm here from the Montreal branch of McCain and Burnbach," he said cockily. He seemed to know most of the individuals seated round the table as they turned to stare at him. "I practice picking out Canadian accents and I know you are not from anywhere near here. Where are you from? Out West?" he asked in an almost mocking tone?

"Moose Jaw, Saskatchewan," she replied bravely.

"So you are a 'Stubble Jumper,'" he said, as he roared with laughter, and everyone around the table, except for Hans, joined in with the giggling. If this story didn't take place in the 60's, Sue would have kicked him squarely in the shins or between his legs where it hurts, with her chunky platform shoes.

"How do you like the big city? And you even blush to boot," he suggested as Sue could feel her face going redder than a bull fighter's cape. "I haven't met a woman who blushed for the last ten years," he boasted.

"Then that's unfortunate for you," she retorted angrily.

"When did you leave the family farm? Let me guess, you must have got your start on writing farm equipment copy, am I right," he enquired.

"Yes, as a matter of fact you are dead right," Sue replied as she was trying to turn this grilling ordeal into a plus. "I know more than most folks about wheat, tractors, combines, grain augers, and harrows. Farming is a big industry in Ontario too," she suggested, trying to sound a bit chipper, meanwhile, her spirits were sinking lower than a single earth worm in heat.

"Maybe we can start a farm division in the Toronto office," he joked, then proceeded to laugh loudly again, and the others joined in unison.

"Excuse me for a minute while I go to the ladies room," she said cheerily as she rose to high tail it out of the main room.

Some sense of decency must have sunk in with the creep as he said, "I'm sorry you're leaving, is it on account of what I said?...ah, I was just having a little fun."

"Fun, my ass," Sue thought as she flew by the other tables enroute to the solitude of a washroom stall, questioning herself over and over again whether she really belonged in the city.

TWO STRANGERS
by Karen Lam

THERE WAS A KNOCK — once, twice, light yet anxious. I was in no hurry to answer the door; I rarely had visitors and wasn't expecting company either. But the knocking persisted and I was obliged to give in — once, twice, light yet anxious.

I was unprepared for the tall figure that stood before me. He looked dishevelled, his shirt half-tucked and gapping, revealing a thin layer of chest hair. I stared at the bottle he held in his hand; the quick gulping sounds he made told me that this was not his first.

I opened my mouth, but only found strange half-guttural sounds, which I stifled. He was starting to make me nervous.

I hold my breath, unafraid. Suddenly, I have the urgency to touch him. I reach out my hand, half anxious to feel his flesh under my fingertips, half afraid that touching him would cause him to disappear. Eyes can deceive, but touch rarely does. My fingers trace the raised flesh on his chin, mapping each stroke to memory.

He winces as if I was opening up old wounds he was struggling to forget. The scar was his only physical tie to his past, a past I know nothing about. He places his hand over mine as if he is about to speak. I hold my breath; we both do. No words come. And then I notice the strange glint in his eyes, every nerve in my body suddenly awash in its electromagnetic aura.

We stood at the doorway of my apartment, both of us afraid to look at each other, both of us afraid to break the spell we were under. Then, without warning, I feel something on my forehead and pull away. He averts his eyes, but I can tell that the connection we had made had

affected him. Whatever he has been running from, whatever old wounds he had reopened, I silently promise myself that I would help him pick up the pieces. "Shhh... it's okay," I soothe, my thumb unconsciously wipes the stray tear from his right cheek.

He stares back at me and leans forward. I remove my hand from the side of his face and blush. There's a strange stirring in my heart; some scent draws us in subconsciously, our foreheads nearly touching. I was about to speak but he didn't wait for my reply. Somehow he took my surprise as an invitation, his lips feel warm and wet against mine, kissing me with a sort of urgency. I now know what his eyes were trying to tell me and shiver with the knowledge of just what will happen, without fail, when lips interlock.

For some reason, without explanation or consultation, we both found ourselves engaging in a sinful proposition. The air sharp with the mysterious sparks of lust, progressing rather than stagnant. I push back every sense of reasoning I have and allow my mind to explore its hidden spaces without restraint. Where our evening in the rapture of a single orange, undressing in darkness and deliberation, tonight was somehow an unmasking of layers, finding vacancies in the growing cracks of our existence. He stops suddenly and says the first sentence since our long period of reflexive movements. He looks at me intently. "You're mine."

I stiffen. This is the first time that anyone has ever claimed me. The first time that anyone has wanted to own me. My mind screams for me to awaken from mental slumber, sense tells me that it will not last and I was letting him use me. But I love him, and whether I am confusing my lust for love, I don't care. Pushing all sense aside, I respond with my lips, pulling him towards me and tumbling into the sheets.

Morning came sooner than I had anticipated, the apartment illuminated by the light of lemons. Now it was the dreaded morning after, and I, with makeup smeared all over my face was hardly glorious.

Stumbling into the bathroom, either from the tainted water or from the consequences of my actions, I prayed to the porcelain god. As I knelt there feeling wretched and confused, it troubled me to think of how quickly I had submitted myself into seduction.

Shaking away the remnants of nausea, I compared my likeness in the mirror to a banshee. Makeup smeared and hair tangled into a horrendous disaster, I could easily frighten children. I was frantic to purge of all evidence. That was until, everything turned black.

It startled me that I hadn't noticed the rustling of sheets and the padding of his soles on the hardwood. "Alright, wise guy, what's the big idea?" I reached up and felt a hand obscuring my view. "Oh, I wonder who

it is," attempting to sound surprised, my left hand slinking up his arm. I stopped partway, "Since when did I agree that we could act like five-year-olds?" I huffed, trying desperately to peel his hand away with my right.

He was not going to surrender easily. "I think the right question is why you are about to destroy such beauty with a facecloth." He finally removed his hand from my eyes, but quickly lunged for the facecloth I had left on the counter.

I screwed up my face in annoyance and raised my eyebrows in disbelief. "I look horrific; you've got to be bloody bonkers to think other-wise." He dangled the facecloth in front of me like a matador's cape. "Either that or you're in dire need of some strong coffee." His belly shook when he laughed. I knew this was revenge for the pillow I had thrown at him days ago. I had almost forgotten. "Ugg," I grumbled, foolishly reach-ing for the cloth in earnest and missing it by centimetres. "Wanker."

"Now, now, there's no need to use that sort of language."

I glared at him through my lashes, arms crossed. "Don't be a blockhead," I miffed.

My eyes grew wide as he tilted my chin towards him for further inspection. "You saw right through me," his lips hovered. "I am a block-head."

The arm that pressed me to his torso soon slid up the small of my back. I shivered, tracing the scar on his chin with my eyes. He took this as an opportune moment to fling the facecloth over my head.

"Argh!" I grunted, peeling it from my face. "Blockhead!"

He leans on the frame of the bathroom door. Crows' feet grace the corners of his eyes. Now that I am finally in possession of my face-cloth, I scrub at my face, harder than it is required. I must look like a child with sunburn.

I catch him looking me up and down more than once. He impul-sively grabs my wrist and spins me around, my chin thuds softly against his chest. It frightens and amazes me at how quickly topics can be trans-formed into a sexual blur; not to mention my own, unthinking willingness to allow things to get sticky. "Loneliness is a spreading epidemic," his eyes dance forlornly over my reddened visage. His lips hover again, this time his whisper barely audible despite the proximity of our intimate con-tact. "Loneliness was the only thing that defined my existence before you came into my life." Shuddering: I float in the drunken pleasure of words. I find him; my own lips ache to meet his blatant lie.

SPEAKING GOD
by Peter Lisinski

IN LATE SEPTEMBER OF 1976, I had just begun to settle into my new job as shipper/receiver at the recently constructed warehouse of a Dutch multi-national electronics corporation located in suburban Scarberia.

Having been employed on a temporary basis since May, I had somehow made a favourable enough impression on the general manager to be offered a permanent position. Bill Stewart was a quick-tempered Scot of medium build, whose thick head of wavy hair had turned completely white long before he met me. He was the only person in the whole place who always wore a hard hat when he ventured out of his upstairs office. It was light blue, the same colour as his frequently bloodshot eyes. Anyway, a couple of weeks later he had approached me about succeeding the incumbent, V.Q. Kim, soon to retire.

Kim, as everybody called him – because nobody could pronounce the name that V.Q. stood for – was a short South Korean dynamo whose safety shoes turned out to be hard to fill. His unstreaked, shoe-polish black hair, combined with his inexhaustible energy and unwavering good cheer, well-concealed his chronological age.

During the two training days, I raced behind him around stacks of crated televisions, climbed shelves of light bulbs, and radio transistors, and dodged bales of bubble-wrap and clingy styrofoam packing peanuts and gained a new appreciation for the agility of the mountain goat. When suddenly left alone to navigate my new domain of corrugated cartons, speeding forklifts, and impatient couriers, I got lost in a wilderness so dense, it took nearly two weeks of twelve-hour days to find my way

back to civilization.

If not for the interference run by Harry Douglas, my immediate supervisor and loading dock foreman, I'm sure I wouldn't have lasted long. A tall, slim man with thinning, light brown hair, he had worked side by side with Bill Stewart for nearly thirty years. One afternoon, near the end of my three-month probation period, the two of them got into a heated shouting match in the lunch room over the latter's expressed intent to fire me.

A vocal and assertive "born-again" Christian, Harry had taken me under his evangelical wing. I was already a believer and lifelong church-goer, but I guess my style of faith left enough doubt in his mind about my "personal relationship with Jeeesus," to make me the target of his Bible thumping.

One day bay door # 8 rolled open with its usual sound like skidding tires on gravel. After the clash and clang of unlocking transport trailer doors, a deep baritone voice called out,

"Aaaargooos!"

I recognized Jack's voice right away. The grizzled veteran trucker's mocking lament always heralded his arrival on those mornings after the Toronto Argonauts had, yet again, managed to snatch defeat from the jaws of imminent victory. And, as usual, from all corners a chorus of invisible voices echoed the greeting: "Aaaargooos!"

Jack gradually bobbed and weaved his way toward me, clutching a bill of lading in his thumb-less left hand. As I snatched it from between his nicotine stained fingers, he lightly punched me in the arm and said, endearingly, "How's it goin', Hippie?"

Like I said, it was the '70s.

After we engaged in a short bout of shadow boxing, he continued his good-natured hobnobbing while I headed over to the loading platform to match the items on my list with the load on his truck.

When I returned to my cluttered desk, Bill Stewart was waiting. I could see by the reddish glow of the broken blood vessels in his cheeks that he was angry. I can't recall exactly what he was angry *about* – nearly four decades later – but his exact *words* remain indelibly engraved in my memory: "This is the second time this month you've made this mistake."

I confessed my sin, repented and waited – in vain as it turned out – for his word of absolution.

"Sorry's not good enough! What I want to know is this: When are mistakes like this going to end?"

I had never pondered that particular philosophical question, and

down to this very day I can't explain what inspired the answer I blurted out. Maybe it was because I had watched the previous night's Billy Graham Crusade instead of the latest football fiasco. Or was it, perhaps, the cumulative effect of Harry's persistent efforts to convert me? But, whatever my inspiration, I looked the plant manager right in the eye and said, matter-of-factly, "Mr. Stewart, mistakes like this are not going to end until the second coming of Jesus Christ, when all imperfect human beings will become perfect in the salvation of God."

He looked as *stunned* by what he had *heard* as I was *surprised* by what I had *said*.

A few speechless moments later, he had calmed down completely, and quietly broke the awkward silence between us: "I have a feeling you're not going to be with us very much longer," he said, quietly. Then he turned and walked away.

As I watched him go I, wondered what that might mean. But there were no immediate consequences. For the next six months the two of us worked together without incident or rancour. And by the time I was summoned to the personnel office the following spring and handed a pink slip, I had already come to the same conclusion. When I left the building for the last time that day, I finally understood what Bill Stewart's words meant – and *who* had *really* spoken to me through him. Shortly thereafter I contacted our church's theological school to explore plans to permanently exchange my work boots and box cutter for a preacher's cloth and soap box.

THE SHOES DONE HIM IN
by John Maar

Northern Ontario, 1977

"ARISTOTLE, OR PLATO, I'M not sure, off hand, which one of the two Greek philosophers had thought of democracy two thousand years ago," said Spud, my hick-town friend, explaining some things he had read in books he got from a local second hand store. "Thanks to him," he said, "I can shoot off my mouth any old way I like."

Usually I was interested in stuff like that, which was probably why Spud sought out my company, but this time a fancifully made up woman, her eyes on us, was approaching us on the sidewalk. She was smiling sweetly, but she was too old for me, and I was relieved to see her heading towards my friend. Spud was a big landowner in Kirkland Lake and was well known; the woman obviously knew what she wanted.

Spud left the sidewalk and crossed the street as though blown by the wind. Pushing sixty, he had never been married, and it was obvious he wasn't going to get involved with this beauty.

The next morning he was at our usual coffee shop, a greasy-spoon hangout frequented by retired gold miners. Broad faced and round in the middle, resembling a typical feudalist Eastern European landowner, Spud was having a few words with his tenant roomers. "You guys had gone through life without having achieved anything," he said. "No wives, no children, no money. You'll have left nothing behind to show that you'd ever existed. If it weren't for the pension you're getting, you would have died a long time ago. Hah, hah, hah!" he laughed. "You're just empty duds."

Spud, I thought to myself. This was so unnecessary and cruel. The wise Greek philosopher surely didn't envision democracy of this kind. Why tell others the first thing that comes to one's mind? To defuse the sudden tension in the air, I called out from the line of customers, "Spud, you want a coffee?

"No."

"He would have one if it had a protective factory seal," one of the miners commented acidly from a nearby table.

What the man said was something that was common knowledge to almost everyone in town; Spud was convinced that the world was out to poison him, and was careful of what he consumed in public places. He ate and drank only at home. Whether this complex of his was the result of having grown up back in his communist homeland, or just an excuse for not having to spend money, I wasn't sure.

Spud took good care of his health. I'd seen him purchase walnuts, honey, fruit and other healthy things at grocery stores. Anything else that he needed, he bought at the local second hand store. Then, a couple of days ago I saw him buy at Woolworths, a brand new eight-track player with a stack of tapes, something I thought a bit strange because he had never been interested in music before.

Spud, one of the wealthiest landowners around, owned a number of buildings, yet he had the appearance of homeless person, almost as if hiding behind a secret veil. His clothing was passable to a degree, but his shoes didn't look like shoes. They had no shape and I couldn't indentify the colour of the leather.

Knowing how, in addition to his other hang ups, Spud was petrified of women, who he claimed were only after him to ruin him financially, I was surprised to see that his eyes strayed to Daisy, one of the newest waitresses. In her early twenties, with a sweet-looking angelic face, she was smiling at Spud openly. "What would you like?"

"A coffee," Spud replied and the entire patronage in the restaurant looked over. "Oh - oh!" someone sang out.

"A large one," Spud said, and taking out his wallet, packed thick with cash, pulled out a $100 bill.

The girl placed the coffee on the counter. "Anything else?" she was smiling at him as a daughter would at her father.

"No thanks." Spud slid the money towards her. "Keep the change."

The girl pushed the bill back. "No, Spud. Your coffee's only a dollar."

"Keep the change," he insisted, and this was the first time I no-

ticed him speaking to someone in a soft tone.

I realized then that Spud for some reason couldn't see the difference between the $100 and the $2 bills that were in circulation at the time, so I hinted under my breath, "You're giving her a hundred."

"Oh," Spud snatched it back. Fumbling around in his pant pocket, he found a handful of change and placed it on the countertop. He was going to leave his cup of coffee there and leave, but then, thinking better of it, he took it over to one of the tables. "All yours," he said to an old timer in the vinyl upholstered booth.

A cup of coffee in my hand, I couldn't help but think how Spud's paranoia didn't make any sense. He had refused to have the coffee, because he thought it was tampered with, so how would he share food with a wife from day to day? The woman he married would have to be really trustworthy.

Glancing at Daisy, I forgot Spud. Not only did she have angelic features, but she seemed to be one. "Bye," I said to her softly, and followed Spud out into the street, all the while keeping her stunning image to myself. Spud seemed to be reading my thoughts. "Daisy's my rent-free tenant. She comes from a dairy farm south of here." On and on he went about how modest she was in everything she did, so that in the end I realized that deep within his old-fashioned soul he was convinced that since he had never been involved with another woman, it was his given right to marry someone as young and pure as Daisy.

I took it in silently. Daisy was a wildflower free for the picking, but whether she was as modest and sweet as she seemed was to be determined. By refusing to take the $100 tip, she had passed the first test, but this could have happened because she was surprised. She hadn't expected to be given such a big tip, and her refusal to take it could have been the reaction of someone who was still green. The next time she might know better.

I had also invested in real estate and was eager to pick up hints about running the business, so I hung around with Spud, often waiting patiently while he would, standing with his feet wide on a sidewalk, admire and scrutinize his buildings on the opposite side of the street. One thing that I learned from him was to own enough real estate so that I could afford a manager who would deal with the tenants. "Some of the young renters can be a handful," he told me. "They will drive you into an early grave."

Spud was lucky to have a reliable person to manage his buildings. It enabled him to spend a lot of time travelling by car all over Northern Ontario. I wasn't that lucky. I had to deal both with the tenants and

the maintenance. The money that was left at the end of each month - after paying off mortgages and everything else - was barely enough to carry me through. A wife was out of the question. Nevertheless, I longed to go back to the greasy spoon and see Daisy.

At noon Spud suggested that we go there for lunch. He would treat me to a hamburger. That was generous of him, especially since he was so tight with his money, but what would Daisy think of me if I accepted? Eating by myself, while Spud sits and watches, would make me seem like a kept boy. "Thanks," I said, "but I better go home. I want to change into a clean shirt."

"Why?" Spud shot me a sharp glance.

"I just noticed a woman that I know from the bank take a look at my collar as she was passing us a minute ago, and by the expression on her face I'm sure she doesn't think much of me."

"Who gives a shit!? When she sees you put all that rent money into the bank, she'll change her mind."

"She might, but she'll never forget the soiled collar on my shirt."

Spud shook his head. "You're just being funny."

It was none of my business, but I'd had the urge for some time to help change Spud's appearance, so I said, "After women size up a guy's face and his frame, they check out his shirt and shoes. If those are not up to scratch, they feel that the guy is not up to scratch either."

By the look in his eyes I knew that Spud didn't like what I said, and I wasn't going to stick around to hear his reaction.

"See you for coffee tomorrow," I said, and then strolled off into a side street where my car was parked.

Was he going to get himself a new shirt and shoes? I wondered. Then, just as I turned my car onto Government Road, the main drag in Kirkland Lake, Spud was entering the local second hand clothing joint.

I squeezed the car into one of the parking spots and sat there waiting for quite a long time. When Spud came out of the store, he was a new man. In fact I could hardly recognise him. He wore checkered bell-bottom pants, and an Elvis Presley collar shirt. His new sport jacket was also checkered with a variety of oversized brown squares. Huge heels elevated his new shoes.

Spud was heading towards the greasy spoon and I followed him at a crawl in my car. The drivers behind me didn't object to the slow speed. They too had their eyes on this man in his weird outfit. And then I started panicking. Daisy will also think he is an old clown. Why didn't he just stick to a new shirt and shoes? I sped up, leaning over to lower the window on the passenger side door. The car was old and the crank

refused to budge. "Spud!" I yelled from inside. "Spud, wait!"

It was too late. Spud had already entered the restaurant. And that was the last I saw of him.

Later that afternoon, someone I knew met me on the sidewalk. "Did you hear about Spud?"

"No. What happened?"

"He died."

"But, how?!"

"He slipped on a potato chip, fell and broke his neck."

I rushed to the restaurant. Daisy was there sitting at a table all by herself.

"He was a nice man," she told me through tears. Ever since she was a teenager, Spud visited their farm. He helped her leave the boondocks and see a bit of the world. She had never been on a train until he took her to North Bay. He also helped her mom and dad on their dairy farm quite a lot. He cut and dried their hay when her dad was too drunk to do it. He paid to repair their tractor. He even bought them a car.

"The shoes done him in," she said. "The soles on them were all smooth and slippery."

Why did I have to open my big mouth about his run down attire? I asked myself later that day. What business was it of mine what he wore? If I ever see anyone with green hair and matching coloured shoes, even if he or she happens to be running for the prime minister's office, I'd pretend to be colour blind. It is none of my business.

When I got home the phone rang. Spud's lawyer knew I was one of the old man's friends and he asked me to take care of the funeral arrangements.

"Send the bill to my office," he said.

A month or so later I started receiving National Geographic in my mail. The subscription ran for a whole year, which gave me enough time to realize who it was that had paid for it.

As for Daisy, she inherited one of Spud's buildings. The caretaker of his estate told me that she was in the office with a hometown sweetheart, who brought her over in his half ton to pick up the eight-tracks. She didn't know what to do with the building and had put it up for sale.

"See the real estate people with whom she had listed it with," the caretaker said. "You can pick it up for a song."

When the time came to erect a tombstone for Spud, I made the arrangements for that as well. The question as to what to inscribe on it was raised, and after a bit of thought I decided on: ALONE HE TRAVELLED & ALONE HE RESTS.

Visiting the greasy spoon restaurant one morning, I found most of old Spuds' tenants. Nobody ventured to mention his name, even though he used to drop off shopping bags with food through the doors of some of the men. Having spent their pension money on booze early in the month, they used to leave them ajar to make sure that just in case they died of starvation, their remains would be discovered before it was too late. I was sure they all knew that deep in his heart Spud was an all right guy. It was his self taught philosophical rant that had distanced him from everyone.

"The young waitress doesn't work here any more," one of the men said.

"I know," I replied. "I know." As it had turned out, I knew much more than they could have suspected. Thinking about Spud, I was aware of the fact that, just like his old tenants, Spud never got the chance to marry, and he had not left a legacy of importance to be remembered by.

I have left the North since, but miss the town and the people I knew, so I take an occasional drive back. One of the things that I do regularly is to visit Spud's lonely grave.

ANECDOTES OF A SOLITARY CHILD
by Victoria E. MacDonald

MY FIRST MEMORY OF our family cottage is through the eyes of a five year old. I recall a small cabin, a front porch, a slamming screen door, a wobbly kitchen table, and a backroom where my parents, my brother and I all slept on cots. I was fascinated by the fact that there wasn't a fridge. Food was stored in a dark underground hole by lifting a small trap door beside the kitchen table. Daddy hauled water up the hill in pails and Mommy cooked over a wood stove. We used Coleman lamps for light.

I was especially mesmerized by a small painting on the wall beside the screen door. Inside the frame, in a shadowy forest, stood a lonely, frightened fawn. I wondered where its Mommy and Daddy were? I worried that it was never going to find its way home.

Two years later, we upgraded to another cottage nestled among fresh smelling cedar and birch trees. It was painted baby blue, with big stone steps leading up to the front door. A large picture window over-looked the small bay. Pine needles, tree roots and green moss layered the ground; and a short walk down the hill led to a small, floating dock, with one tethered rowboat.

My older brother avoided me, so I often had to amuse myself. I was allowed to swim in shallow water, and endlessly splashed about. My dark blond braids never had a chance to dry, and smelled like clothes left too long in a locker. For company, I loved to catch little toads. I would build them enclosures made of sticks and moss. I would tenderly place lush green moss in their homes and attempt to feed them ants. They would either escape or die. When I sorrowfully shared my losses with my

mother, she explained that the baby toads needed to be with their mommies and daddies, just like the little fawn in the painting. I briefly felt sad and guilty, but was unwilling to give up my newfound companions. Defiantly, I continued collecting. When my father discovered what I was doing, he got very cross and forbade me to torture the poor creatures. As a result, I had to acquire my little playmates on the sly, and hide them behind the outhouse. When this cache was discovered, I was spanked, shamed and sent to bed. Feeling rotten and alone, I plotted my next capture. I couldn't bear the thought of giving up those little bumpy creatures that crawled down my shirt and peed on me when they were scared.

A few days later, I was exploring the shoreline. I spotted an enormous, lumpy, brownish gray toad. He was sitting on the sand, breathing in and out, facing the other direction. I assumed he couldn't see me. I lusted for him. I crept up stealthily behind him and slowly bent over to grasp him around his fat white tummy. He suddenly jumped straight up in the air about two feet, landing this time to face me and stare at me ferociously with his beady eyes. A ripple of fear warned me, but I persisted with my plan of capture. As my greedy hands again lowered, he lunged and grabbed my thumb aggressively in his mouth, hanging on for dear life, and kicking his fat hind legs frantically. He had no teeth, but he valiantly succeeded in changing my attitude permanently. Never again did I terrorize toads. Nevertheless, I felt empty inside without my collection of unwilling hostages.

I found a new pastime. I sat patiently at the top of the cottage steps with popcorn kernels in my outstretched palm. Resisting the urge to swat mosquitoes, I didn't flinch. I was finally rewarded when a chipmunk tentatively crept towards me and furtively snatched the morsels out of my hand. Eventually, Chippy would routinely come scampering to the sound of my clucking tongue. I adored his fat little cheeks, and giggled when he jumped on my shoulder. He would disappear down a small hole beside the roots of a nearby pine tree with his stash. I wondered if he had a family, or if he lived alone in the dark.

One day, when I had depleted my popcorn supply, I decided to watch ants. I was captivated by the sight of a large, black ant dragging a dead beetle uphill towards the cottage. The beetle was three times the size of the ant. There were tree roots, pine needles, rocks and crevices blocking its way. It persisted on its treacherous journey with amazing strength. At one point, after struggling uphill for about twenty minutes, it came to a huge impasse. It dropped the beetle and scurried in circles near the edge of the precipice. Suddenly, to my amazement, several other ants arrived out of nowhere. Together, they flipped the beetle to form a

bridge, and crossed over in single file. Safely over on the other side, they flipped the beetle again, with amazing coordination. The original ant continued on its mission, no longer needing assistance. I was fascinated. I watched until the ant dragged the beetle under the cottage. Then I wrote a journal about my observations and saved it for school. I proudly showed my notes to my father, and was forgiven for my sins against toads.

When our new black Labrador puppy arrived, I was elated. Mike was a round, quivering, enthusiastic bundle of love with beseeching brown eyes. I attempted to win his love and special allegiance by feeding him raw hot dogs and cookies. Nevertheless, he had an annoying habit of scampering off to neighbouring cottages in search of new adventures. He would eventually return, and sooth my hurt feelings by diving off the dock to retrieve sticks and balls.

As the summer wore on, Mike's absences became longer and more frequent. One day, he went missing for the whole afternoon. I pouted on the dock, miserable, waiting impatiently for his return. My father circled the island in our motorboat, calling his name. He was nowhere to be found. As evening approached, my parents, my brother, and I, sat anxiously on the dock, squinting at the reflection of the setting sun.

From the east, we heard the increasingly loud roar of an engine as a huge, sleek, gleamingly white, high speed motorboat zoomed by, full of people. On the front deck, ears flapping in the breeze, was Mike. We watched in shock as the vessel sped off into the distance. I lay awake grieving much of the night.

The next morning, Mike mysteriously returned. He was scolded by my father, and lay on his special mattress, looking apologetic and guilty. He acknowledged my secret commiseration when Dad wasn't looking by peering up at me and thumping his tail. He was finally forgiven and toddled off in the boat with my dad to go fishing. I waited jealously for them to return.

THE RED MAPLE LEAF
by David Mandel

THEIR BLACK BOOTS CLOMPED up the concrete steps, slowly, one by one. From the bottom, I watched as the men in blue uniforms carried her up towards two wide open doors, my eyes drawn to the red maple leaf in the center of her coffin. Beside me, my dad squeezed my hand tightly. Behind us, my grandma and grandpa.

"You're being a very big boy today," my dad told me, and I could tell he was sad cuz his eyes were all red, only not thick and ketchupy, like the maple leaf; more like runny tomato soup.

"A flag. That's what she died for," my grandpa muttered, but as I looked one more time before it got too far inside, I could not understand what he meant.

It was all very confusing. First, Dad came to my school just to tell me, then he took me home early. I remember the red of the maple leaf standing out to me then, from the flag pinned over LMNOP on the alphabet sign that stretched all the way round my classroom. I knew what it stood for, of course. It stood for my country, Canada. But to me, that was only a place where we lived.

"Mommy's been hurt in an accident," he explained when we got to the hallway. I stared back at him, but I'm not sure he could see me. His eyes seemed to be looking inside his own head.

"Did she go to the hospital?" I asked, but I don't think he heard me.

"She died." His throat closed on the word, like he shouldn't have said it. Then he coughed it clear. "She'd dead."

The church was much bigger than I expected. My eyes caught up with the red maple leaf, almost to the front, where more steps led up to a stage and a podium, plus some curtains and other stuff. The windows were all different colours, transforming the sun from outside into dusty beams of red, yellow and blue light that fell down on us all as we followed the men up the aisle. I held onto my dad's hand the whole way until it was finally time to sit down. We sat right in the very first row, probably cuz we knew her the best. Grandma and Grandpa slid in beside me, squishing us all close together. It was uncomfortable, but I didn't say anything.

I looked back to watch all the people coming in with their noisy conversations, coats and cell phones. Soon, a priest came and everyone got quiet. He stood at the pulpit in front of my mommy, who I could not see because she was asleep inside the shiny wood coffin. Asleep for the rest of her life.

Most of what he said made no sense to me. Some words I knew though, like soldier, and sacrifice, and bravery. I even heard my own name a few times, which made me feel funny, then, when people looked at me, kind of embarrassed. Everyone seemed to be listening really closely, like he were telling the best story they'd ever heard and I wished I could understand it better. My mommy used to tell me good stories too, like the one where she had to do drills in the rain and some people threw up after, but not her – so I thought about that for a while – till he was finished.

At times I got bored. I tried not to, cuz I knew it was bad, but I just couldn't help myself. I looked around at all the wood carvings and candles and pictures of Jesus and other people I couldn't recognize. Some looked sad. Others were smiling, but not like they were happy. There was other stuff too, but I can't remember.

Some other men said things. They wore blue uniforms like my mommy wears, and said stuff that I know meant they liked her a lot. I could hear everyone crying and sniffing like they all had bad colds. Then a lady went up and talked about Afghanistan, the place where my mommy went before she came back dead.

After that, my aunt talked about when they were sisters and little, like me, but she was crying too much for me to hear most of it. At the end, we all stood for a moment of silence, but I couldn't hear that very good either cuz my mind kept on talking, so I thought about the way she made really good French fries from the bag in the freezer, which had a maple leaf on it too, but I'm not sure if it was red. I hoped my dad could make French fries as good as her. If not him, maybe Grandma.

There were lots more people outside, way more than the church,

which got stuffy and hot after so long. When we came out, they all parted like the water in that Moses movie I watched once at Christmas, right before she had to go away. The coffin that had my mommy in it was carried through and my dad and I followed after, along with Grandma and Grandpa. They put her in a car with a square at the back, then we got into another one right behind it. I could see a lot more going far down the street and I wondered how we would all fit in the cemetery.

Our car had room for more people but just me and my dad and my grandma and grandpa went in it. A man, that I didn't know, was driving. He sat way up front and every now and then, I saw his eyes looking back at me in the mirror. I'm not sure but I think he was smiling.

"Sure do go all out," said my grandpa, looking out the dark window. There were police cars parked at every stop light with their coloured lights flashing really bright. "See the horses?" he nudged me with a smile, and I did. The people on them saluted when we went by.

I began to count all the red maple leafs on the flags and signs people held in the sidewalks. There were tons of them, maple leafs *and* people, and seeing them all made me feel special.

"Want a candy?" said my grandpa, who was watching me, still smiling, and slipped one from his shiny coat pocket into my waiting hand. 24, 25... no wait, I lost count.

The candy was caramel.

I was still sucking it when the car finally stopped. The cemetery was really nice. It looked like a big garden with green grass everywhere, flowers and lots of trees in all different colours because it was in Fall. I wished for my mommy to get up so she could see it. But she didn't.

I saw plenty of red maple leafs there too; not just on flags and stuff, but on jackets and pins, even on some people's tombstones. I could tell it was important to everyone cuz lots of the men in blue uniforms, and some ladies, stood real stiff when they looked at it, flapping high in the breeze at the top of a very tall flagpole, and gave it the same salute as they did on the horses.

My mouth got pretty dry from the caramel and it made me want something to drink. I told my dad a few times, and my grandpa, but both told me there was no place to get one, and no time, cuz the funeral was about to start. I thought it was finished.

The priest did more talking while they put her on this machine that went over her grave. The men took the flag off her coffin and folded it into a square, then they gave it to my dad, who said thank you and we watched the machine lower my mommy into the very deep hole in the ground. It was the only time I ever wanted to cry cuz I thought she would

be lonely, and scared, and cold. It was so dark. My dad squeezed my hand even tighter and it hurt so much, I thought I could feel some bones breaking. But they didn't.

Next came the part when we threw lots of dirt on it. I only did it one time with my dad holding onto my hands over the shovel. It was scary and I didn't like it. After that, my grandpa took me for a drink at the fountain down a little stone road, and when we came back, the men in blue uniforms all had their guns out and they stood very straight. A different man stood in front of them and called out words I could not understand. They sounded sort of like grunts, or dog barks. The men heard him, I guess, cuz they started shooting bullets into the air. It was loud and I jumped every time, even when I knew one was coming. After that there was smoke for a really long time.

At home, I went up to my room, but I didn't feel sleepy so I stared at the ceiling and listened to all the people downstairs. Some had loud voices and coughed a lot. Others were too soft to hear properly. I pretended one of them was my mommy and that they were having a party, but I still knew the real truth inside.

I wondered if she could see how much I missed her, and that I was sorry my room was so messy and had so much that was blue in it with pictures and cartoons everywhere but not even one maple leaf. I hoped she wouldn't be sad about that from Heaven.

Then I guess I fell asleep.

I stayed home from school some more after that, and when I got back, the whole class gave me a speech with the principal, and a gigantic card that they made with their names on it. It looked just like the flag except there was no maple leaf in the middle. It was nice. I was still pretty sad though, and so was my dad, cuz we missed mommy a lot and wanted to make sure she was okay.

On the weekend I went apple picking with my grandma and grandpa near their farm up north. My dad couldn't come because he had to work, but I think he was also sad, still. I asked my grandpa about whether mommy could see me and he said she could. "She can hear ya good too, when it gets nice an' quiet."

I didn't know but I guess I believed him.

In the woods, I went to a spot where there were no more apples, only bare trees, dirt and dead stuff on the ground, and lots of quiet, and I asked her if she was okay. But she didn't answer. I thought I would always be sad for the rest of my life, cuz my mommy was gone and would never come back.

Then some wind blew right in my face so I put my head down

and saw lots of dirt swirling all over the ground. When it stopped, I saw something that was not there before.

Something not dead, but alive.

"Plenty've ripe ones, I see," said my grandpa as we walked to the car, though he did not look closely. "And what else've you got there?"

I showed him, and his eyes got all watery, but I think he was happy, not sad, cuz he said it made sense, "seeing as it's what she loved most," besides me and my dad.

That time, I did understand.

I held onto it all the way home, eager to show my dad what she'd left for us both to remember her by. On the card my class gave me, there had been one thing missing.

What better place for a perfect red maple leaf?

An excerpt from the memoir "Broken Compass"
FRAGMENTS
by Maria Pia Marchelletta

I OPEN MY EYES to the cold concrete floor and strain my back to regain my balance. Have I stumbled into a black hole of the universe? Why am I on the floor?

I feel a ripple of panic percolate inside my chest and try to control its expansion with several deep breaths. I reassure myself, there must be a reasonable explanation for this, refusing to be overcome by total fear, knowing that if I do, this burst would expand and infest every inch and part of my being.

"Can anyone see me? Can anyone hear me? "

I picture myself walking up the west corridor made of concrete toward the office area, hear the heels of my black leather shoes slide along the ground like a slippery rubbery snake on its back.

What has happened here? I can't move...

"What the hell is this?" I say, and then the ripple in my chest rises into my throat, impeding me from speaking. I try to lift myself up using my hands but I can't. I try to move my feet, but I can't. They feel numb and rigid. Is this happening? Is it just a nightmare? I could have spared my-self all this grief and wasted energy. The only thing I have to do is wake up from this bad dream. *Come on stupid idiot. Wake up from this torment.*

I can't remember waking up, but I must have. The day started with the usual routine. I awaken at 6:00, prepare breakfast, then read the daily newspaper while having my oats, and head out the door for work. So, is this a dream? How can I remember all these details?

"Hello, can anyone hear me or see me?"

Why can't I move? I now realize, as new fear grows in my stomach, I am alone in this and not imagining things.

"Please someone, get me off this floor," I cry.

My words reverberate in my ears and resonate in the hovering silence around me. I lay on the ground as in a dank hole waiting for mercy.

I know they can't leave me here on the ground like an invalid. They can't walk away and presume I don't exist.

I hear the sudden opening of the library door. Someone is coming through. Hey lucky me.

"Oh, my God, Maria. What's happened?" says Kathy, eyes bulging.

"I slipped and fell."

"We'll help you off the floor. Just hold onto my shoulders and Miriam's for support."

"I'll try but it's tough."

Can't you tell what's happened here? I'm in distress. And I'm in terrible pain. But who cares and who's going to listen to me anyway!

Miriam and Kathy serve as my crutches till we get to the staffroom.

"There, do you feel more comfortable on this chair, Maria," Kathy says.

I'm not comfortable at all and I'm in a lot of pain, damn it. Can't you tell?

"*Maria*, we'll get you some ice for the swelling." says Miriam.

"That would be good."

Wait a minute, here. Please don't leave me alone. I'm scared. Is this all a big nightmare. Is this really happening. Oh, please God help me. If you do, I'll be a better teacher. I'll be a better mother, a better friend. Oh, please God, tell me this is not happening. I don't want to live in this pain. And to top it all off, my leg has gone numb. I want to see my children and hold them tight and be able to joke with them. Is this for real? Oh, please. No. No. I feel dizzy from all these thoughts pouring out like a parachute floating in thin air.

Anita, my principal, comes out of her office and enters the staffroom. Her office door leads into the staffroom. She volunteers to drive me to the closest walk-in clinic near the Morningside area, just a short distance from the school. This is a big chore in itself. I have to drag myself feeling like a big piece of lead all the way to the parking lot and then I have to try being jovial with my boss and put on a fake smile, and you know, all the rest. After what seemed like an eternity, we finally arrive at

the walk-in parking lot. Once again I have to lug my leaden body into the waiting room and onto the chair. What an enormous ordeal. The doctor is not busy so he takes me immediately.

Dr. Lamb is an energetic male, probably in his mid-forties who manages to balance friendliness with indifference. It's typical of the medical profession that I just can't get accustomed to. Probably he has his reasons for this approach, this impersonal tenderness, but the only thing I can think of is, that whatever he says is only an estimation when it comes to figuring out pain.

I also get the feeling that Dr. Lamb wants to promote his weight loss program instead of dealing with me. He spends a few minutes examining my knee and asks me a few questions.

"What happened here?"

"I fell."

"How did you do that?"

"I slipped on an unnoticed puddle of water."

"I'll order an x-ray next door here. And I'll give you a prescription for Tylenol 2's. But it's not broken."

"That's great to hear."

I toddle like a one year old to the car and now we are headed for the x-ray department near the Neilson Rd. area. Once again, I am forced to put on a mask — a cordial and polite external demeanour. Make small talk. Meanwhile my knee and thighs are burning up like a hot pancake from the darn pain. I dare not tell Anita what I'm feeling. She just couldn't grapple with this. She just wouldn't understand. I keep my tough composure like the outer shell of a tortoise, durable and persistent. Pretend everything is alright. I recall the words of Shakespeare: "All the world's a stage. And all the men and women merely players; they have their exits and entrances." I feel just like an actress on stage just pretending, faking my happiness. Shakespeare's echoing words bring some clarity to my confusion.

I stand proud as a peacock as if not injured. Remember the faking part of it. I fill out the forms with all my personal information. And then the waiting game begins and the superficial talk with Ann. Finally my turn is up for this damn knee x-ray. "Thank God," I say, if there is one. Right now I'm doubting this very thought.

"Can you manage to get onto the table," the technician says.

Well can't you tell? Something is seriously wrong. I'm not flexible and mobile.

She helps me onto the cold surface. I hate x-ray machines, and remember the experts warning about radiation exposure being bad for

you. In this case it is inevitable. I swallow my pride and hope God will spare the verdict; if there is one in store for me.

"Your results will be sent to your family doctor by Monday," the technician says.

Ann drives me back to school and asks Miriam, the grade five teacher to drive me home in my car as she follows us in her car. Once again, I force myself to engage in insignificant talk. I'm in such distress I can't distinguish my head from my toes, let alone remember what the conversation is about. It's probably about the weather or how to get to my home. With composure we arrive at my place. I finally say good bye to them.

And boy oh boy am I glad to get rid of them. Now I can peel off my teacher mask and wear my injured masked and sink into my misery like a ship at sea. But I can't swim. So how do I tread water?

I hobble like a lame horse onto my leather sofa and slouch into its comfort. My thoughts are racing a mile a minute. What the heck is causing all this pain? Even childbirth did not cause such agony, although, my first emergency caesarean was a nightmare. But that story is for another time. The nanny, Amy, takes care of my six year old son, Mauro. He must be wondering what his Mommy is doing home so early today.

"Mommy, mommy," Mauro shouts jumping happily, embracing me with his small tender arms. His angelic face temporarily fills me with some joy. I love little children especially if they're one's own. I guess it's the teacher in me. Standing before me is what I should be grateful for. I have a healthy boy. He is affectionate. He is happy and good-natured. Not like his mother who is very miserable and lost.

The night is long and eerie. The silence looms. Moaning and groaning fills the dark night. It must be the werewolf moon. Am I stuck in a dank hole of the universe? In Dante's purgatory, lamenting. It feels like there are little sharp claws or creatures grabbing at my tender limbs. Agonizing screams fill the stillness of this ebony evening. Will this saga have a happy ending? I question what's going on and mumble, "What lurks in the heart of men, only the shadow knows."

And to think my family doctor, Dr. Wasser doesn't work Fridays. So what do I do? Go to the emergency room in this damn pain and wait and wait, say five hours, for some painkillers. What are my alternatives?

Are we not all afraid of change? Resist challenges like I do. I guess so to some extent. We are all humans. This is disappointing and I deal with it grudgingly.

How long will I be off work? Is it going to be a week or two weeks? What will happen to my job or is my health more important? This fall has

taken my future away from me.

There is a story in *Sky and Telescope*, my amateur astronomer husband, Maurice, tells me that the other day a new comet was discovered. It just appeared from the far reaches of the solar system and it is still very faint. But astronomers have calculated an early trajectory that shows the comet will graze the earth. There is a major worry that the comet will fall into the gravitational pull of the earth and ultimately strike our planet. Early predictions are that the comet could cause catastrophic damage to the earth. It might wipe out life on earth as we know it. Would this event be a recurrence of the 1908 Tunguska explosion in Siberia, a thousand times more powerful than the Hiroshima bomb, or will the world end in December, 2012, with the end of the Mayan calendar?

I have trouble getting these thoughts out of my mind. I Google search this and find to my surprise that Maurice is not lying about Tunguska. But the end of the world for me has just occurred today.

Maybe this is the break the whole world needs. This could be very cool, the whole human race sucked in by a wicked comet. Nobody excluded. Everyone eradicated by the same fate. How cool is that! I wouldn't be around to compare my pains with my neighbor. In a perverse way, it would put an end to my misery.

But at breakfast, my husband reports that this comet is not coming our way after all. As it got closer new calculations by astronomers indicate that the comet will just miss the earth. I laugh it off since I really am in need of some good humour to lift my spirits. I feel denied the chance to be part of the end of the world. Instead, I can't kid myself any longer. I am stuck in this dilemma and need to see Dr. Wasser tomorrow morning. Can I survive another grueling twenty-four hours? The Tylenol 2's are not doing the trick.

THE RIVER: CAR TON BRAS SAIT PORTER L'ÉPÉE
by Louis Massey

THEY SAID 'JOIN AND see the world' and indeed, the Navy had delivered. However, after nine years, I had enough of the flat limitless intensity of the oceans. I loved the work, but despite positive discrimination programs, I was still negatively discriminated against. I was allowed to grow my hair and that apparently annoyed fellow sailors. Furthermore, I had lost my wife to the successive missions to fight far-away invisible enemies. I was not going to loose the rest of my life. I cashed in my pension and one morning I started walking towards the sun in search of light in my life. Perpetual movement appeared to define me because nothing else successfully did.

Now, I am tired of the land. Every hill, each field, all roads look alike, just as the ocean did. Perpetual movement may be insufficient if it becomes the imposed norm. What is movement if there is no change? Am I running away from something that I carry within me?

Some days I wish I had a car. I would get to destination faster. If only I knew where I was going. Maybe the other ocean? Or the other one? Today is one of these days. I see all the imperfections in the road. The small cracks, the loose gravel, the discarded cigarette butts. People have no respect. Cars zip by, probably on an emergency to line up at the nearest Tim Horton's drive thru. They spray me with oily water caught in a vortex inexorably trying to catch up with the speeding vehicles that created it in the first place.

Despite its annoyances, walking leads to interesting discoveries. For instance, I found that the short dotted yellow lines one sees dashing

by when driving are actually quite long. Perceptions do strange things. We assume so many things. Sometimes, I discover less interesting, but more useful facts. Sometimes, discoveries are much more than that: they are life changing.

Halte routière. Everything is French here. *Halte* is familiar enough and I obey the command. I need to rest my feet. One car is parked, wiper on intermittent. The driver is wearing a hooded yellow raincoat distorted by the pearls of water nonchalantly suspended on the side window. The licence plate says '*Je me souviens*'. I remember. What do Québec people want to remember so much to put it on their car plate? Oil change, maybe?

There is a small gazebo with a view on the river. I take my backpack off and feel as light as a bird. When I was a kid, my recurring dream was that I was flying. I would wake up and be so proud of my nightly achievement, certain that I could indeed glide in the sky like an eagle. After all, I had gone over the mountain peaks, touched the clouds: I was sure of it! I'd done it by the pure force of my mind; there was no need to flap winged arms. A certain sense of balance was required, so the skilful positioning of my extended arms and legs was necessary. To this day, I remember exactly how I did it. I remember how I changed direction by a slight shift in my arms and legs. The dreams felt so real. I would tell my mom all about it in the morning, a mouthful of Rice Krispies distorting my excited words.

I take my boots off. The soles are worn out. I can imagine the millions of microscopic rubber particles they have shed on the asphalt along my journey from the West Coast.   My socks off, I put my feet up on the damp wooden bench. My bums feel uncomfortable, so I sit on my gloves, and pull my raincoat down to add a layer of protection. Humidity is a killer; cold you can always handle for a short while to let the skin dry. My maternal grandfather had taught me well.

It feels good to rest, my eyes wondering in the slow current of the unknown river and my feet taking a bath of fresh autumn air.

"*Salut*"

A woman stands under the drizzle beside the gazebo, watching the river. She didn't turn her head when she continued:

"*Tu vas où comme ça?*"

French: vaguely familiar. My dad taught me as we paddled the bays and hiked the valleys. We fished and we collected game in our traps. We ate what we needed and sold the rest. We had just enough money to buy sugar, milk, eggs, flour and Rice Krispies at the general store. The bureaucrats in Ottawa said they wanted to help us, but, for mysterious

reasons, they kept us in a state of dependence and misery to reach that self-valorizing objective.

I guess she is asking where I am going, so I risk an answer in the best French I can muster: I have no idea.

"*Je pas savoir?*"

It did sound like a question. She smiles, still contemplating the brown-greenish water that kept moving, apparently having no time to stop by and take a break with us.

"Where are you from?"

She had switched to English. I had met a few people since venturing into Québec, and "*les Québécois*" — the Quebecer as we call them — all had this extremely accommodating behaviour. Contrary to what we were told back home. Will someone call Québec's evil language police? They must be hiding somewhere. We can be so easily manipulated.

"I'm from Vancouver Island. Do you know?"

"I do, it's a beautiful place."

A yellow raincoat hood covering her head, she and her eyes were immobile in the rain.

"You have been there?" I was always curious about people knowing my homeland.

"No, I saw pictures on the Internet. Would love to go. I love nature."

"I love nature too. I am Native."

I thought this was a suitable explanation for the origin of my love for nature. I might as well volunteer this important information about my ethnicity right now. Even thought I was only half-blood. My father originated from a small Québec village, Saint *Something* as everything is called here. Maybe that is where I am going unconsciously. Is it home? What is home?

I need silence — as if I don't get enough of it on the road. People usually develop tongue paralysis when they find out I'm an 'Indian.' I keep hoping this is because they are ashamed of having stolen our lands, but I am realistic and I know it is because of fear. Fear of the difference.

"Aren't we all?" Surprising answer. The desired effect of my answer had failed to materialize.

"Aren't we all *what*?" I responded, as a fish goes for the bait.

"Natives... our ancestors exchanged more than goods." Her dreaming eyes flowing with the water, she replied almost before my interrogation was uttered, as if she completely expected my question. I join her in a contemplative silence, while I continue to analyze her answer.

I do not know how much time passed before the implicit peace

treaty was broken. Her voice warmed my blood, so I forgave her.

"My mom was Italian and my dad Irish."

"A true Canadian, heh..." I meant it to be a kind comment reflecting my openness to multiculturalism, yet it came out sarcastically. She evidently tuned to the vibes of the unintended meaning.

"You have no idea what it is to be Canadian." Abrupt. Hurting. But bull's eye, lady: Why the hell do you think I am on a cross-continental walk?

The lady in yellow interrupts my self-justifying thoughts, her eyes drawing from the invisible energy of the river.

"Look at this river. It's named Richelieu for the 17th century French cardinal and politician. Because it connects to the Hudson and provides a navigable waterway to the U.S. East Coast, the English, and later the Americans, repetitively used it in their multiple attempts to invade this land. You didn't know that, I'm sure. The source of the river is in Lake Champlain, named after the French founder of Quebec City, the 400 year-old walled city. Maybe you know that, right? That city was bombed into ruins in the summer of 1759 before the English finally took it in September. But then France abandoned us to the English even though we took back the city the following year. The road you were walking on, the road bordering the river, is known as *Le Chemin des Patriotes* – the Patriots Road — in remembrance of those who gave their life to rid this country of the English invader back in 1837-38."

She spat it all out in one breath, with the utmost passion, her eyes incessantly observing the passing liquid History.

"So this is why your licence plates say '*Je me souviens*'?"

"*T'as tout compris. Presque.*" I apparently understood everything. Almost.

"We are not that different, your people and mine. Living in the past-perfect; crying the lost land; cheated by History. "

Was this the key to my identity crisis? I am walking the land of my ancestors. The Asian hunters crossed the Bering Sea. The First-Nations people roamed the vastness of North America. The French voyageurs, les '*coureurs des bois*,' criss-crossed the continent. And all those who continue in the tradition, unimpeded by illusory borders and differences. What is it to be Canadian? It is perpetual change, movement, and construction. It is a mosaic of ways, of interactions and overlapping cultures and Histories to form a dynamic, unique Nation. This is our strength, our beauty. My ecstatic thoughts were short lived, shattered by a new History lesson.

"Yes, but no. *Car ton bras sait porter l'épée*... Because your arm

can carry a sword. The French version of the national anthem says it all..."

"But we have a tradition of peacekeeping..."

My objection is rejected with furor. I can imagine the fire of her eyes evaporating the rain, even the river itself.

"How long does a Nation have to do something, for it to be elevated into a tradition that supplants other traditions? Do you forget the thousands of Canadians who died in wars here and all over the world over the past century? Do you forget that Canada became a Nation in the mud and blood of Vimy Ridge? That it re-affirmed its stature on the beaches of Normandy, in Italy and in the Netherlands? It seems convenient to forget the past, to build the new myth of a peaceful Nation. But how can we forget the more recent sacrifices? Do we forget the Medak Pocket? Do we forget the first Gulf War? Do we forget that my brother just returned from Afghanistan in a box draped in red and white? That is what it is to be Canadian. *Car ton bras sait porter l'épée.*"

I should know better. In my defence, I could claim national amnesia. After all, we must distinguish ourselves from our trigger-happy neighbours to the South.

"I'm sorry. For everything. You know, I was in the Gulf with the Navy..." An attempt at reconciliation by showing that I truly understand.

We return to a meditative state of peace that was only punctuated by the trickle of the lazy rain. Without warning, she finally turns to face me.

"Are you continuing your journey?"

"Always, but I think I will stay here for a while."

She smiles, a drop of water holding heroically at the tip of her nose and a river of tears flowing down her cheeks.

MY PATCHWORK LIFE
by Corinne Cast McCorkle

I OPENED A BOX today. I thought I knew what was in it, so I hadn't bothered to open it the last time we moved. Now we had moved again, this time to Canada from England, and had gotten the remainder of our household goods back from years in storage. I wanted to consolidate my sewing supplies, so it was time to sort through the "quilting projects" hidden for many years in this small box. Surprises lay in this box, though. Look, here are the sewing machine needles and the bobbin box I haven't been able to find and have had to replace! Packers, I thought in exasperation, they do the dumbest things. Then I picked up the unfinished quilt squares, which I hadn't seen for several years, and suddenly I found myself, twenty years ago.

The young woman that I had been then, coping with living in the first foreign land she had ever seen, was vividly present in the room with me. My thoughts rocketed through the intervening years ... the babies who were now young men, the lost pet dogs and cats, the departed, dearly loved father and grandmother, the different countries, the many houses, the new communities, the strong friendships... I was stunned. I had not expected to find so much in this box.

Strong images of the year we spent in Germany arose as I looked at these quilts. Who knows the paths that will be taken in a lifetime, the unexpected turns, the lengthy byways that become the destination? I had made these quilts in the home of an American "military wife" in the middle of Frankfurt, Germany. I had spent a long time selecting the fabrics in a German department store, trying to find prints that most nearly

matched the American calicos I pictured when I thought of "quilts." The things we will do to try to make a foreign land feel like home! These fabrics still looked pretty German though, I thought, as I lifted them from the box. Somehow these little quilted cushion covers and the process of making them encapsulated the experience of being an expatriate, living away from one's own country. These bits of fabric evoked the sense of dislocation, the attempt to recreate a bit of home while still exploring and absorbing a new land, the new activities one tries, in order to fill the suddenly long days of no friends, and no real purpose.

I no longer recall the name of the woman who taught me to quilt, though I can still picture her and hear her Southern accent, so different to my Midwestern ear. The class in her home had been my first experience with the amazing and elaborate organizations that American women create to support each other in foreign countries. I had moved to Germany determined to make friends with only German people. After a few months in a country where I didn't speak the language, I finally admitted it wouldn't work. My husband's company had no information about local American resources, and I was the only "trailing spouse" associated with the Frankfurt office at that time. So I went to the American consulate, which was just around the corner from my apartment. Surely they would know about such things. They only knew of the American military officers' wives club, so I gamely went along and joined up. I didn't expect to be the only non-"military wife" in this large organization.

It was odd to find myself in a foreign country, learning about a group from my own country whom I had never before encountered. Even though I was a teenager and college student during the Vietnam era, I knew only one boy who had served in the military. Learning about American military life was not an experience I had expected to find in Germany. And yet, this is exactly what life overseas has given me: experiences and ideas that I have not anticipated. Of course, back then I looked forward to learning about my new country. I had expected to learn another language. But, I also found myself learning unexpected things, such as about other regions of America, even when I was so far from my homeland. I gained knowledge of other countries, too, even though I wasn't living in them, from the other lonely foreigners I encountered.

Most importantly, though, I learned about myself during that year in Germany. Coping with living in a foreign country was revealing for the young woman I then was. I had never been out of the United States before I moved abroad. We moved from Chicago, a city I had lived in all my life, where I had a group of friends who had been close for many years, a very egalitarian marriage, and a job with a title, a staff, and a decent

salary. When I first arrived in Frankfurt, I felt as if I had left behind all that had defined me and given me an identity. I suddenly had no value of my own, but had been demoted and submerged into Mrs. Mike, the stay-at-home wife doing ALL the housework and ALL the laundry and ALL the bookkeeping. I felt I was a blank, a void, all alone with my cat, in a flat with no phone, very little furniture, and very little husband. It was a shock.

Obviously, I wasn't as much of an unformed blank as I felt in those first days. However, moving overseas gave me the chance to discover parts of myself that I hadn't recognized before. In this foreign land where I knew no one, I did that most American thing -- I recreated myself. I found I had outgrown the persona I had been assigned in my group of long-term friends. Much to my surprise, I was an outspoken, even argumentative person, not quiet, and shy, and given to giggles. Even more surprising, as our moves came and went, I found myself taking charge of things, running committees and serving on organizational boards. Most important, though, those long lonely early days revealed strength, resiliency and a sense of adventure I never suspected I had.

Most days in those first weeks in Frankfurt, I found myself sitting on the floor of my empty flat, hugging the cat and sobbing. On those same tearful days, though, I also ventured out to explore my new land, buying meat from the butcher, figuring out how to read the signs for the *strassebahn* or streetcar, or exploring the local museums. I found that I enjoyed being by myself. I discovered enough depth within myself to survive the loneliness of living in a place where I didn't speak the language in spite of those last minute lessons, and where I didn't know a soul except my husband. As we explored other countries, I found I thoroughly enjoyed discovering the wildly different ways of doing simple, everyday things, and the different manners and social customs that have developed around the world. I discovered that kindness does not recognize any language barrier, as strangers reached out to help me resolve momentary difficulties. I even found I had the courage to mangle my new language in public and yet make myself understood. I still laugh over the poor lady behind the bread counter in my local German grocery who began flapping her hands in bewilderment and frustration whenever I showed up to order "bread rolls," whose German name, *brötchen,* has one of those impossible umlauts in it. My face would be bright red, but I got my bread rolls eventually.

I looked again at the quilts in the box, remembering the German living room where I sat and stitched them in the endless afternoons, watching our cat lounging on our balcony, our fifth-floor aerie in the tree-

tops. What a journey I had taken since then. The 70s tan sofa these cushions were supposed to match (which then was, of course, in storage back in the U.S.) was long gone, and anyway, I had never really liked brown. I had moved them so many times since that single year in Germany, always thinking I would finish them up when I was less busy. They had journeyed with me from Germany to three different houses in London, a suburban Chicago house not far from Lake Michigan, a mini-mansion near Dallas, and back to England, where we lived in two other houses. Now here they are in the Toronto suburbs, the latest stop on my life's journey. Perhaps I should just accept that I was never going to finish them, and quit moving them around the world. Time to get rid of them! Yet these little quilted pillow covers have so much to tell me about my past and the journey I have taken. They effortlessly recreate a wonderful year of my life, a period of great difficulty and huge excitement and joy. A year I love remembering. Maybe instead of tossing them out, it was time to find a quilting class in this new foreign country, and finally finish them up.

CHESTER AND GRACE
by Cassie McDaniel

GRACE WAS SOAKING IN a half-filled bathtub. Her breasts floated to the top of the lukewarm water like sand dunes smoothed by constant wind. With her whole hand she pinched the dimpled side of her thigh. "Dumplin'," she said. She looked at Chester who sat on the floor beside the tub, his boots pressing black marks against the base of the toilet. He didn't seem to be paying attention.

"Am I always gonna be like this?" Grace asked.

Chester looked up from his reverie, seeming to register his place on the floor for the first time. "Dumplin'?" he wondered out loud then shook his head. "I think you'll *always* be like this."

Grace's eyebrows furrowed. "You don't understand anything!" Her hands slapped the water and splashed drops onto the walls. She gathered soap bubbles to hide her body but the flesh of her lower stomach capped the water and her nipples pierced the iridescent bubbles with dark mauve. Chester looked away. Despite what Grace believed, he was listening, and he had meant to say *beautiful*, that he knew she would always be this beautiful to him.

"What do you like about this place, anyway?" she asked.

Chester knew what she was talking about now. This was his trailer, his home, and she hadn't wanted to come here in the first place. He sucked in his breath and tried to say again what he'd been meaning to say all this time. "This is perfect for us. We got so much land, Grace!" Chester motioned toward the window. "We can have fresh corn, grapes, even if they ain't s'posed to grow here. Endless stars. Don't it seem like

everythin's alive?" But that was the wrong thing to say. Grace slipped further into the tub as if cringing. Chester's voice picked up again.

"Grace I don't mean to say that you gotta love it here like I do... Maybe it's just hard times right now."

"Maybe I ain't got it," she creaked.

"But Grace, I think you could be happy here."

"Chester, I ain't in love."

"Grace... You ain't gotta love it back, not right away. It takes time. Besides..." He paused. What she had said was finally catching up to him.

She too was thinking hard about what she'd said, but all of a sudden she didn't know what they were talking about. "I don't know, Ches, I gotta get outta here." She pulled the plug with her toe and the drain began to chug the water down. She stood and reached behind him for a towel hung on the rack, her breasts swinging dangerously close to his face. She rained soapy drops as she arched her back and pulled the towel behind her like a grizzly against a tree. Chester clumsily unfolded himself from his tight spot on the floor then stood in the open doorway looking down. Grace dropped one end of the towel and with her free hand pulled it between her legs. He had never seen a woman be so rough with herself before – somehow it didn't seem right. "Grace..." Chester tried.

"What, Chester?" Her dirty-blonde hair clung to her forehead and neck. Any patience left seemed to have drained with the water.

"I.... I..." While Chester stuttered, Grace pushed past him through the doorway and while she dressed he stood alone, eyes still averted to the floor.

Chester stepped outside in time to see the pickup truck speed away, dusting the dry plants that grew by the road. He watched until the truck had become a fly on the horizon then he turned and walked back inside. The front door shut behind him with a soft thud. The air was heavy and dull. There was always room for more disappointment, Chester thought to himself. He wondered if he might ever stop expecting things to stay the way they were.

Inside, he stood by the window. The cloud of dust could still be seen hanging over the cornfield in the east. The sky was the color of an overripe peach and the smell of flowery suds lingered in the air as he thought about how she hadn't said goodbye.

Grace didn't come back that night. At first Chester hoped she would return for dinner, not fully understanding what had happened. Finally, he fell asleep on the couch.

He spent the next morning wandering around outside, nudging piles of dry sand into the cracked earth with his boots. He sat on the porch and looked across the still yard, shadows tumbling across the wooden angles as the hours passed. He watched from inside, eating supper alone, as a dog missing a hind leg limped across the distant field. He felt a sadness he had never known before.

In the evening, Chester lay in their bed staring up at the ceiling. "Open up, Boy!" hollered a booming voice from outside, a fist rattling the screened front door. Chester didn't get out of bed. The door handle gave easily to the man's large palm and he barged in. "Chester what are you up to, Boy? You got any beer?" His voice reverberated off the plastic walls. The man left the door open as he walked to the kitchen, shouting across the room, "I heard Grace ain't here and I could use a drink!" The cat bolted through the front door, frightened.

Chester saw the flash of animal from the bedroom and stood abruptly. "Dammit, Gainer! Tipsy's never comin' back now! Grace is gonna kill me."

"Chester, don't you worry about Grace. Let's you and me go for a drive. But first I'd like a beer if you got any." Gainer sat heavily on one of Chester's vinyl kitchen chairs. He planted his elbows on the table, marking it with mud from his work shirt but not noticing. Chester grimaced.

"Fine, no one else is gonna drink it." Chester went to the fridge and pulled a can from the plastic ring. He set it on the table then crouched at the front door where he called for Tipsy.

"What's the matter, Ches? Freedom too much for ya?" Without pausing for an answer he repeated, "Let's go for a drive. I need some air." He popped the can open and swallowed the beer in large gulps. "I wish my wife had taken off with Grace, you lucky bastard!" Gainer laughed loudly. He stood and finished his beer, crinkled the can, then went to the fridge for another. Chester stayed where he was clicking his tongue but Tipsy wouldn't come.

"Anyway, let's go. I'll drive."

"Fine," Chester said finally. "Whatever you want."

Gainer wedged the can into the cup holder between the two front seats and drove them to the creek that ran off Brownwood Lake. They parked the truck and Gainer got out; he lumbered toward the water through sharp brambles and yuccas. Sitting in the cab alone, Chester could hear coyotes howling far away. He remembered when Grace had let him love her just how she was. He couldn't remember the last time they had been apart.

He watched a gust of wind heave a billow of dust across the land-

scape, moving like its own weather system, independent of the rest of the sky. It darkened the creek and gave the land an antique veneer. Gainer returned to the truck, his sleeve pressed against his mouth, coughing. "Let's go," he said, looking at the sky. "It's gonna rain."

They rode the short distance back to the trailer in silence. It didn't rain, but Gainer left anyway, taking the remaining beers with him. Chester felt that he could blink and everyone would disappear.

He went to bed early and dreamed of dust storms that blew in strangers from distant lands. They stayed long enough to play a hand of cards. Then the dust blew them away again, leaving in their wake small, congealed balls of dirt that soon dried out and disintegrated back to dust. He woke a little past midnight, feeling that the land he lived on was ephemeral, like love. He couldn't hang on to it. He closed his eyes and tried to sleep again.

It was hot the night she left. Grace's thighs stuck to the plastic seat. Holding the steering wheel with her left knee, she ducked below the dashboard for an old rag that she shoved underneath her legs. She drove for several hours not knowing how long she would be gone.

She pulled into her grandmother's driveway and switched off the headlights. The porch light wasn't on, but Grace knew this path by heart. Nothing much changed out here. If her Gran had still been alive, she would have been asleep in the familiar, flowered nightie, her teeth foaming in a glass beside the bed. Tonight Grace crept in as if she was seventeen again. She knocked her shin on something hard in the entryway, cursed to herself, then collapsed on the sofa.

In the morning she opened her eyes, her neck stiff. Sunshine poured in through oversized windows across Gran's sewing magazines and boxes of string and ribbon. She looked around the house, but it was still. Her fingers trailed along the walls of peeling wallpaper as she wandered from room to room. In the bathroom she picked up an expired medicine bottle and without thinking dropped it into the waste bin. She knew now why she was here.

She gathered momentum in the kitchen where things were easiest to discard – deflated onions in milky-brown liquid and skillets caked with grease and charcoal, both empty and unused tins of Ovaltine. She moved to the back room, sifting through drawers of linen and cabinets of keepsakes, boxes of yellowed magazines, letters in faded ink. She continued filling garbage bag after bag until the last space to clear was her grandmother's bedroom.

She took a deep breath and entered the room. The heavy muslin

curtains admitted little light and the room smelled of baby powder and damp wood. The bed was made.

Grace sat on the floor and began to weep, understanding she had never believed Gran would ever die. After awhile she went to the closet and pulled the clothing off the hangers, hugging the blouses and sweaters as if they could conjure up the missing body. Grace pulled a dress down and rubbed the fabric between her fingers. By then she had made up her mind.

When Grace returned to the trailer, the moon had positioned itself high in the sky. The plants in the yard glowed neon blue as if lit from within. She walked to the door and almost turned the handle but at the last moment decided to knock. She wanted Chester to know that she was asking to be let back in, not demanding it.

Chester came, his hair in sleepy disarray. Grace spoke softly. "I don't know how to explain," she said, but Chester shook his head. He opened up the screen door and pulled her to his chest, his hand wrapped gently around the back of her head.

"I went to Gran's," she explained, speaking into his shirt. "It's not home anymore."

"That's okay." His voice was soft, tired.

"I missed you."

"I know. You're home now."

Chester held the door for Grace and they climbed straight into bed where his hand stayed on her all night, and Grace did not try to escape. For a long while he lay awake listening to her breathing, but soon enough he slept, and in the morning just before the sun had finished rising, before either of them woke, Tipsy emerged from behind the sprawling yucca. She placed herself on the porch in front of the door to the trailer, licking each of her paws, waiting to be let in.

A BLACK SNOWBALL
by Braz Menezes

THICK SNOW BLANKETS THE park by the Toronto Island Ferry dock. After days of gloom, a bright sun in a clear blue sky lazily burns away the crispness of a winter morning, even as the chill penetrates every inch of my made-in-the-tropics body. I clasp my Tim Horton's cup of hot coffee with both hands, determined that any escaping heat must pass through me first. A mother is hugging a paper bag, from which her five year old, warmly bundled in 'Vancouver Winter Olympics' designer wraps, feeds the hovering gulls. These desperately clamour for the dried breadcrumbs, while a few feet away, a flotilla of ducks is engaged in its daily swim class. This morning the lake has a raw beauty. An overnight snow flurry has dumped white stuff over the previously iced surface and the early morning Island ferry has cut a wake of crushed ice fragments that sparkle like huge diamonds, as refraction and reflection transform each piece.

Around me too, everywhere is absolutely white except for the long grey shadows of a winter sun. I spot a black snowball about seven meters away... whoever heard of a black snowball? I look again, as the snowball comes to life. A tiny head peeks up, and a furry tail whisks back and forth. The squirrel chatters angrily, as if I shouldn't be sitting on this particular bench. I stare right back in defiance, but I give in. I stand up and stroll away along the boardwalk. I figure it too, like the gulls, must be desperate for food, to have come out on a cold January morning. Once when I was young and lonely, my really good friend was a squirrel.

The memories are vivid. It was 1950. I had just turned eleven at a Jesuit-run boarding school in Goa, India. My family had embarked on a steamer back to Kenya, and I was left with the priests to hone me

on the three Rs: Religion, Routine and Repentance. Fortunately for me, within two months, I found the love of my life. My friend Pedro and I, in our world of perpetual hunger, routinely roamed through a grove of cashew trees behind the school. Sometimes we were lucky and found a cashew or two or some berries to tide us over between meals. But alas at the end of the season, there was nothing to be plucked. As we had been warned to look out for snakes, we stepped cautiously, listening for the possible movement of a snake among the fallen leaves. The relative silence was only broken by the sounds of birds above, and the rustle of leaves and cracking of small twigs under our feet.

Suddenly Pedro freezes, signalling me to stop and listen. I hear the gentle, yet painfully squeaky whimper of a young creature. We inch forward. I see it first — a baby squirrel in a nest of leaves, tucked into the crevice of a cashew tree. In Nairobi, my friend John, and I had experienced such scenes often. We would pick up little fluffy chicks, baby pigeons, puppies, squirrels, and other animals. Now I instinctively reach out, squeezing my palm through the opening and cupping it to gently scoop the tiny squirrel out. Its big round eyes seem frightened.

"Snake! Snake!" Pedro shouts so hysterically, that I nearly drop my prize. He is jumping in a panic. "Snake! Lando! My heart is beating so fast...here, put your hand here and feel it. It was that thick," he says, holding up his index and thumb, "orange-brown with black marks." We realize the snake had been stalking the squirrel, and those panic squeaks were the baby sensing danger. Pedro tells me it was about three feet long and was slithering down the cashew tree just as I was putting my hand into the nest.

"You scared us both," I tell him, holding my pet, now cowering in the warmth of my hand. "I bet its little heart is also going boom, boom, boom, inside." I hold the squirrel to my ear like a wrist watch, and I can hear its fast heart-beat. "It's so cute. Feel its fur, see how soft it is."

"By the way, it's not an 'it', but a 'he'," Pedro announces. "So what are you going to call him?"

"It's the colour of a dik-dik in Kenya," I tell him. "I'll call him Dik-Dik."

"I've never heard of a dik-dik before. Is that a bush or a bird or something?"

"It's like a small deer," I tell him, as I carefully place Dik-Dik in the side pocket of my shorts. Dik-Dik seems instantly at home and stays quiet and content as we walk back to our dormitory

"It's scary to think that if we'd been just a little late, Dik-Dik would have been half way down that snake," Pedro says as we walk back

to school.

It never occurred to us at that time that it was wrong to take a young one from its nest. In a way, we ourselves had been removed from our own parents' nest at a young age, and had been sent off to boarding school, had we not?

Several of my friends in our dormitory already had pet squirrels of their own. With their help, I learned the basics of parenting baby squirrels to adulthood. Dik-Dik responded quickly to my affection, and to his training, so we bonded easily. He made no big demands — all he wanted was just a few crumbs of food daily and a cuddle; he was just like one of us.

Within three weeks, Dik-Dik could run all the way across my outstretched hands; he could manoeuvre himself around the back of my neck and crawl down my back. He sometimes walked slowly, moving first the right front and right rear legs simultaneously, and then the left set. When he moved fast, he almost skipped, moving the front legs and the rear legs alternately. Within a month or so I could walk around the school campus with Dik-Dik perched on my shoulder, just like Long John Silver and his parrot in 'Treasure Island'. Dik-Dik was beautiful at three months old. His body was about four inches long, not including his big bushy tail, with dark streaks along his tan sides, and with big black eyes.

Dik-Dik made St. Joseph's bearable, but one day he got me into deep trouble. The rules said no pets were permitted in classrooms. In practice, however we pet-owners felt we could not really keep them in their boxes in the dormitory all day. So each morning at breakfast, each owner would put aside a few crumbs of bread in an envelope, to take into class. We had individual wooden desks with a hinged lid that became our worktop when down. Under the lid, we placed our books; pens, pencils and erasers; our pet squirrel and the bread crumbs. The desks had a little hole, about an inch and a half in diameter; the ceramic ink-well effectively plugged any escape for our squirrels during class. One morning, I placed Dik-Dik as usual into the desk, spread the bread crumbs, and added an extra treat – half a cashew nut crushed into tiny pieces. Dik-Dik looked up so pleased. His big dark eyes radiated affection. I put the desk lid down just as Fr. Damien, our Latin teacher, walked into the room.

Latin was one of our most boring subjects. The older boys joked that Fr. Damien was completely celibate in both mind and body; neither sports nor other extra-curricular activities seemed to interest him. He lived for and loved Latin.

"Good morning, class," Fr. Damien says as he gazes over his wire-rimmed spectacles, "today we will continue with Latin grammar and syntax.

We will review the four verb conjugations and five noun declensions, and then we can move on and spend time on the irregular verbs." The class gives a collective groan, which he characteristically ignores. My friend Ben is summoned first to the blackboard; he scribbles the conjugations of the first class of verbs, ending in '*are*'. Then it is Musso's turn to spell out the conjugation for verbs ending in '*ere*'. The class drags on. I open the lid just a little bit. Dik-Dik perks up; I quickly close the lid. It makes a gentle thud.

"Lando, let's see what you remember from last week," Fr. Damien says. His keen ears have picked up the sound of my lid closing. I walk to the blackboard.

"Please write down the present indicative, active singular and plural for the verb to love... *amare*," Fr. Damien says. I visualise in my mind a simple table I had prepared the previous day, and start scribbling with the short piece of white chalk that he hands me: *amo, amas, amat, amamus, amatis, amant*... and then pandemonium breaks out!

When class got unbearably boring, which often happened, someone would quietly remove the ceramic inkwell out of a colleague's desk, if there is a squirrel in residence. Then events usually took their own course. On this occasion, my colleague Celso 'got even' with me; he quietly removed my inkwell. Dik-Dik, sitting on a pile of books, sensed I was not at my desk; the lure of escape was irresistible.

In a flash, he was out. A hand reached out to grab him. Dik-Dik leapt across two desks, and then across to a desk in the row behind. My ceramic inkwell crashed to the floor, splattering ink all over. The class was enjoying it. Somebody removed another inkwell. Everyone was yelling and laughing. Eddie's inkwell was removed. Within seconds Armando's too. There were now four squirrels chasing each other and being chased around the room. We were lurching forwards and sideways to catch our own squirrels, or any squirrel for that matter. Boys that did not own pets, did all they could to escalate the level of chaos. The class was already out of control. Fr. Damien had learnt from experience as a novice at the school, that the best way to resolve things was to leave the room; he could then return to extract a bigger toll from the class. Experience had taught him that conjugating Latin verbs ad nauseam can tame the wildest spirits. So Fr. Damien quietly slipped away, closing the door behind him to contain the noise within the classroom.

Eventually, the squirrels had exhausted themselves and surrendered one by one. They returned to their respective desks. The pieces of ceramic were swept up; the spilt ink of two broken inkwells mopped up. We waited in absolute silence for that door to slowly creak open and for

Fr. Damien to appear.

Perhaps, at one time, Fr. Damien himself has had a small squirrel as a pet, or he may have been denied the opportunity to have a squirrel as a pet. Whatever the reason, retribution was not as severe as we had expected. The class paid a collective price staying late to complete the work; but for the class it had been a successful session. Time had just flown by. For some months after the incident, I harboured a suspicion that one day, sooner or later, retribution from Fr. Damien would still come my way. I made it a point to be especially nice to him. Dik-Dik too, behaved himself. Then about a year later, I was hastily summoned back to Kenya, and Dik Dik was released into the dense growth behind my grandmother's house. He was constantly seen in the neighbourhood until one day he disappeared forever.

I have been the length of the boardwalk and am back to the park bench, which has been abandoned. On the lake, a ferry boat seems to be returning along the path of diamonds. The mother and child have moved somewhere else; the gulls are gone; the ducks dispersed. I see my little 'black snowball' quickly scurry up a maple tree. Only the long winter shadows remain, as they follow the sun; soon they too will be gone for the day, as it seems, has the black snowball.

SERENDIPITY
by Michelle Monteiro

FEELING THE BLOOD RUSH through his body, he checked for the third time to make sure his helmet was firmly placed on his head, confirming that his curly chocolate hair was neatly tied back. Anticipation revved up his anxiety as sweat dripped from his forehead, down his nose, and into his mouth. Straightening his seatbelt, he counted the seconds until the flag signal was given to start.

Intoxicating cheers from the crowd sounded like muted echoes from a far away mountain, reverberating against the 750 horsepower gas engine roaring in his ears. Hands shaking, jaw trembling, he steadied his hands on the steering wheel, waiting for the track marshal in black and red to drop the checkered flag. His hazel eyes narrowed when he sensed a flash of movement and he saw the track marshal thrust the flag into the air for barely a second before it swung back down. This was the awaited signal; he jabbed the gas pedal as hard as he could. Travelling at two hundred and twenty kilometres per hour, his adrenalin pulsed even harder. He wanted to win the race; he was going to win the race if only ...

Twenty-four-year old, Helio Romano's head jerked up as the sound of the SUV's horn behind his pickup vibrated through every nerve in his body. Snapping back to reality, he remembered he was on the 401 trying to get back to his garage, *Helio's Speed-Way,* in Toronto. The heavy traffic appeared to have subsided since the last time he was paying attention to his surroundings, so he managed to pull to the curb while cursing at the old woman who ruined his day dream with the bark of her car horn. Putting the car in park, Helio removed his seatbelt and rested his

head on the steering wheel.

Life wasn't supposed to be as boring and pathetic as this. The five foot, seven inch mechanic who fantasized about becoming the next professional NASCAR driver shouldn't spend the rest of his life fixing cars and getting paid a little over minimum wage to do so.

Fantasy over, Helio lifted his head and glanced at the side-view mirror. His eyes widened at what he saw. A reflection of a red Viper caught his attention, erasing any thoughts of his day dream. Sticking his head out of the open window, he squinted his eyes and stared at the car. Undoubtedly, the Viper was there, seducing his imagination as he tried to absorb every detail. He always wanted one, even if he couldn't afford it, but he never seen one this close until now. He fantasized about the type of person who actually has cash to buy one of these beauties?

Wiggling back into his seat, he wished there was something he could do to stop the driver of his future car from escaping from sight. Eyes fixated on the Viper driving away, he inhaled deeply, and staying focused on the red vision, he saw the right turn signal flash. Unexpectedly, it veered into Helio's lane, made a sudden halt and backed up closer to his muddy pickup. Yanking the keys out of the ignition, he swung the door open and stepped out. What was happening? Did some unnatural force give into his desires? He stiffened when he saw the driver of the Viper staring back at him.

Her jade eyes caught his attention as she unfolded her slim body, with impossibly long legs and slender arms, as she exited the Viper. Under a 1977 Toronto Blue Jays baseball cap, was an enchanting face smattered with freckles and framed by long blonde hair hanging past her shoulders. Her plain white t-shirt and jeans, clearly emphasized her physical attributes.

"Hello, did your car break down?" she asked, lips curling into a smile. "Would you like some help?"

"Nice car," was all Helio could mutter, pointing his index finger at the Viper.

"You mean the Fourth Generation Viper SRT-10? Yeah, I guess it is pretty *nice*." Mouth wide open, he could not believe what he was hearing. How could this woman possibly know what model she was driving?

"You know about cars?" he sputtered not expecting to hear a squeak echo in his voice. Grinning, the woman casually flicked at her nails.

"Oh, I know a lot more than model names. I recognize a good engine when I see one," she smirked. "And the 150 horsepower you got in your 1968 Ford F100 pickup is pretty lame for a truck."

Helio was once again stunned. So this woman also knew what model he was driving when not even he knew? The only thing he could remember about it was that his own father had bought the pickup when he was only a child and was given to him as a birthday present when he turned twenty-two.

Fumbling, the keys in his hand, Helio sarcastically laughed. In truth, his mocking was meant for himself because he knew his truck was garbage.

"Wait, you think this piece of junk is mine?" he chuckled leaning against the pickup. "This belongs to my friend." The woman's eyes narrowed, suspecting him of lying. Helio saw this, gulped and looked around nervously.

"I'm serious," he assured her. "There's a crack in the rear bumper and I was asked to fix it for a lower price." Pausing for a moment, he grabbed his wallet from his jacket, took out a card and gave it to the woman.

"You see," he added, gaining his confidence back. "I have my own business, *Helio's Speed-Way*. It's very profitable."

"I'm sure it is," the woman smiled as she put the card in her pocket. "So I assume your name is Helio? I'm Olivia, by the way." Helio studied the woman as they shook hands, his eyes lowered, his lips dry. Skin touching skin, he felt a tingle race through his nerves, followed by quick-paced heartbeats. Stomach tossing and turning, he hoped Olivia wouldn't notice how clammy his hands were becoming.

"You know you can't fool me," she snickered, breaking the silence. "There was never a second when I believed your story. I hate it when guys lie about their cars; I think that's probably worse than cheesy pickup lines."

"I... I –"

"Hold on, let me finish. Gosh, weren't you taught not to interrupt people?" Olivia laughed. "Anyway, have you ever thought about replacing the engine in your pickup?"

"Replace it?" the puzzled mechanic asked.

"Yeah, you take out the bad engine and put in something better." In response, Helio rolled his eyes. This woman was surreal, thinking she knew everything about cars.

"I get it," he replied. "I *could* buy a new engine, but I rather save up the money. When I've earned enough, I'll be packing my bags and leave Toronto to pursue my dream."

"What's the dream?"

Helio smiled as he remembered his latest day dream. Recollect-

ing the images and sounds of the fantasy, he got himself lost in a trance and it took Olivia to repeat her question again to bring him back to reality.

"I plan on moving to Tennessee to become a professional NASCAR driver," he mumbled with some self-doubt. Arms crossed at ease, Olivia's gaze on Helio lightened, intrigued by his hopeful future.

"You like to race?" she simpered. "Have any experience?"

"If street racing back at home in Ecuador counts, then yeah, I do have some experience." Helio boasted as he failed to hold back a cocky smile. "I love to race. I guess it's because of the rush you feel when you're speeding and your eyeballs feel like they're popping out of their sockets." Eyes focused on Olivia, his mind was blown away by her expressionless face.

"Oh sorry," he paused, blushing. "You probably don't know what I'm talking about."

"I know what you mean," Olivia snapped staring at her running shoes. The drastic change in tone of her voice caused Helio to flinch.

"I can't take this anymore," she snorted. "I've lasted this long, but you surprise me, Helio. I mean, you say you want to be a NASCAR driver and yet you can't even recognize one when she's right in front of you."

"What?"

"Still haven't figured it out?" she gloated. "Boy, do I pity you. Allow me to reintroduce myself. My name is Olivia-Elizabeth Parker, last year's Sprint Cup Series champion." Having nothing to say, Helio froze, such reaction made Olivia laugh hysterically.

"You're O.E Parker?" he gulped recalling seeing the Sprint Cup Series last year. These particular races were most memorable. He had spent hours watching them on television, in between breaks to retrieve more popcorn. Parker was in the lead most of the time, and won the final race by a tenth of a second before anyone else.

"That's what they call me in the tracks." Olivia smiled.

"I had no idea it was you."

"Clearly."

Neither one said a word, both waiting for the other to speak. Listening attentively, both could probably hear each other's breathing, if not for the cars passing by.

"You know," Olivia paused stepping closer to Helio. Flicking at her nails again, she kicked a pebble out of her way. "I recently fired one of my pit crew members. I'm still looking for a replacement." Eyes widened, Helio stood up from resting his body against his pickup. Were unnatural

forces making his fascinations come true?

"I'm a mechanic, a pretty good one if I might add."

"I thought you might say that!" laughed Olivia grabbing a pen out of her pocket. She reached for Helio's hand and began writing on it.

"This is my cell phone number, call me if you're interested in the job. It pays well," she added. "Now if you step back, I can fix your pickup in a couple of minutes."

"About that," Helio muttered scratching the back of his head. "My truck never broke down."

"Then what have I been doing here for the past several minutes?" she giggled, heading back to her Viper. Pausing for a moment, she turned her head back and gave Helio a wink.

"I better be going now," she smiled. "Hope you'll think about my offer."

"I will."

Opening the door of his pickup, Helio glanced at the number on his hand. This was real. This wasn't his day dream again, he was actually living it. Sitting in his truck, he took his cell phone out of the glove compartment and dialed Olivia's number out of impulse. She answered after the second ring.

"Hello?"

"Hey Olivia. It's Helio," he mumbled. "I'm calling about the job offer."

"And?"

"I'm one hundred percent interested!" he smirked. Gazing at the side-view mirror again, he heard Olivia laugh at the other end. This made him smile.

Maybe life *was* supposed to be boring and pathetic, at least for only a while.

A BLUE FISH
by Yoko Morgenstern

A FRIEND DIED. HIS 1400cc grey Honda crashed into a six-ton dump truck, right between the tires as he tried to overtake a car in the wrong lane. The police found a crushed can of Ginger Ale behind the brake. An intern at a junior high school at that time, he was on his way home from school. He knew his girlfriend was waiting.

Makeup couldn't mend his damaged body. The small window of his plain-wood coffin was covered by a white cloth, and we couldn't see his face for the farewell. We only made a pile of white chrysanthemums on the coffin.

Right about then, we heard a thud. Rei, his girlfriend, my close friend, fell down on the floor. Immediately, the crowd of black clothed people formed a mountain over her. Picturing her small body lying on the floor under the tens of faces, I couldn't even go to talk to her. Whatever I would say would sound fake, I thought. It wasn't me who'd lost my love. Not knowing what to do, I left the funeral.

"Thank you for the letter," said Rei to me a few weeks after the funeral. I wrote to her that I'd regretted I hadn't said anything to her, and that I would be always there for her.

"You don't know how much I appreciated it. People who I didn't even know came to me and said *I-know*s. I mean, it was nice of them, but," Rei closed her eyes, "...I just wanted to be left alone."

"...I know," I said. She opened her eyes and looked in mine, and we both laughed.

"Now, I'd like to ask a favor of you," said Rei.

"Which is?"

"I'd like to go to his forty-ninth-day ceremony in his hometown. Can you give me a company?"

He, she and I, all lived in Tsukuba city which was about fifty kilometers north-east of Tokyo. The city was built only for a university and some governmental institutes. An artificial landscape, boulevards, crossing at right angles, like squares of a chess board, the uniform height trees lined the streets.

We were students of the same university, and waiters at the same pub. We had all come from different parts of Japan to this city. Going to his hometown in Kagoshima prefecture meant going to the most southern prefecture of the most southern island of Japan's four main islands.

A university girlfriend wouldn't have the same legitimate powers as a wife would do. His body was brought back to his home, and for Rei, *c'est fini*. I sensed her hesitation to visit his family in this delicate time. I did quick mental arithmetic to see if I could afford flight tickets from the month's saving. "... Sure," I said.

September in Japan is a Typhoon season. Flights were often canceled and we missed the forty-ninth, a Buddhist ceremony for the dead to leave for *the other world*. We finally had a chance to fly, though at the check-in counter we were informed about a possible change of the route due to an approaching typhoon to the Kyusyu area.

"What do you think?" asked Rei.

"Why not take chances? We are here anyway," I said.

Our flight landed at a small airport instead of the Kagoshima main airport, as expected. We decided to rent a car for the detour. As we were lining up in front of a rent-a-car company counter, a big man behind me asked us, "Where are you two going?"

"To Kanoya city," answered Rei.

"I'm going in the same direction. Why don't you let me rent one and give you a ride?"

Rei and I looked each other. Her eyes implied yes.

"Sure, why not?" I said.

The driver's seat of a white Suzuki Kei car seemed too cramped for the man. I sat in the front seat, so I was in charge of being social to him.

"Were you on the same flight?" I asked.

"Yes," the man turned his face toward me.

"Where are you going?"

"To Fukuoka."

"Fukuoka? That's like a half-day drive from here!"

"My flight to Fukuoka was cancelled, and ours was the only one available today. I have to go back to work tomorrow."

"What do you do?"

"I'm a prison guard on the death row."

Thousands of questions came up in my mind. Still, I only asked, "What is it like?"

The man didn't turn his face toward me. "...well, I sometimes get chocolate boxes from their families."

Blown down trees oppressed the highway from the both sides. "I hear it was really stormy around this area yesterday. Some even died," the man said.

He dropped us off at the address we gave, and drove off, not accepting our offer to split the cost of the car.

It was an old, traditional Japanese wooden house. The teak walls had turned into silvery grey over the years, yet the black tiles of the gabled roofs still remained lustrous. No sooner had the car left than the front door of the house opened. A graying-haired, middle-aged couple appeared. The woman stretched her neck like a crane in the direction of the car left and said, "Oh, has the taxi already left? We wanted to pay the fare..."

We explained there had been no need.

His mother was short and chubby, his father was tall and skinny. The pair looked just like those old couples in picture books of Japanese folk tales. A traditional wife and husband, who called each other "*Okasan,* the mother," and "*Otosan,* the father." They never forgot to put smiles on their faces.

The father led us to the living room, while the mother made green tea for us. When we sat down on the tatami floor, I noticed its mint-like smell.

"We feel so bad for not picking you up at the airport," the father brought up the topic again.

"We didn't know which one we were landing," said Rei, "Really, please don't feel bad. We were fine."

While they make small talk, I looked at photographs of the family on the shelves. The mother and a boy. Three boys and a dog. I knew his elder brother was also at our university. They were soccer players, and our university was famous for it.

The mother came into the living room with a tray of tea, and noticed that I was looking at the pictures.

"Do you have any siblings?" she asked me.

"No. I'm the only child."

"Oh, then," *you must have been spoiled,* was what I expected to follow, because people had been telling me that millions of times. An only child usually doesn't wear old clothes or has old toys, but this doesn't tell anything about being spoiled. People judge people by what they have, not by what they don't have. "...you must have been so lonely."

I raised my brows and said, "Yes."

"I was still not satisfied when I got two kids. Two was too few. So we made three," she said, and gave a half smile.

The father told us that the third son was also going to Tsukuba the following year. "They all have to go so far, just to play soccer," he said, and gave a half smile.

"I think the bath is ready," said the mother. Japanese family members share the same water in the bathtub, and guests usually take *Ichiban-buro*, the first bath. Rei was too tired to take a bath, so I was the first to go.

I cleansed my body thoroughly in the washing space, and then soaked myself in the bathtub. Sunk in the hot water until the chin, I felt as if I had been peeping into someone's life when that very person was absent.

"We'll take you to a *Satsuma-age* restaurant tomorrow after-noon," said the mother in front of our guest bedroom. *Satsuma-age,* a deep-fried fish cake. Nothing fancy; there are many factory-made items in the chilled section of supermarkets. But I got a craving when she said that in this restaurant, cooks fried them in the open kitchen in front of guests. *Satsuma* was the medieval name of Kagoshima prefecture, I sud-denly recalled. I went to bed, dreaming of golden brown crispy skins and spongy white fish meat of a freshly fried *Satsuma-age.*

The restaurant was closed the next day. His parents decided to take us to the coast instead. When we were waiting for a bus at a stop, I saw an old shed right in the middle of the yellowing rice fields. One of its walls which faced us was occupied by a huge billboard. Jodie Foster was smiling at us with a coffee beverage in her hand. An advertisement from years before. The billboard had been in the sun and rain the whole while, and had lost its colours. It almost looked like a black and white picture.

The bus went uphill, and began to go downhill. From the windows, far below through the darkness of pine tree woods, I saw the seawater shine. The bus threaded through the woods, and reached to a beach.

It was a sunny day, but the water was grey. It wasn't like white-sand beaches of Phuket Island, or like black-sand beaches of the Canary Islands. It was a typical Japanese grey beach. We strolled to the rockiest

part which was exposed because of the low-tide.

"Where are you from?" the mother asked me.

"Tokyo."

"Oh, then, the life here must be so different to you."

When I was about to answer, Rei called me, "Hey, come over here, look!"

The mother and I went up to where she was. She was on the ground, her knees bent in her chest, looking into a pool between the rocks.

There was an inch-long, neon blue tropical fish paused in the water.

"A tropical fish? I thought we have them only in Okinawa!" I said, because Kagoshima still belonged to the temperate zone. When I lowered my head toward the water with a slight excitement, I heard the mother shout, "Otosan, where are you going?"

Rei and I looked up. The father was standing on a rock which was a meter away from the shore, his hands on his back, one held the other's wrist. He was looking down at his feet, his shoulder stooped. And then he jumped onto the next rock, and onto the next.

"Otosan, don't go so far! It's dangerous!" cried the mother, yet the father didn't turn around. He kept leaping, like a little boy hop on a foot, and went farther and farther from the shore.

"Otosan, Otosaaan," she kept calling. The father didn't turn around. "Come baaack!" Her cry echoed in the air. I looked at her face. I saw tears run down on her cheek. And then I looked at the father. He was still jumping over the rocks, hand in hand on his back, his head down, his shoulder stooped.

ME?

by Diksha Pal Narayan

EAVESDROPPING, THOUGH NOT MY profession, is my favourite pastime. Unlike most people who like spending their free time daydreaming, I prefer to be an eavesdropper. I feel I learn most about myself, by observing myself in relation to others.

At work I eavesdrop on conversations of a group of ladies who think of themselves as out of reach of the normal person. This 'elite' group consists of women who are usually cold to anyone who is not a part of their friends circle. As hard as I try, I cannot see myself a member of this group. I lack the tact it takes to ridicule not only others, but their own friends within this circle.

These women pretend to live the smooth, controlled, trouble-free existence, where, the kind of nail polish to wear is the biggest problem of their lives. How can I accept that a life like that exists? Besides that, as much as I try, I cannot learn to appreciate my painted face. The remainder of my adolescent years, those few pimple marks, make me feel more pretty than any lipstick or eye shadow would. I guess, I don't belong to this set of women.

During lunch hour I prefer eating at a restaurant near my office, where the food is edible, cheap, but most importantly — interesting. Regular visitors like me, are a group of three girls who prefer this restaurant to their college canteen.

All they ever talk about is there is the love of their life...a movie actor. Their faces light up when they read a new article about him. They spend most of their time quarrelling over a man who they might never

see, let alone talk to.

"Why do you love him so much?" I once got the courage to ask one of them. She looked at me in such disbelief, was it not obvious? He is very good at what he does... infact 'the best.' Acting is a profession, right? So why is it that the plumber, postman or the dentist...who are also good at their jobs, do not attract these girls' attention?

I got the privilege to meet this fellow, courtesy a journalist friend on a popular website. I had to feel all the excitement those girls felt while merely talking about him. I had thought my face would light up like theirs did each time they saw a new photograph of their idol. Ironically, as hard as I tried to get that reaction I just couldn't. My heart didn't thump any faster, nor did I skip a heartbeat, at the sight of their idol. All I saw in front of me was a man... a normal man with a fatuous smile on his face. Even when he sat next to me for the photograph my journalist friend was insistent on having taken... I felt nothing.

How am I to feel anything for a man I really do not know? My curiosity had placed me beside him - not any emotion. Maybe I have outgrown the Mills & Boons stage of my life...

Quite contrary to my lunch companions, are my travel companions. As I travel along with this other set of women on my way home in the overcrowded bus, I learn of the latest in music & fashion. These girls are the milder versions of the 'elite group' as they let anyone join in, as long as they are fashionable, have an absurd accent as well as fool themselves into believing that they are the centre of every one else's world. They are loud and their activities provide the much needed entertainment for all us fellow travellers.

I have sincerely tried to appreciate their music - which I can't understand more than the initial 2 lines-ever - their choice in boy friends ,their fashions , and their jokes; all, I can't seem to understand. The concept of 'small in size-big in price' clothes that they wear also confuses me.Just when I think I have learnt the way to live, my life changes. When expected to feel a portion of the excitement I knew the star-struck girls would feel, I felt, nothing.

I actually learnt the lyrics of the new Jennifer Lopez song...but it did nothing to my soul. Fancy clothes and painted faces make me feel like an object put on display rather than an individual. I can't see myself as the shy-obedient kind either. I think, but I am not a thinker. I believe in religion, but I am not religious. I like movies, but I am not a movie buff. So who am I?

Will I ever belong to a specific group? What group does the other person place me in? Can a group and its members be termed as good

or bad? Are we all just different? Why is it that I desire to be someone else?

The most powerful desire within me is to be more than I am now, at this moment. I want to be more, learn more, grow more, and experience more. Is that the reason I push myself into being someone else? Is that how, in seeking to be someone else, I realize more of what I want to be? Is seeking them releasing the 'me' inside of me?

WRITERS' CLUB
by Peta-Gaye Nash

LILLIAN USED TO BE a poet. She's not anymore, not because she gave it up but because she's dead. Or expired as my Punjabi friend says, expired, as if she were a plastic tub of yoghurt that has gone all curdled and runny. All that I have left of Lillian are two of her books of poetry and a dim memory of the time I went to visit her and tell her how much I liked her poetry. I also wanted to see what her house was like. It was in a gated community and I knew her son-in-law was wealthy. I can't remember much of her place but that's because I'm not a sensor, the personality type where you remember things, details around you. I'm a perceiver. I notice relationships. Keith, our workshop leader, told me that's the problem with my writing. He said, "Lizzy, you don't notice the natural world around you and how the sunlight coming through a window can cast a glow on someone's face." Now I always include the sunlight in my writing but I never know if it sets in the west or rises in the east and when I find out I always forget and it doesn't matter because I don't know directions. If I'm straight ahead, it's always north for me. I walk with my head down oblivious. One time in the country, I had my head down walking and staring at the ground, my head clouded with a thousand thoughts and I walked smack into a low branch of a tree. It surprised me somehow that a branch should be so low. I resolved to walk with my eyes straight ahead from then on, but it didn't last. Habits. As soon as I put my chin up, some magnetic force pulls my head down again.

I remember that Lillian's life and house seemed idyllic. It didn't matter that she'd been married four times and had divorced and outlived

all her husbands. She was sitting on the veranda with a cup of tea in her hand and the shadow of a maid in the background dusting or doing some menial task. It was a scene from plantation life. Lillian wore a long, loose flowing dress and even though she was hunched over, she still managed to look quite the diva, her thinning black hair cut short, her body slim and her eyes bright blue. Back then, she was at least eighty-five.

"Elizabeth, my dear, welcome and do sit down. Would you like a cup of tea?"

I felt old world - comfort and luxury, and then she called to the maid who came and brought me a cup of tea and the maid smiled at me in a friendly way, as if there was nothing more she'd like to do than to bring me a cup of tea. Not like these insolent young girls nowadays who are from the city, begging work, their eyes shifty and hard, their dark skin blotchy with black spots, signs of hard ghetto living. If you ask them to bring you something they practically throw it at you, their downturned mouths and angry eyes unable to hide their resentment. It oozes out of them, this anger, at being poor and black. They mix up colour in all this, never seeing that being black doesn't mean you're poor and being white doesn't make you automatically rich. They hate me and I hate them.

I can't tell you that the sunlight dappled on anything or that it cast a beautiful glow on Lillian but I can tell you it was a sunny day. It usually is in Kingston and I wouldn't have gone out if it had been raining. I would have laid on my father's king sized bed with the remote in my hand channel surfing, or I'd fall asleep with the sound of the heavy raindrops splattering on the pavement outside. So it was sunny and I had nothing to say so I said what I had come to say. "I really love your poetry." It was true. I didn't like poetry before but Lillian's poetry had fuck and bitch in it and I could see that she hated her mother until she, Lillian turned forty but then it was too late because her mother was dead. "Thank you, my dear," she said. What courage, I thought, to write a poem with the word fuck in it but still manage to make it beautiful and deep and thought provoking so that I kept reading it over and over again and when I went to bed, the words haunted me so I couldn't sleep. The poem was about a failed marriage, a fiery, passionate, jealous, angry marriage.

"And you, my dear, Elizabeth, are a gifted writer. I'm your fan." I couldn't believe it. Lillian liked my writing. Lillian said she was a fan. My spirit soared and my head felt giddy.

"Really," I gushed. "Thank you. That means so much to me." I vowed I would go home and write story after story in the hope that Lillian would read them.

Then I migrated to Canada. I asked Keith about Lillian, now ninety.

"I took her out for her birthday," he said. "She is fine, feisty as always."

"Like how?" I asked fishing for gossip.

"Like a woman. You have to compliment them or they get cranky."

I wanted to attend Lillian's funeral but I couldn't. I was thousands of miles away, separated by sea and credit card debt. I was a limb severed from the body that nourished my creativity, cast off and apart from where I should have been. Keith said this would happen to me. "A lot of writers go abroad and find they can't write. They don't know the lay of the land. It's not in their blood. Then they try to write about home and there's no depth, or they write about a home that existed twenty years ago."

"I will never be that type of writer," I insisted. "Never!"

But I became a worse type of writer, the type of writer who isn't writing at all and uses every excuse to blame it on someone or something else.

Glenn used to be a writer. Keith said he would probably be one of the best new young Caribbean writers. Glen's stories were rich in detail, like an exquisite tapestry. I read with envy, devouring the words. Glen was the cliché: tall, dark and handsome but I wasn't interested. We just connected as artists connect. We had great conversations, moments of mild flirtation, and he'd send me the occasional e-mail. So when I received a mass e-mail one day that requested that none of the writers of the club contact him and that he would no longer be attending club meetings, it was quite a shock. How could someone so talented give up writing? I thought Glenn felt like me, that life without writing wouldn't be a life at all.

"What happened to Glenn?" I asked Keith.

"Glenn found religion." Keith waved his hand impatiently, like he had no time for nonsense.

"Elizabeth, promise me you won't find religion. Don't get saved. It ruins the writing."

I didn't see how religion and writing were connected but there is always some cult that says you can't do this or you can't do that and it's usually something like not dancing, not wearing makeup, not celebrating birthdays, eating or not eating some type of food and I guess in Glenn's case, not writing. I bet God is laughing at how stupid we all are.

I tried to contact Glenn after that, to show that we could be friends and I wanted to ask why he would write off a whole set of people he'd been close to. The writing club had been meeting for years. We'd shared so much. He wrote back saying he was going away for a while and that he was severing contact with the writing club. He asked me not to write him

because he would be unable to keep in touch. So I didn't. I deleted his name from my contact list as if he'd never existed. That's one bonus of living in this age. No ratty tatty address books with names and numbers crossed out.

I kept in touch with Keith for a long time after I moved to Canada. It's a different way of life as everyone knows, but what some people don't know is how hard it can be. My Punjabi friend said she is nothing here but someone over there.

"Why did you come then?" I asked. She tells me she came for a job. She complains that there is no one here to do her housework.

Keith asks me by e-mail if I'm doing any writing. I say I'm working on something even though I'm not and I say it's hard, what with the laundry and the cooking and the working. He tells me to remember that I'm a writer and if I don't write, it's a waste of my talent.

"What you need, Lizzy, is a rich husband who understands your need to write and then lets you do it. That's all that matters, you know darling, the writing." I tell him half seriously, half jokingly, that I'm following in Lillian's footsteps. I'm on my second divorce.

"I'm sorry, darling," was all he said.

One cold fall morning I sat down to write. The windows were frosted with ice. Mouldy, rusty water settled in the window panes. I sat at the computer and checked e-mail. The urge to wipe the floor became stronger and stronger as I sat there staring at some black spots on grey and blue tile. There was no sun. The day was grey and gloomy signalling the start of another winter. It was imperative to change over the clothes – put away the shorts and summer dresses and pull out the sweaters, the scarves and the hats. Four hours later, the house was spotless. Small handprints that had smeared the walls for weeks were gone. Because the fact is, if your house is not 'company ready' and someone happens to stop by and see that mountain of paper, the laundry strewn over the sofa and the dishes piled in the sink, well, every woman knows that's a failure of another kind.

Keith came to Toronto one summer. He was lecturing at the university so we met for lunch. I was on husband number three and took my new baby with me. She slept through it all, her tiny head full of dark curls was tilted to the side and her button nose was adorable. "She's lovely, said Keith. You are still full of the maternal glow. Maybe you should concentrate on being a mother, for now."

Was this the same man I knew from ten years ago? I didn't want to hear about maternal instinct. I came home and tried to write but the baby kept crying and in response, my breasts filled with milk, my nipples

grew hard and erect and leaked down my shirt. I wanted to hold my baby and throw her away at the same time.

Keith used to be a writer, a club leader and my mentor. It's not that's he given up any of those things. It's because he's dead. I kept meaning to call him but I was waiting for inspiration. I wanted to have an answer for the question he always asked, 'are you writing?' and that answer would be yes. They say pancreatic cancer takes people fast. Keith didn't tell me he was sick and I was too broke to make it to his funeral.

Sometimes, I dream I'm with Keith and Lillian. It's always the same dream. We are in a large plantation type house. Lillian smiles and welcomes me. "Elizabeth, my dear, do sit down for a cup of tea." Then we get down to the serious business of prose and poetry. After all, it is the writing that matters.

TOANCHE OR ANACHRONISM
by Gord Pannell

I AM ALWAYS AN early raiser. At the cottage, I got up long before anyone else. I meandered down to the beach and stood with my feet in the lake. I stood there looking out over the lake and turning to look over my land and cottages and thinking to myself, "This is my land." Proud as punch and wallowing in my success at having been able to acquire such a beautiful piece of land and saying to myself, "Yes this is all mine." And then it dawned on me, that I was an unsophicated bit of flotsam floating in time and that at another time some other man could have stood in the same place and felt the same way.

He stood there and watched the sun slowly creep down the trees on the far side of the lake, enjoying the dawn of a new day, with the breeze rippling the water, which was lapping at his toes as they were snuggled in the sand at his feet. With his lean-to behind him, and a smoking fire, which, while it flamed, had kept him warm during that night, he looked out to where he would have to catch his morning meal.

His birch bark canoe sat quietly on the beach. His dad had helped him build this one many years before. Now it was a means to go out and catch his next meal. The hooks and line he had for fishing were obtained from the French in Montreal. He and his brothers had paddled, one spring, all the way to Montreal and back, getting Axes and tools made of iron.

He quietly picked up his canoe and slid it out into the lake. He knew where the fish were because he had watched the ducks diving. Within minutes, he had caught two beautiful pickerel, one of the tastiest fish in the lake. Back to shore, to stoke up his camp fire, he pinned his

cleaned fish to a piece of birch bark, leaning it close to the fire, and in no time they were cooked.

Now that his belly was full, he had to get food for his family. Back out onto the lake, he slid with his canoe and over to the far side of the weed bed. The gentle breeze would blow him down the outer edge of the bed where the big fish would be chasing their food. All day long he had to paddle back up to where he had started and drift down the lake. He could look down on the shaded side of his canoe and see the weeds just a few feet under the bottom of his canoe.

As soon as he dropped his line in, he started catching all kinds of fish. His favorite kind was pickerel but there were others in the lake, bass, sunfish and sometimes lake trout, a real delicacy. He kept these fish alive, on a line, he had dangling at the side of his canoe. He strung them through the gills and out through the mouth. This would keep them fresh and still alive until he paddled back to shore that evening. On shore he found a long straight branch, wadded out waist deep, and using a rock, drove it down into the bottom of the lake and then tied his catch to it. It was far enough out so that the resident foxes, raccoons and wolfs would not sense them and destroy his days work.

Stoking up his fire and snuggling back into his lean-to, he prepared to spend another night at the lake. There was no setting sun that night. It was blocked by heavy clouds. The wind was picking up and had started to lash the trees. He picked up a rock and waded back out into the lake and hammered down his stake, making sure that his fish would still be there in the morning. Now he was wet and soon he would be cold. He had to get that fire going and hotter than it was, so to dry out his clothes. Buck skin takes a long time to dry and the clothes his mate had sewn for him had to be dried out. As the wind kept picking up, he had to let the fire almost die or the sparks could cause a forest fire. He was cold, even if it was summer. Now he pulled his clothes under his blanket because the rain had started and the light of day had gone. Tired, he drifted off into that land that we all know.

He awakened cold and damp at the crack of dawn, crawled into his still damp clothes, looked at his water logged fire, and wanted the warmth and comfort of his home. Pulling his canoe up by the lean-to and throwing some boughs and leaves over it to hide it, he wadded back out into the lake to reclaim his fish. A muskrat had taken one but the rest was his to take home. Still fresh and jumping, he threw them over his shoulder and marched dripping wet out of the lake and headed up the hill, back to his lodge, in Toanche village, where his mate and babies would be looking for him and the fish.

As I stood musing, I felt that he had been there.

An excerpt from the novel "The Gospel of Now"
THE BC CRIB
by Brandon Pitts

IT WAS THE DAY I quit taking Ritalin that I first saw the Gospel of Now engraved into the faces of many men, women, queers and types. It had come about from the desire for clearer thought and had left me in a strange meditative state recalling the days before the psychologist's prognosis.

I remembered how it happened, back when I used to feel good about myself, back when I was happy. Lying on a medical bed, EEG diodes attached to my head, people with clipboards taking notes and then the bottle with the pills that had the CG/202 engraved on buffered tablets.

This will help Deacon to concentrate. This will help him to spell. He can now show his work in math and be able to focus in class.

The medication did its job. I got through the school day, sitting still, without complaint and within a week, I had accepted the fact that I was stupid and this was how things were going to be.

By the time I got off the school bus in the morning, it was like the whole world was weighing down on me as it rushed past. Did you ever feel so low you could almost collapse inside yourself? I hadn't realized I had grown so dependant on the meds. I had it so bad; it was pushing down upon my bones.

I entered the school's dark hallway, lined with deep green lockers and the students who loitered around them, steeped with a paranoid trepidation. Laboring through a sigh, my dopamine receptors screamed out for the Ritalin I had deprived myself.

My eyelids were still dope heavy from the pill I had taken last night but I was cognizant enough to see Douglas "Bone" Reinhold primping in the mirror that hung in the faux tiger fur lined locker that we shared during our senior year.

Bone was the most stylish fellow in school. Not that anyone recognized this, not even the self-proclaimed fashion diva, Adonai Garcia, but in my heart, I knew it was true. His approach was new and untested. Permed hair, pencil mustache like Clark Gable, Indian chador around his neck and a leather sport coat he came across at the Salvation Army. He was as decadent as he was genius.

He took me in, as if examining my aura, frowning.

"You look ill," he said, pushing up his eyebrows, left hand on his hip, right arm bracing his weight as he leaned against the wall next to our locker.

"I quit taking my medication last night," I said, laboring to push out the words. "Told my parents they couldn't make me take the shit anymore. I'm eighteen and I can do whatever I want. They can all fuck off, especially the school. Those pills make my head spin."

"It must be tiresome, living in a fog so you can rise up to society's expectations," said Bone, slowly shutting the locker. "I don't know how you ever let them talk you into taking that crap in the first place. I always say; if you're going to alter your mental state, do it *au natural*."

"I must've been seven or eight when I started takin' it." I squinted at him, headache cinching my brow. "Everything since then has been clouded in strange memories. I can hardly recall the past ten years, like I was a ghost floating through it. It's as though I've been violated. They've taken something from me."

The warning bell rang and students began to bustle in all directions to make it to class.

"Well I better get to math."

After class, my math teacher stared over her ancient bifocals and purple polyester frill, hair as stiff as her demeanor, and glanced at me with a strange mixture of suspicion and satisfaction.

"Not so fast," she said, opening the drawer of her desk, handing me a note.

"You're to meet your father by *the Bomb* out in front of the Councilor's Office to discuss your eligibility for graduation."

She smiled for the first time all year as I took the note. *What now? What could this be?*

The town we live in is famous for two things: The Hanford Site, the world's largest radioactive waste dump and out there at the *B reactor*, they made the plutonium for the *Fat Boy* that they dumped on Nagasaki Japan back in 1945. Other than this, we're a community surrounded by miles of desert and vast expanse of sagebrush. This isolation causes us to develop a little different culturally from the rest of the country, that

and the incredible mixture of Ph.D., science, and back woods bumpkin logic, gives the area a surreal quality, backed by conservative values.

If it weren't for the Hanford Site, we'd probably be a small farming community or an out of the way place where Congress might put an Indian reservation. But glowing tanks and split atoms hath made us important.

I sat down on the green bench facing the Councilor's Office, looking at that damn bomb. Or was it just an explosion? I don't know. It looked like an explosion to me, a mushroom cloud- Japanese killing blast. But everyone called it, "The Bomb."

The mushroom cloud was our school's logo and mascot, a stylized R- for Richland High, emerging from the fiery sun that leveled Nagasaki. It was a thing to behold.

Our logo of death was tiled into the floor in front of the councilor's office where I was sitting on a green bench, waiting for the thing to go down, my future, blown to particles by my school's lust for atomic annihilation.

We were the *"Richland Bombers"* and had the best damn high school football team in the State of Washington.

If you walked on the Bomb, especially if you were a freshman, the members of the varsity football team, those bastards who'd won the AAA state competition would beat you with conviction. They'd done it to Reese Whittaker and he was a senior; even shaved his head in a blaze of school spirit, right in front of the whole school and select faculty. Everyone watched those blonde curls fall over the tiled mushroom cloud. Most of them cheered, even if they didn't want to.

Reese had done more then walk on our school's mascot; he'd stepped on our parent's livelihood.

I looked up and there was my dad, standing over me, hands on the hips of his blue-gray suit. The radiation dosimeter id badge that gave him security clearance hung over his wide styled tie. He looked a little mad.

"Hi Pa."

"We're early," he said, looking at his watch.

I could tell he wanted to loosen his tie but did not. He'd driven all the way from his office out at the Hanford Works.

"Having a bad day?" I asked.

"Well Deacon, in addition to being called down here to talk to these folks at your school, I got some bad news about the *BC Crib*."

"What's the BC Crib?"

My dad took a deep breath and tilted his head back, hands still

on his hips, pushing back the sides of his sport coast.

"Well son, back in the days of the B-Reactor, they ran out of single shell tank space for a sizable batch of nuclear waste. So they dug a few 6x20 trenches with a backhoe, made them about thirteen feet deep and poured the glowing sludge into those trenches and covered it with about six feet of soil, calling it the BC Crib."

"That sounds pretty stupid," I said, sitting with my elbows on my knees, fists under my chin.

My dad was still standing.

"It was stupid. But that's how they did things back then. They weren't enlightened about things like we are these days. Well, they fenced it off with chain-link, topped it with razor wire and just left it there to radiate."

"So what's so bad about that? Didn't it happen in the forties or fifties?"

"Well it turns out," continued my dad, holding out his hand to animate his story, "that they paved a lot across the road from the chain link and I've been parking my car there for the past three years."

He reached down and rubbed his kneecap.

"Since I moved out to the 200 area, my knee's been acting up. I call it my Hanford knee."

"Didn't your radiation badge pick it up?"

He ignored the question.

"I don't know dad, seems pretty crazy. I heard they had some guy living out there for years because he was so full of radiation that he was dangerous to others. They even had to properly dispose of his piss. I wouldn't work out there for any amount of money."

"Well you'll do a lot worse if you don't start taking your schooling a little more seriously."

"Yeah, I know."

The councilor's door opened.

"Come in," said Mr. Ryers, the senior class councilor. "Mr. Jones, Jeff Ryers. How are you?"

"Doing good, thanks."

"Hello Deacon."

"Mr. Ryers."

He sat down at his desk, in front of a mural, portraying a football victory. "Go Bombers!" was painted in gold letters above it.

"So Mr. Jones, I've called you and Deacon in here today to inform you that Deacon doesn't have enough credits to graduate."

My father stared at him blankly.

"Seems he's missing freshman health. Mr. Ropeman failed him. And that time he was expelled two years back for forging attendance notes, that caused him to fail sophomore P.E."

"So I have to take health and P.E. to graduate?"

"Yes Deacon," said Mr. Ryers. "I'm afraid you're on the *five year plan*. I have another appointment so you'll have to excuse me. Deacon, good luck with your life."

And that was just the beginning of the day I quit taking Ritalin.

An excerpt from the novel "The Rani's Doctor"
ARRIVAL IN CALCUTTA
by Waheed Rabbani

1855, January: Calcutta, India

IT WAS THE MOTION of the ship and sounds of shuffling feet on the deck above that woke me. From the bright sunlight shining through the cabin's porthole, I realized I had overslept. I noted Mrs. Willoughby had already left, and her trunk and other boxes looked packed and ready for disembarkation. I had packed my sea chest earlier and just a few more things remained to go in there. I went to the tiny washbasin in the corner of the cabin. Mrs. Willoughby had thoughtfully left fresh water in the jug. I quickly washed myself and put on a clean blue dress. Running a comb lightly through my hair, I made sure the ringlets still held in place. I put on a straw bonnet—I'd bought it at a bazaar in Alexandria—for it was already stifling hot in the cabin and likely hotter outside in the sun. Packing the remaining things into my sea chest, I locked it. I placed my portmanteau on top of it and with reticule in hand, strode out of the cabin. The aroma of brewing tea guided me towards the dining room, for I felt hungry even for the watery soup, biscuits, salted pork or beef, and the usual dried fruits for dessert.

After a refreshing breakfast—or lunch, rather—I went up on deck to join the crowd at the railing. All were eager for a first glimpse of Calcutta, as the ship gently manoeuvred its way up the Hooghly River. Very slowly, the scenery along the banks changed. The continuous rows of mud huts with thatched roofs and fishing ports gave way to sizeable buildings. Just as the Colonel had predicted, the waterway swarmed with vessels of all types, from small bobbing dinghies, manned by near-na-

ked natives, to sleek launches—obviously owned by the rich gentry who, sipped glasses of wine and waved at us—to large British naval vessels. Finally, the buildings of Calcutta loomed ahead. Beyond the onion-shaped domes of mosques and pyramid-style temples, stone structures of larger edifices were visible. They reminded me of London's skyline, which I had seen when travelling up the Thames Estuary, from Canada with my dear Robert — lifetime ago, it seemed.

A shrill sound startled me from my thoughts, the likes of which I had never heard before. I looked at the other passengers' faces, wondering if they knew what the problem was. Had our vessel run aground or something? They all seemed calm as ever, as if this was a common sound one heard regularly.

"It's nothing, Mrs. Wallace," a familiar voice called out to me from behind. It was my mentor, Colonel Humphrey. "It's only the sound from a conch shell being blown by one of the priests in the temple, yonder. Listen, there it is again."

True enough, the strange shrieking noise came again from one side of the docks. I peered in that direction and noticed a priest, wearing only a loincloth and white paint marks over his forehead and arms, standing at the embankment. Behind him, a rose-coloured temple was situated at the top of wide stone steps leading up from the water.

"Thank you, Colonel. I believe my introduction to India is now complete, is it?"

"It never is. India is a fascinating country. It's full of different customs, religions and novelties. You will encounter something new every day." He withdrew his pocketbook and, opening it, took out a card. "Mrs. Wallace, in case I do not see you at the wharf, here's my card. Do look me up whenever you are in Calcutta."

"Thank you, sir... err... Colonel Humphrey. I will." I accepted his card, although I did feel a bit anxious about him paying me so much attention.

The ship anchored in midstream and passengers were ferried across in tenders that plied to and fro from the ship to the wharf. I tried to spot my parents among the throng of people lined up at the quay, waving at us. After a while, I gave up, for it seemed a futile attempt to locate them, and joined the line-up for the ferryboats.

There was a tap on my shoulder. It was the portly Mrs. Willoughby. "Aww... Margaret, I've been lookin' all over for you." She sounded out of breath. She handed me a slip of paper. "Here's our address in Delhi. We are in the Civil Lines. I know it will be a while before you get there, but as soon as you are, do visit us. Frank and I will be delighted to see you."

I took her note and, opening my reticule, got out a paper and pencil. "Here, Mrs. Willoughby, let me give you my parents' address in Futtehgurh."

"Aww... not to worry. I know exactly where they are. My Frank goes to the station there ever so often."

"Good. Please do look in on us, whenever you are there."

"We surely will. Now let me find a porter. Do you want your luggage brought up, too?"

"Yes, please. Here, let me pay you for him." I fished for some coins in my reticule.

"Aww... not to worry about that. I know how to bargain with these lads." She kissed me goodbye and hurried off.

Soon enough, the tender with my baggage and me gently hit the side of the wooden wharf. The boat rocked as the passengers scrambled up the dock's steps. I trudged my way up, holding the hem of my dress in one hand and the handrail with the other. Eventually I emerged onto the pier, followed by two red-turbaned porters who carried my sea chest and portmanteau. They placed the luggage at my feet and, putting their palms together, bowed—I later realized this was the Indian way of saying thank you—and scampered back to the tender. I cannot say whether it was due to the bright sun or not getting my land-legs yet that a feeling of extreme tiredness overcame me. The sea chest looked inviting enough and I tried to sit on it, but could not stay there and slipped down onto the ground. I do recall hearing shouts and screams and sound of feet running around me, but nothing else before passing out.

The next thing I heard was someone calling my name. "Margaret, Margaret! Are you all right?" It was dear Papa. Squatting down beside me, he held me in one arm and with what looked to be a bottle of smelling salts in his other hand.

"Papa!" I cried and, putting my arms around him, sobbed.

A crowd had gathered around us. Seeing me revived, they clapped and cheered. A gentleman who looked to be in his early forties, dressed in a white suit and a pith hat, stepped forward. "I see your daughter seems to be all right, James. Shall we get her into the carriage?"

Papa kissed my forehead and asked, "Are you all right, Margaret? Can you get up?"

I nodded and both Papa and the other gentleman helped me up. There was more clapping and cheering from the onlookers as they led us to a waiting carriage. Helping me onto a seat, Papa sat next to me while the gentleman took the seat in front of us. My baggage was secured at the back, and the landau rolled forward.

I put my head on the side of the padded seat, and rested. While I had regained full consciousness, I was overcome with too much emotion to speak. Papa looked just the same. Despite the heat, he was still dressed in his dark suit, although he now wore a beige pith hat. We looked at each other for a while. I believe he was also speechless, likely from seeing his long-lost daughter faint before his eyes.

"You look funny in that hat, Papa."

He laughed. "Your Mamma makes me wear it! Now are you sure, you are well, Margaret? Shall we get you to the hospital?"

I shook my head. "I'm all right, Papa. It was just the heat."

The gentleman, who had also been observing me, said, "We will have to get you one of these hats. Although it is the cold weather season here, the sun is still fierce."

Papa said, "Of course, can't have one of your staff fainting on you, Edward, can you?" Then, quickly turning to me, he continued, "Margaret, meet Doctor Edward Stewart."

"So pleased to meet you, Margaret." Doctor Stewart extended his hand.

"Likewise," I shook his hand. "Have you come all the way from Delhi, sir?" I asked, rather astonished.

"Oh, no, no. I'm with the Calcutta Medical College here. The new hospital in Delhi, which you have been recruited for, is under the Indian Medical Service, and we are part of it. It's all due to the efforts of our Governor General, Lord Dalhousie."

Papa asked, "Isn't he due to retire?"

"Yes, unfortunately, after doing so much good work here."

I remembered the not-so-good-work the Earl had done, which Colonel Humphrey had mentioned. But I bit my tongue and simply nodded.

Doctor Stewart continued, "I am not exactly your supervisor, Margaret. You will meet him in Delhi. I am more like a liaison officer, shall we say. When we heard of your arrival, we telegrammed your father. I know Reverend James is anxious to return to his work at the mission, but my wife, Moira, and I, would be delighted if both of you would spend some days with us to help you recuperate from your long journey. Also, may I offer my heartfelt condolences on the sad loss of your husband."

His kind words brought tears to my eyes. I could barely whisper, "Thank you, sir."

Feeling tired, I rested my head on the side of the cushioned seat and looked out of the window. We were travelling in a southerly direction, on a road that wound its way along the riverbank. It seemed I was

going back the way the ship had arrived, for the scenery looked familiar, only now, the masses of pedestrians in different clothing, the passing carriages, and bullock carts, all looked real, not like those in a painting. We passed by a large fort, with octagonal-shaped thick walls of brick and mortar. It looked strong enough to repel even a combined armada of the French and Spanish fleets. I looked inquiringly at Doctor Stewart and he informed me, "It is the famous Fort William—but the second one, mind, built in 1780."

"Really! What happened to the first one?"

"That one is in the city. It's a much older—1701, I believe—mud structure. Most of it has crumbled by now. They are planning to replace it with a post office."

"Is the Black Hole still there?" Papa asked in a solemn voice.

"Yes, a bit of the jailhouse and some walls are still standing. A monument erected by Clive disappeared quite mysteriously. The native groups are all denying any involvement." He smiled. "Government House seems to be at a loss on deciding how to preserve the memory of those hundred and twenty-three souls who perished there."

"Did that many people suffocate in there?" Papa asked.

"Yes, that number was reported by Holwell, the fort's commander at that time. Although some dispute his count. I can take you there, if you wish."

"Yes, I would very much like to visit there, since so much has been written about it."

While they engaged in a philosophical discussion on the causes of that incident, I continued to look out of the window. It seemed we were approaching a more affluent part of the city. Rows of well-constructed, single-storied houses appeared, each having wraparound porches like those in our southern states. Their manicured lawns and attractive gardens gave the neighbourhood a distinct European look. Although smart carriages drove in and out from the homes, few persons walked in the streets.

GOD AND THE COUNTRY
by Elana Rae

I WAS FIVE THE first time God abandoned me. My family and I were making our way down the path from our cottage to the ocean beach below. I had run ahead straight into a nest of angry wasps who stung me all over. By the time my family rescued me I was quiet, altered. Covered with calamine lotion, I sat in our rocking chair and whiled the day away. I knew I'd lost a protective lens through which I'd viewed the world.

Certainly I felt His absence the many times I hid and prayed that He would save me or my father or brother and sister, from the alcoholic rages my mother spewed with regularity. I never gave up on God, and he and I have been in conversation for as long as I can remember. I was sure if I kept trying I would earn His Love.

And then, at age forty-two, I had a one-day reunion with my first-born son, Kent, whom I'd placed for adoption twenty-three years earlier. Our connection was immediate and intense, our first ever. He said he needed some time to process our meeting, and what kind of relationship if any, he would like to have.

I was between jobs, when Kent and I met. I'd lost the work I'd loved at the urban teaching hospital, during the downsizing of the nine-ties. My social work position had enabled me to work with women in all stages of pre-and post-pregnancy. The months came and went without word from my son, and I sensed what eternity might feel like.

Finally, a community hospital invited me to interview for a part-time position I'd never applied for — a start-up of a paediatric diabetes clinic. I never wanted the job. It was too far away, and I'd never wanted

to do family work — too many players and complex layers of relationships — way over my head. Nonetheless I went to the interview. Being new to reunion, and still somewhat naive and wanting to acknowledge Kent as my son, I said that I had three children.

I took the job in spite of my reservations. They wanted me and I so needed to be wanted, to belong somewhere. The environment and the people bespoke a kinder way to keep my finger in the professional world as I tried to manoeuvre the daily battle with waiting and grieving. The hospital sat in a large open field, which is how I came to refer to it as "The Country."

We worked as a team, giving genuine meaning to the well-worn term. We spent our days together, initially designing and developing the clinic and then working with the children and their families. Children with diabetes, who've completed their initial teaching and who are managing their routines, came to the clinic every three months, until they reached the age of eighteen.

The core of the team included two doctors, a nurse, a dietician, and myself. All were dedicated professionals, who also loved fun. Dr. Bruce spearheaded the development of the program. Rumoured to be tough and at times arrogant, he filled most of our days with unconditional support, and leadership. Dr. Sari was the most beautiful woman I'd ever met and she knew how to connect with the child, and the dream, in everyone. Margot, our dietician, was our resident caustic as well as our very own culinary Martha Stewart. Alice, our nurse, was the heart of our team and clinic. She made it all happen, giving of herself tirelessly.

I worked in "The Country" for five years. I spent most of them trying to run away. Initially I didn't know how to deal with wholesome, healthy people, and the intimacy of the group. They'd talk about their families, introduce us to the characters, and I'd do likewise, but I felt like a fraud. None of them came from families with gun-toting mothers, or had children missing, given up. Every time I talked about my children, I was painfully aware that I'd not raised Kent, that I had no memory of his first steps, his first words, his first day of school. But the hardest part to deal with was the way they each valued and respected my work and myself. They included me in everything, sought my input, consistently showed with words and actions, how much they appreciated who I was and what I brought to the team. I didn't understand it, and wondered how long it would take them to discover that I wasn't worthy of their high regard.

The first two years in "The Country", I spent in acute grief. Year one I mourned the original loss of my son — something I'd not been able

to do fully until I had met him. My relationships with the people who'd been in my life at that time, and not offered me help, came up for review and scrutiny. The pain was beyond anything I'd ever thought was humanly possible to survive. I learned to quilt, and designed a story quilt depicting my experience of adoption. I started to write again, to put words to what I was going through. It's like I had to work and rework it in a variety of mediums to try and integrate what had happened to me. Year two was even harder — the grief was less intense, but it held a more permanent dead quality. I understood that Kent might never choose to be in my life — confronted the possibility that I might forfeit my grandchildren. At the same time our eldest daughter Sally left home for university and this additional loss weighed heavily.

I started to look for a new job. I had to get out of "The Country". I had to get back to serious work in the city. I longed to be autonomous, making my way anonymously through each day. I didn't want to be close to people. Couldn't they see I was dead inside? Why did they insist on bringing me in to everything, showing me how much I mattered to them? I'll show them. I'll tell them about my son. At least our relationship will be more honest, and they'll know I'm not one of them. And still they loved me.

Life seeped slowly into my bones during years three and four and a funny thing happened in "The Country". The children and families I worked with began to weave tentacles around my heart. I cared about them. I respected the daily courage required to live with diabetes. I became involved in their stories, and every three months we'd add a new chapter. I was witness to moments of great poignancy, pain, love and celebration.

I tried to view the loss of my son through a wider lens. What, if anything, had I gained through the loss? Although a much sadder person, I felt wiser, and more real and whole than I had ever been. I no longer lived in shame, and was more open about what my life had been about. After the grief and pain, the potential for healing old wounds with others became possible. I'd discovered my creative self, as I quilted and wrote, and formed new and supportive connections.

But I believed that God had truly forsaken me this time. On some level I felt entitled to have my son in my life. I thought I'd paid my dues, endured my measure of suffering. The fact that Kent was choosing not to be in my life was simply too cruel, and could only mean that God had left. I knew other birth mothers, women in close connection with the children they'd placed for adoption, welcomed for tea and included in family functions by the adoptive parents. I wasn't a mean-spirited person;

my children and I had only love and good things to offer Kent. Eventually I had to accept that for whatever reason, God had decided that "no, this too shall be denied you." It wasn't part of His plan for me — I wasn't worthy enough.

My dance in "The Country" continued. Every time I faced a major challenge in a relationship, or I had to negotiate a new transition, or confront difficult emotions, I looked for work. As our youngest son Brian learned to drive, I felt my last useful purpose as a parent slipping through my fingers. Visions of empty-nest stared at me and I was terrified. If I wasn't mothering, what would be my purpose? Writing stories held magical, transformational moments, but it was the hardest, loneliest work I'd ever done. I needed more.

The timing finally seemed right; it was time to move on. And sure enough an opportunity presented itself at another urban teaching hospital to work in obstetrics. The day I accepted the new position I called Drs Bruce and Sari, and Alice to let them know. My heart pounded as I spoke to each of them — now they'll get it. They'll be angry; they'll see they were wrong to love me, that in the end I've betrayed them. And still they loved me and continued to do so right out the door with affection, reminiscence, and tears.

I was in the kitchen doing the dishes the evening I called my team. I was shaking my head at their responses, feeling blessed to have had them in my life, when a wave of something passed through me. I threw the dishtowel over the chair, raced up the stairs to our bedroom, and buried my face in the bedcovers. "Oh my God. The whole time I thought You'd left me, turned Your back on me for good, and there You were, each and every day, in each and every one of them. At the lowest point in my life — bereft, rejected by my son, a shadow of myself, lacking confidence, self worth and self esteem - You sent me these people. And slowly with patience, consistency, and unconditional positive regard, they held up the mirror. They said, "...look. We don't see what you see. Come a little closer and look again. We care for you, and the gifts you have to offer."

"Forgive me, God, I didn't see."

UNFAIR GOODBYE
by Elizabeth Carina Ramos

"I WISH I COULD have something sweet to eat with my tea this after-noon," his mother would say; and before she pronounced the last word, he would already be outside looking for a bakery. By the time the tea was ready, he would be back, not with just something sweet, but with her fa-vourite Danishes. She would smile and give him a long look into his eyes, showing how pleased she was.

"Thank you, dear."

To see her happy was all he wanted, all he needed. When the snack time was over he went away, not without kissing her and asking her if she needed anything else.

"No. It's OK. I'm fine, thank you for asking," she said, although it was not true.

She always needed something else from him, but not all at once. She didn't like to overwhelm him. There would be a chance to ask him for another special favour the next day. He never skipped a date for snack with her after work, disregarding his jealous wife's complaints.

Working at the family's business gave him the chance to leave early enough to have time for that Monday-to-Friday date. It also allowed him to become her driver. He didn't have to worry about taking the day off to take Mom to the doctor. "I have an appointment for Tuesday afternoon, at 3:00 p.m.," was all she needed to say; and he was already re-arranging his schedule to accommodate that duty.

"Oh, no, I can take a taxi," she played; but she knew from the very first second that he would drive her there without making excuses to avoid the task. She loved it and he enjoyed it.

He drove her everywhere since he turned eighteen and got, as a present, a small second hand Fiat, his first car twenty years ago. Ever since he got behind the wheel, he provided her with all the rides his father, her husband, eluded: a few trips a year to her beloved beach resort, evening tours around the city after a difficult day, and trips to that far store which sold the unique merchandise she liked so much and couldn't get anywhere else.

Many of those things changed when he married: the drives were just to the doctor and the little favours were done - not so often. But the love between them grew stronger over the years. They both knew his marriage was just right. They had enjoyed that close mother-son relationship for too many years. He was twenty-six when he met his fiancée and thirty-two when he finally got married to her. The triangle was not easy, but never an issue.

He was the perfect son: caring, loving, patient, smiling, helpful... unbelievable. Even married, Mom would ask him all kinds of small things to keep him closer; and he always found time for a lawn trim, a light bulb change, a drive, a kiss. They loved each other as everybody should do.

His sister loved him too; although Mom confessed to her that he was the favourite, "You will understand me when you have your own son." She still loves him. It is an easy job. The perfect son is also a great brother.

He was born with that incredible patience that made him nice to everybody; and that resignation sometimes was annoying for her. She always talked back to Mom and Dad, he just couldn't. Maybe he could but he didn't need to. He belonged to that rare kind of people that still believe you shouldn't argue with your parents, even though they could be wrong. Moreover, he was happy to believe his parents were always right. It didn't matter how many times he bothered her with that attitude. She grew up with him and knew his true nature: he was a good guy. She didn't hear him gossiping or making stories that could get people into trouble. He always tried his best to smooth a dispute between parents, friends or neighbours. If anybody needed a small repair or a little push, he didn't say 'no.'

It wasn't something new. He had been that good since he was a young child, since she could remember. He didn't swear; at least not as much as her. He shared his toys. He was a pleasant teammate.

The only thing he did wrong was soccer. He was an awful soccer player. He used to wait aside, biting his nails and watching how 'The Best' chose other boys to play in his team. He kept waiting, his nails getting smaller, his eyes bigger, until he was picked too: goalkeeper, again.

That soccer rivalry built no resentment. Over the years, that

fabulous player became his best man; and the wedding was gorgeous: The family's fairy tale. Nobody went through all those details and special treats to organize such a big outdoor party totally uncommon in his hometown.

At the catholic ceremony, his father-in-law was the godfather; and, of course, Mom was the godmother. She was radiant. Her endless smile spoke of her happiness. That event was one of the wishes she treasured all her life and she wouldn't miss it for any reason.

"We don't need to operate now," she said.

"Of course not," her cardiologist helped to avoid conflicts that could worsen her condition. "We'll make it after the wedding." It was January 1993.

In October, Mom's youngest brother died. She was very close to him and everybody was worried about her reaction; but she did well. Her grief didn't cause further damage to her health; although the short breath that comes with heart disease almost didn't let her walk.

"If I have to live a few years more, I don't want to do it in this condition. I want to go for the surgery," she told her daughter. The operation was scheduled for December.

The valve replacement was successful. Despite the lack of vision in her right eye -old sequel of the same disease and the post-surgery anti-coagulating treatment, Mom recovered soon and was strong enough to celebrate the first Christmas at home with her new daughter-in-law.

New Year's celebration was not that good because this time the traditional family reunion was incomplete for Mom. She ended 1993 without her son. After passing by with his wife to wish her "a happy 94," he went for dinner to his in-laws'.

Birthdays, anniversaries, father's and mother's days passed and helped to get things reorganized. Mom adjusted to her new reality of having one person less in the household and a new in-law in the family. Among smiles and serious faces, mixed and intense emotions were always brewing, but they hardly developed into a turmoil.

Her son was now a man. His responsibilities multiplied and he started exercising his sense of humour, that had never been his strongest point to say "no" to her when he was busy and she wanted to prepare some extra snack to spend more time together.

Dad started driving Mom. Together they harmonized the family, enjoying that their son had grown healthy and had gone away from home, but not so much. He was still there for them, working with him, taking her to the doctor, sometimes. They also felt proud of seeing him becoming a good husband that soon would be a great father.

A couple of years after his marriage, his sister started joking

about a nephew. Mom had always been asking for a grandchild. His wife got pregnant just three months after his sister. Mom was in love with the babies. They brought her back all the satisfaction she used to feel at her favourite job: motherhood.

As a Grandma, she took care of her eldest granddaughter and became very attached to the little girl. She fed her, changed her diapers, taught her how to speak, and how to walk.

Late in July 1998, Mom waited for her daughter with pride over-flowing her smile.

"Look what she has learned with me today," she said and ex-tended her arms to the baby. The little girl smiled and fixed her eyes on her Granny; then she started toddling. She had turned one, just two weeks ago, and her penguin walk was Mom's precious achievement.

The eldest granddaughter stayed at Grandma's everyday when her Mommy went to work. Friday July 31 was not different. The daughter came from work and had dinner with Mom. They were chatting when he opened the door.

"How is my niece? Are you taking good care of her? You're lucky that Mom looks after her," he said while holding Mom's shoulder.

He had come from the senior's club across the street, where he was spending some time with Dad after snacking with Mom to pick up something; but he heard his sister's voice in the kitchen and dropped by to say hello and tickle the baby. After the small talk, he kissed his sister and said "Goodbye."

"What about me? Give a kiss to me too," said Mom. "No, not to you jealous lady, I'll see you later before going home," he doomed himself with that joke and left. He was at the club where his father still spent his days, planning to go back to kiss her as promised, when she called.

"Please come to drive them home. I'm getting tired," she said to Dad.

When he learned about that call, he changed his plans. Waiting for Mom to come back from his sister's to give her that kiss would take quite a while and he would be too late for dinner. He went home and saved the kiss...

Without notice, Mom's heart gave up that night. He would have never missed that kiss, if he had known how bitter it was going to be to hold it in his lips forever.

When the chapel closed and she lay alone with her two children, I saw his impotence. Before shutting down the coffin, I kissed her marble hands. He stepped back and couldn't kiss her corpse.

DISPLACEMENT
by Anu Rao

SHE COULD PICTURE IT in her mind's eye.

A massive wave of gray foam moved up in between the little rick-ety houses with an unimaginable power and devastating speed. In its wake was a lot of debris, uprooted palm trees, broken bits of wood from the fishing boats, bits of thatch from the fishermen's huts, all unravelled by the fury of the storm, plastic bags, assorted bits of garbage – a motley collection of flotsam and jetsam.

She could see the masses of people running away from the un-stoppable juggernaut, down the narrow alleys. Then as if in a movie frame she zoomed in on Deven, Yamuna, Tara, Suni and little Sree. Yamuna had Sree strapped to her hip and in a desperate bid to move faster had firmly anchored the baby using the folds of her saree.

The crowd surged ahead but the black water was gaining mo-mentum. It smelt strongly of sewage and rotting fish. The alley came to a dead end and the wall that blocked their path was too high to scale. All at once mindless confusion erupted, some tried to turn back and run the other way, some milled around trying to get onto rooftops and some jumped at the wall and tried to clamber over it. All of their efforts were hideously impeded by the panic-stricken thronging crowd. Then the first piercing screams were heard as the cold, angry water caught up.

He could picture it in his mind's eye.

Roads with perfect tarmac, smooth and clean, the lanes marked with neat white paint. Cars whizzing by scarcely emitting noxious fumes, drivers very civilized and not cutting into your lane or gesturing obscenely.

Rows of clapboard two-storied houses with green manicured lawns and dazzling flower beds. He supposed in winter all would lay in white in pristine snow.

There would be no power cuts, one didn't have to stand in agonizing queues or travel in horrible congested buses. The shops were clean, well-lit, well-stocked, and more importantly they wouldn't rip you off like Rashid did, substituting dried papaya seeds for pepper corns and spooning copious amounts of *dalda* in *ghee*.

Then other things. Tara and Suni were growing up – it was an ongoing battle getting them to dress decently and do up their hair properly and not talk to those dratted boys. The neighbors would talk.

"Deven's girl you know, found behind the shed with that no-good lout, his hand was up her..."

"Oh my God did she...? Have they...?"

"One can never tell... can you? Who knows?"

And the prospects of marriage would be forever doomed. He supposed in Canada she would be bound to mix with boys, have boyfriends even, but that was an accepted norm. Ironically, that very fact would keep her pure and unsullied, for he had been told it was always the forbidden fruit that was tempting.

He would say, "Yes brought up in Canada but very decent girl, knows our culture and traditions." They would all nod knowingly, and silently calculate that even if the girl wasn't as decent as he claimed they could square it off against a passport to foreign shores. A deal would be struck and the girl married off. And they wouldn't dare ask for more than token dowry.

All this would be possible with the generosity of his distant cousin Kannan. Kannan had gone into business. Over cracking long-distance telephone lines he said he had opened a laundromat. He explained at length what a Laundromat was and why it was popular in Canada.

There was something vastly amusing to think of those foreigners lugging dirty clothes in huge black plastic bags, dumping them in the machines, patiently waiting and then putting them in yet another set of machines to be dried and then finally folding and putting the clothes back into those bags and lugging them home. Kannan added that they were some people either too busy or too lazy to do their own washing and for an additional charge he would wash, dry and fold the clothes for them. This amused Deven even more – were the foreigners so lazy that they couldn't even put clothes in a machine and press some buttons?

However their sloth was turning out to be a blessing for Deven. Kannan was over-worked and he needed a helping hand. Kannan's wife

held a very good job at the Post Office and there was no question of asking her to give up a secure well-paid job. Their children, two daughters, were all grown up and busy with their own lives. Kannan needed someone reliable, someone who would not cheat him when his back was turned and had thought of Deven. He would organize for Deven to come to Canada and urged Deven to get a passport as soon as possible.

"Bribe someone if you have to, I will send you the money," he said.

Lately the back pain had worsened.

At first the pain had been intermittent – no more than an occasional twinge. However, it had steadily gotten worse. Sometimes he barely slept thorough the night yet stubbornly resisted all efforts to go to the local walk-in clinic let alone see the family doctor. But when the dizzy spells started, compounded with shortness of breath and inability to eat, he reluctantly drove himself to Dr. Silver, and even more reluctantly, to get his X-Ray taken and the mandatory blood tests.

The Specialist was matter-of-fact. "Pancreatic cancer is never easy to detect and you compounded it by coming in too late," he admonished. "You should have come several months ago. All we can do now is to do a round of chemo and radio and hope for the best."

Kannan at first raved and ranted and then seemed quite resigned to his fate. He stopped raging and instead became intensely practical. He set about updating his will and sold off the Laundromat.

"Poor Deven," he told Selvi, "I built up such hopes for him – I feel quite consumed by guilt. You should make it up to him, by sending him a good chunk of my life insurance - be generous."

"Yes," Selvi agreed, "I had spoken to his wife before we came to know about this dreadful disease and she was filled with wonderful plans. She is pregnant you know – I'll wait till the child is born before we tell them. We don't want them upset right now."

Everything was smashed to pieces; cars and buses were overturned and on top of each other; the houses and shops were completely gutted. Broken remains were piled up everywhere; peoples' possessions were no more.

When Deven came to, he was lying on a sheet stretched out on the floor of what appeared to be a canvas tent. A row of people were lying on the same sheet. A young man in jeans was moving slowly, pausing to check on each person.

Deven sat up suddenly, the floor and tent swan in a frightening circle.

"Sree, my little Sree," he shouted, ignoring the black spots and

bright lights dancing before him.

The young man came swiftly to his side.

"Are you alright? Lie down for a bit, do you want *something* to drink?" The Red Cross volunteers had trained themselves not to mention the word "water."

"My Sree, my girls, my wife. Where are they? Where are they?" Deven shouted again. His ribs and chest hurt and the floor continued to wobble.

"Sir, you must lie down. Your family is probably in another tent. If you will calm down we can try find them." The young man's measured tones did calm Deven down and he gratefully sank down back on the floor.

Deven was amongst the few that learnt about the fate of their family fairly quickly. The violent tsunami had claimed the lives of Yamuna and his teenage daughters, but by some miracle, his baby, his little Sree was unharmed and being cared for by an elderly aunt. Deven himself had sustained a few bruised ribs and a broken ankle.

Little Sree clung to the new aunty with a passionate love. Totally uncomprehending about the disastrous events that had suddenly erupted around her and her own miraculous survival she had naturally whimpered for her mother. She had floated away from her mother's grasp and had landed unhurt on the beach, where a rescuer had recognized the child and had taken her to Deven's aunt.

Deven's aunt was old and severely traumatized by the tragedy. Being suddenly landed with the task of caring for a thirteen month toddler was more than she could handle. She just about managed to feed and clean the child, but consoling the weeping the child or providing the affection the child was so obviously craving for was quite beyond her.

When Selvi arrived and took over, the child readily responded to her gentle concern and reassuring hugs and allowed herself to be smothered by lavish kisses. Here was someone who sang lullabies, someone who changed her diaper immediately and didn't let her wallow in wet discomfort, someone who gently coaxed milk and food down her little throat.

"Can not tell that lady has lost her husband quite recently," the aunt confided to her neighbour. "She says she knew Kannan was dying so it didn't come as a shock. She feels that what we are suffering, families suddenly coping with loss and grief, no homes, no jobs, no money, is far worse."

"Like Mother Teresa,' the neighbor said and then added maliciously, "It would be perfect if she didn't spend so much time with

Deven."

"She feels responsible for him," the aunt explained. "If Kannan had not died, Deven would be happily settled in Canada by now."

"Doesn't she already have children?"

"They are all grown up, in fact they don't stay with her, and anyway she is older than him."

"Doesn't look it, let us see what is cooking there, anyway she is a Canadian madam, they are bound to have different ideas from us."

True she was older than him, but at their respective ages a four year difference would hardly matter, she reasoned. Besides she would continue to live in Canada and he would come and join her, not even the most inquisitive of her friends or acquaintances would ask for the finer details. Above all there was Sree, precious, adorable little Sree.

No doubt adopting a motherless baby was the best thing she could do but it wouldn't be fair to deprive that little child of a father. As well the old guilt of failing to keep their end of the bargain in bringing Deven to Canada continued to haunt her. It was time, she decided, after days of fruitless vacillation and in a kind of curious gender reversal, to make an honest man out of Deven and start a new life.

The paper-work for Deven and Sree took an agonizingly long time. Every time she followed up she heard the maddeningly prosaic "Your file is being processed, we will get in touch as soon as everything is complete." the cool impersonal voices of the authorities all sounded alike.

Deven walked on the beach, the sea was a beautiful cerulean blue, the waves gently crashed on the shore. In his hand he held a post-card from his daughter - rows of clapboard houses in the gently falling snow. He angrily tore it to bits and let them scatter on the sand.

"That's Deven," the neighbors whispered. "Lost a wonderful chance of going to Canada and marrying a rich lady. He was found behind the shed with that good-for-nothing slut, his hand was up her..."

"Oh! My God...then what...?"

"I tell you that lady may be a Canadian lady, but she knows our culture and traditions. She wouldn't stand for any of such kind of nonsense. She descended on him like a veritable tsunami I tell you, departed with his daughter but left him high and dry."

Deven picked up the torn post-card and began flinging the pieces one-by-one into the sea.

HAPPY MOTHER'S DAY
by Larry Rodness

I HATE WAITING IN line at the bank, probably more than you do. The lines are always too long and the people ahead of me just seem to dally at the teller's cage while I wait impatiently to get my business done. It used to be that you could stand in a separate line to get your favorite teller – the good looking one or the polite one, but these days the bank has us all corralled into a single queue leading us like cattle to the slaughter, just one more way the 'big 5' have depersonalized the banking experience while they shake every last nickel out of our pockets. It's a crapshoot as to which teller you get. I hope it's not the one with the bad breath.

Meanwhile, standing in line gives me time to go over the coming weekend's activities which will center around Mother's Day, a day originally designed to allow people to express their love and appreciation for the women in their lives but whose meaning has been drowned in the deluge of manipulative advertising that guilts me and every other husband into spending even more of our hard-earned cash on cheap chocolates and expensive perfumes. Perhaps 'bah-humbug' is more suited to this holiday than Christmas. After the bank I'll have to slip next door to the drug mart – another corporate monster with its own nefarious designs on how to separate me from my money by forcing me through a labyrinth of cosmetic counters before I get to what it is I really came for... if I haven't already forgotten by the time I get there. After picking out some eight dollar, over-sized card along with it's under-sized envelope, I'll have to stop at the local florist to buy their pricey flowers (which will be half-price on Monday).

Today, against all odds and in spite of the bank's best laid plans, I get my favorite teller. She's not my favorite because she's the prettiest or because she has the nicest breath. She's a handsome woman in her fifties and it's her sense of humor and sunny disposition that has won me over, far outshining the smug-looking models whose faces smile at me from the corporate posters on the walls.

"Afternoon, Dahlia. Here's some more of my hard-earned money for you."

"Thanks, Mister R. I'll put it in this drawer for now and as soon as you leave I'll go out and spend it on a new dress."

We chuckle until an 'ahh' escapes her as she looks past me.

"Aren't those beautiful flowers?" she comments wistfully.

I turn around to see one of the bank staff at the door giving a red rose to every woman who enters. The Ebenezer Scrooge in me wants to scream, 'Those roses were paid for through the outrageous bank fees you people charge me every time I walk through that door! Those women should be thanking me, not you!' But instead I bite my tongue and turn back to Dahlia who is busy recording my deposits.

"You'll be getting your own soon enough," I offer.

"I don't think so." she replies offhanded. "So what are your plans this weekend?"

I run through my litany of errands for the upcoming Mother's Day festivities and confess that I gave up trying to surprise my wife with a gift long ago after I came home one Mother's Day with a silk kimono that was meant more for me than for her. Now I buy her what *she* wants. In any case Dahlia's previous remark has piqued my curiosity.

"But it's Mother's Day." I joke, "Your husband has to buy you flowers, it's the law."

A tiny smile creeps over her face, not the kind filled with amusement, but the kind that belies a darker truth.

Now I know she has a husband and that she's been married for over twenty years with two offspring of her own because one of the things we joke about is how grown children of this generation prefer to live at home as long as they can. I've even shared my nightmare with Dahlia of the not-too-distant future when I wake up one morning to find my wife and I sleeping in the basement and my kids occupying the master bedroom. In truth I can't blame them. It's not like when we were their age and could afford to move out. With the cost of living in this city these days, not to mention the banks with their exorbitant fees... anyway, where was I?

Dahlia confirms she won't be getting flowers this weekend nor will there be any Mother's Day celebrations in her home.

"We don't have family gatherings. My husband doesn't like my family very much, or my friends either for that matter. I work at the bank during the week and at a medical clinic on the weekends...there's not much spare time... we don't go out often... so when I'm off work he likes me to stay home with him,"

"I guess he loves you so much that he wants you all to himself."

Now I'm not a nosy guy and I don't like to spend any more time in a bank than I have to, but that Mona Lisa smile she responds with begs me to push it a little further.

"I don't understand. That's still no reason not to celebrate Mother's Day."

"Oh I am going to celebrate this year, at my mother's home."

"You mean by yourself? Without him?"

Then in a soft, conspiratorial, voice Dahlia whispers,

"My husband doesn't want me visiting my mother because he is afraid there might be a man waiting for me there, a lover."

She shakes her head as if to say that that's the furthest thing from the truth. And then it dawns on me that this is not just a visit to her mother's. This is an act of defiance and bravery.

"Well if it's such a ridiculous accusation, why do you listen to him?" I ask.

"It's no use to debate." she replies. "It would only lead to an argument or worse."

Any humor present a moment ago has fled the conversation like a nun who has stumbled upon the telling of an off-color joke about a priest and the alter boy. All that's left is a creeping sense of dread over what I am compelled to ask next and what she might answer.

"What do you mean 'worse', Dahlia?"

"Do you remember last year when I came to work wearing sunglasses for two weeks? He smashed the bone around my eye and the bank said I couldn't come in to work with bruises. I need to work so, the glasses."

Now I know how that nun feels and it wrenches my stomach. A story like this is meant to be read from the comfort of your kitchen table over the morning newspaper so you can shake your head and cluck your tongue at the outrage and then turn the page. I am not prepared to hear this from the actual victim standing a mere twelve inches away from me.

"Dahlia, this is Canada, you don't have to take that kind of abuse. Have you thought of reporting him, leaving him?"

She nods and with a sigh explains that her husband has turned their children against her, warning her that if she left they would remain

with their father. She won't risk that.

My transaction is done, my money is banked, and other people are waiting behind me as impatiently as I was a few moments ago, moments when I stood in ignorant bliss, consumed over my world-crushing worries. I have no answers and no solutions for her. I don't even know what to say next. My first instinct is to walk over to the bank manager and give one of those roses to Dahlia, but what if it gets back to her husband and he believes she really does have a lover? My noble gesture could have serious consequences.

In the end all I can muster is, "For whatever it's worth, Dahlia, Happy Mother's Day."

"Thanks, you've made my weekend." She says with a smile as warm as the sun.

Then I add, "And if you do steal my money from my account, buy something nice for yourself."

I leave the bank to buy my card and flowers for my wife without hesitation or self-recrimination, and with a little more appreciation of what Mother's Day means in our home.

TWO OF A KIND
by Philomena Saldanha

"THERE ISN'T A SINGLE empty shoebox in this place!" I announce as I stand in the living room of my new condo apartment.

The spare cables that had been lying in a tousled heap in my closet now are neatly bundled and if I could just find a box to put them in, I would be happy. But I can't seem to find a box. I also wish Adam would get off his laptop and talk to me. But he seems oblivious of me talking.

"I wish I hadn't thrown all those empty boxes after we moved from the old house. Now there isn't even a little shoebox. Maybe it's time I bought some shoes."

Adam looks up from his laptop smiling. Oh, he is listening. A freshman at University, he is visiting me for the day. Adam is tall, dark and handsome. He had decided to lose his long locks of hair no sooner he graduated from the twelfth grade and seemed in awe at having peripheral vision again. He had been quite cute with his long hair and straggly beard, though. Now he looks like an average kid. And Adam is anything but average.

"When do you want me to drop you to your dad's place Adam?"

The haircut had uncovered his ears but had done nothing for his hearing apparently. But I know he had heard. He seemed to always put a lag in his response, as if he was conserving his energy and allowing himself the option of not having to respond at all. Clever, but I know my son.

"Adam?"

"Oh, I don't know Mom, tomorrow after lunch would be okay I

guess?"

Another half-day for me! I thrive on these small morsels of precious time. The cables in my hand remind me.

"I can't find an empty shoe box."

"Mom, can you stop talking about shoeboxes or the lack thereof. Talk about anything but shoeboxes, for goodness sake."

"What would you like to talk about Adam?"

"I don't know...I have to do my laundry soon and I never seem to have enough for a load of whites!"

"That is because you hardly wash your clothes sweetie. All your whites have now become almost black."

"Seriously, Mom, I need help here."

"Do you have lots of blacks?"

"Yes"

"So make a load of blacks and put the whites in with other stuff. Why is it that the whites always have to be kept separate? Let's keep the blacks separate for a change."

"That sounds like some racial segregation!"

We both laugh.

The one minute conversation clearly over, I am on my own again. All these cables still in hand and no place to store them, I am reminded of my mission.

"Where can I find a shoebox?"

"Mom, can you please stop talking about shoeboxes......anything but shoeboxes... please?"

"Ok...ok...what should we talk about?"

Adam looks up, pauses, and with a smirk says,

"Calculus."

"Ok. Let's talk about calculus," I rise to the challenge.

"What is calculus? Let us start with the word. It should clearly be calclueless considering how clueless most people are about calculus. So yes, the word should be calclueless. What do you say? Just makes sense don't you think?"

Adam is now laughing his head off.

"Oh Mom, I love you. Why are you so crazy and why do I love you so much?"

Standing up to his full 5 feet 11 inches height, he wraps his arms around me. Love enfolding in a bear hug, cables all squished around my waist, he plants a warm kiss on my cheek.

My baby is all grown up!

1991

There seem to be clouds in the room.

"WHERE ARE MY SHORTS?"

"They are in the first drawer of the dresser" I say politely while my mind screams, find your own f...ing shorts. Peter changes to his shorts. He has such scrawny legs, I realize. I wonder what it would be to not see or hear. I close my eyes and plug my ears. Peace. But not used to peace, I open my eyes and my ears to see Peter pacing up and down and sniffling. Hope he is not getting a cold. He will blame that on me. Four months pregnant, here I am in Jackie's guest bedroom, with pillows propped against my back on the bed, my mind depressed. I close my eyes again.

We must move out and find a place of our own soon. Jackie seems tired of us. Peter must find a job quickly. I should never have come here. It has been a month now since we came to Canada as new immigrants. I had been ecstatic and brave, leaving a familiar world, heady with the excitement of new adventure that would fix all flaws in my marriage. Oh my back! It hurts! I wish I was dead.

I hear a rustling. Peter is fumbling for a cigarette. Good, he will leave this room and take the clouds with him and let me just breathe.

If I was not pregnant, I would leave Peter. I would be free. I would go back to India. I don't want this baby. No! No! It is Peter I don't want. But how will I take care of a baby on my own. I have no job. I can't drive. I hate taking three buses to go to the doctor. Peter won't even drive me to the doctor. Take the bus he said the other day while sitting in Jackie's backyard, cigarette in hand, reading the papers to find a job. The first page is not where you find a job, you bastard! Oh god, help me. Do something.

Peter accompanies me to the next appointment. No, it is not because he cares, but because Dr. Price had asked both of us to be present.

"Mrs. Fernandes, we have a standard test called amniocentesis we offer to women who are over thirty-five, to rule out any birth defects. Here is a brochure that provides information on the procedure. I must warn you however that this test carries a risk of miscarriage, 1 in 400. But I strongly recommend you take this test as soon as possible.

He opens a book and continues, "Fortunately, we have an opening due to a cancellation tomorrow at 3 p.m. May I book you?"

"Yes, but what if there is an abnormality, then what?" I ask.

"Then you both will have to make a choice."

A choice? How could I choose to have a child with a birth defect?

How could I possibly take care of a child like that? Surely no-one could ever blame me for making the only logical choice.

I glance at Peter. He is staring straight ahead.

"Peter, are you.... coming with me... for the test tomorrow?"

"No, I have to go for an interview tomorrow. Go with Jackie."

I lie on the table feeling insignificant. I am cold. Everything looks very long... the table I am lying on.... the picture on the far wall... the doctor's nose.... and the needle that is being positioned to go right through my abdomen. Is this the 400th needle? Jackie holds my hand as I start to shake a bit. And then the doctor puts the needle in.

Back at the house, I wait for Peter with Jackie at the kitchen table. My body is aching... for a hug.

Peter walks in. Sitting himself on a chair next to Jackie, he talks about his interview with great enthusiasm. I cannot see his face as he has his back to me. Ask me about the test, damn it. Ask me how I am. But he goes on and on. The noise! I can't stand it! I quietly leave to go to the bathroom upstairs and sit on the toilet seat my bare feet on the cold grey tiles. I wish I could just lie down and die. I am tired. Enough of this! My baby and I both, just need to die.

The sound of fluttering wings brings me back to the moment. A robin has just hopped on to the window sill directly in front of me. I have never seen a robin at such close quarters. Orange-red breast, snow-white belly, brown head with a fluff of red at the top, he is a beauty. With his neck sticking out, he peers at me, one little foot ahead of the other. He then settles on the sill, his beak nestling on his handsome breast as if he were hatching an egg. He holds my gaze for what seems like a minute suspended in time. I feel the kindling of a fire in my heart and glorious warmth spreads throughout my body. My beautiful little robin then flies off leaving me in bliss.

I am now very familiar with the long hallways of the hospital and no longer worried about losing Peter who always walks many paces ahead. My eyes drift to a man with his arm around his pregnant wife. They are laughing. She looks radiant. He looks proud. He takes his arm off her only so that he can move ahead and hold the door open for her. I pick up my pace as Peter seems to be waiting impatiently outside the doctor's office. Is he waiting to hold the door open for me? I chuckle at my own joke! He looks concerned when he sees me smile.

Dr. Price looks tired and does not look like he wants to be here.

"The fetus has an unusual arrangement of the chromosomes. The chromosomes are all there but it's just an unusual arrangement. If this is normal or not, I can't tell unless we do genetic testing for both of

you. If either of you have the same chromosome arrangement we may assume that the fetus is normal."

I really do not like waiting at the doctor's office any more. The white walls with pictures of frogs, playful children, and happy expectant couples make me angry. It is a relief when my name is announced.

"As you know, the genetic tests are back for you both." Dr. Price pauses as he opens the file.

God help me. Help me. Please do something.... please.

"Well let's see what we have here. Mrs. Fernandes," says Dr. Price looking straight at me, "I am pleased to tell you that the fetus should be okay because you have the same chromosome arrangement as that of your unborn child."

"Who? ME?"

"Yes."

Wow!

I want this child.

I want this child.

He is mine and mine alone.... Not Peter's.

An excerpt from the memoir
MY HOUSE IS HAUNTED
by Mel Sarnese

"YOU WOULD NOT BELIEVE what's been happening!"

"Why, what happened?"

"Your door from the garage has been slamming all night! When I went to check, it was locked!"

"How could that be? That's ridiculous."

My husband, Alan and I had recently had a baby–girl we named Leanna. The year was 1988. We were happy about the birth but also sad at the recent passing of Alan's grandmother, Nanna. We thought an evening out would be fitting, and as my sister, Mary, hopped at the chance of a couple of hours alone with our baby, we felt relaxed about going.

"Daddy's home!" My one year old shouted out towards the door leading to our garage from the laundry room. I put the last spoonful of mashed carrot into her mouth when I heard the door slam again.

"Alan," I called out as I walked towards the door. The door was closed. I looked up at the dead bolt. It was locked. I felt my heart jump into the pit of my stomach. I remembered what my sister told me the week before about her night with the slamming door. I felt bewildered.

During the following months, I heard the door slam several times a day, every day. As always, my daughter would call out to her daddy when she heard it. Mary often came to visit, where together, we heard the door slam. Alan was the only one not hearing the strange goings-on. I didn't know what to make of the whole thing.

One afternoon, while Leanna took a nap, I walked past the door

with my basket of folded laundry. I stopped – not sure of what I heard. I placed my head on the metal door and gasped. From my garage came the white noise of a cocktail party. I heard the clinking of glasses, men and women talking, and the pleasant and polite exchanges one hears at large social functions. I heard no one particular conversation– just many going on at the same time. I slowly opened the door to find nobody there. The party noises got louder. I decided there must be a rational explanation, and perhaps there was a large group of people walking by in front of the house.

I closed the door and walked out the front door to the sidewalk. There was nobody there. I paused to look at the house with the garage in front. There seemed to be nothing unusual. In a mental stupor, I walked back into the house, and ran to the door leading to the garage, to find the still-existing party noises slowly fading away to nothing. I stood there in disbelief before closing and locking the door. The door did not slam that evening.

It was now 1990, and we were happily expecting our second daughter, Julia. I was bringing in groceries from the car into the house through the garage. As I entered, I was stopped by a growling sound. At first thought, I was sure a fox or a coyote had gotten in, as they were spotted many times in the many ravines in the neighbourhood. I put down the groceries and grabbed a broom from the closet. I reluctantly did a room search to find nothing. I dismissed the growling, as I convinced myself my ears were playing tricks with me.

Mary came for dinner that evening and decided to spend the night, as she often did.

At three in the morning, I was awakened by my sister screaming in our room.

"There is a beast in my room!"

"What do you mean a beast?"

"I heard a growling sound at the foot of my bed!"

"A growling sound?"

"Yes, and there was nothing there!"

My mind finally fully awake, I recalled the growling sound I heard earlier the previous day, and proceeded to tell Mary about it.

"I am not sleeping in that room!"

That night Mary slept on the sofa at the end of our room. She left early the next day, and didn't return for awhile. After that, when she did come to visit, she left late at night but rarely slept over. When she did, she slept on the couch in the family room. One night after returning home, she was about to fall asleep, when she heard crackling sounds

coming from outside her window. She got up and looked out to find her garage up in flames. The fire roared high until the garage and its contents were burned to ashes. They said it was arson.

I laid out the cream, lace and silk christening gown my mother made, and Leanna wore at her christening. There was excitement in the air as we prepared for Julia's christening. I ordered a whole smoked turkey from a local deli, my mother offered to make her famous potato gnocchi, and I made side dishes. We planned to have the party in the large recreation room in our newly renovated basement – complete with wet bar. We put out tables, white linens and white and pink roses. I found myself at my kitchen table in the early hours, putting finishing touches on party favours I made, when I looked out to the lit patio to see what appeared to be a human form of white, cloudy vapour. With my eyes wide and mouth gaping, I studied the apparition, paralyzed in my own curiosity. It was transparent, and it had no legs or feet, the vapour ended bluntly, like the hem of a dress. It was a clear August morning,

The moon was still out, and there was no fog in the air– except for what stood before me on the other side of the glass window. I decided it was a ghost haunting. After all that occurred in the house, it seemed a reasonable explanation. When fear took over the cognitive side of my brain, I bolted up the sweeping staircase. I could hear my palpitations through my ears. I could feel moisture over my top lip as I licked its' saltiness. I woke Alan from a deep sleep to tell him what I had just witnessed. He mumbled something, and went back to his slumber.

I picked up the phone to call my sister, Mary. She believed me. The door leading to the garage from the laundry room continued with its daily slamming. I never heard the party sounds nor the growling again. I often thought of employing investigators of the paranormal to come do a search but never got around to it. I wondered if they would be able to explain the unusual events. I have done some reading on the topic, and have discovered there seems to be a correlation between electricity and the spiritual world.

There is talk about a possible port hole between our physical world and spiritual dimensions. That perhaps electrical currents fuel or makes possible the collision of the two worlds. In front of our house – in front of the garage, sits a green, municipal electrical box which provides much of the electricity for the street. At a recent dinner party at our home, my friend who also lived on the same street, told me that she too, experienced unusual things, and believes her house was haunted. I wondered how many others on our street shared similar happenings.

Of course, few would admit their home is haunted, and fewer still

document stories about it, but I found out when I started to verbalize my experiences, others came forth with their own stories.   Do I truly believe in ghost hauntings?   After all that happened, it would seem unreasonable not to believe in a spiritual world.   I do believe in an afterlife – that there is a world after we pass from this earth. I guess I should believe in ghosts to make it consistent.

One sunny afternoon, I was in my bedroom speaking with my mother on the telephone as my daughters had quiet time in their rooms. The door was closed when I looked up to see the brass knob turn. I waited for the door to open, and for my two year old to dance in at any moment. The door remained closed, I rubbed my eyes as I walked towards it before opening it. There was nobody there. I quickly walked down the hall to look in on my daughters. Leanna was quietly sitting on her bed, reading a picture book, Julia was asleep in her crib. Alan was outside doing yard work.

"I don't know how you could stand living in that house with all that's been going on," my mother told me in her native Italian. She then continued to tell me stories of old hags appearing in the bedrooms of ancient Italian farm houses, and of apparitions of dead people on All Saints Day in village churches.

"I know. I guess I'm used to these things now," I calmly stated. "Maybe we should move. I feel kind of funny raising the girls in a haunted house."

We put the house up for sale, and moved two blocks away a month later. Alan thought it would be better to move to a quieter street for the girls. I agreed.

I packed the cream christening dress my daughters wore in the same box my wedding dress was placed. I very carefully sealed the box with good packing tape, and felt secure the garments were safe from air exposure which, over time, might cause them to yellow. I used a whole reel of tape.

Recently, both my daughters left for university, our third daughter, Genevieve was still in middle school when I felt a need to go back to the preserved box, which housed many fond memories in a wedding and christening dress. I went to my closet, lifted the large box from the top shelf and placed it on the floor. The tape seemed undisturbed, and appeared to be tightly wrapped around the box. The corners were especially covered with tape – two or three layers, as I remembered it. I looked into the plastic window on the front of the box. The familiar white dress lay with its beaded sleeves folded neatly in front. I could feel the corners of my lips curl up into a slight smile as I excitedly removed the

adhesive strips. Layer upon layer, I removed the tape from around the box. I grinned at the mound of it sitting in a pile, and I thought about how wonderful it would be to hold all our precious memories in a box or in a bottle, to untap and unwrap, anytime we like. How great it would be to relish in every memorable moment of our past. To once again, see the young faces of our grown children in a memory box – a box which holds every milestone, every smile – recalled when we liked.

I lifted the top portion of the box. My wedding dress seemed almost sacred. I gingerly picked up one sleeve, and brought it to my face as if to kiss its wrist. It smelled of seamstress and white almond confetti. I remembered dancing with my new husband, and posing for the cutting of the wedding cake. I lifted the garment, my hands palpating through white tissue paper.

The christening dress was gone.

An excerpt from the memoir "Till We Meet Again"
THE UN–BEAR–ABLE ROAD TRIP
by Suzanne Schmidt

IT WAS A BEAUTIFUL spring day, and a little over a week since my mother, my friend, my soul mate was diagnosed with acute leukemia. She was given only two precious months to live. Instinctively I knew I had to take her to Sturgeon Falls, the place where my mother, her sister Fern, and I were born. My Aunt Fern still lives in the house that my grandfather built after he sold the farm. Throughout the years it had been a custom for my mother to go there for her annual retreat in an attempt to escape her demanding life.

My three sisters Kathy, Janet, Pat, and my daughter Tessa decided to come along. We packed our bags and as I helped Mom into the SUV, I was reminded of the many Saturdays we spent together and how I would joke and say, "Get that side of beef in there," every time I helped her into the car. I had to struggle to lift and push her into the seat, because she was so short and heavy, and we would laugh every time.

I decided to do the driving, which I often did, when I took Mom on road trips every summer for the past few years. This time no one seemed to mind the fact that it would take us four hours to get to Sturgeon Falls because as soon as we got in the car the adventure began. We talked about our lives and sang Mom's favourite songs in both French and English. Music was a big part of her life and ever since she was diagnosed with cancer, we seemed to sing all the more. When I asked her why this was so, she said "Turn a bad time into a song."

After crooning a few of Mom's favourite tunes like; "You are My Sunshine," "Le Festin de Campagne," and "Jambalaya on the Bayou," we reminisced about the many family road trips we had taken when we were younger. All six children were crammed into our car, and the little

ones, Kathy and Janet, usually sat in the front seat between Mom and Dad. I was the unfortunate middle child who had to take a turn sitting on my older brothers Jim or Harold, or my sister Judy's knees in the back seat. The trips were so long that I would fall asleep and usually end up peeing on one of their laps. They would get so annoyed and we would start fighting. Dad always threatened, "Do you want me to pull this car over right now? You keep it up and YOU WILL ALL GET IT!"

For some reason, my brothers loved to hear me whine, especially in the car when Dad couldn't see what was going on. They would tease or tickle me and my father would reach his big hand back, while he was driving, to slap whoever was unlucky enough to be within his reach. Imagine, we didn't have to wear seatbelts back then and my brothers enjoyed offering me up for a slap or two. You certainly didn't want to make my father angry. He was under so much pressure, trying to make enough money to put a roof over our heads and food on the table. Dad really did do his best, but it was always an uphill battle, and on those trips, our car would usually break down and cost him money he just didn't have. He would end up making some sort of deal with the garage owner and after hours of waiting, we would be on the road again.

We couldn't afford to go on regular vacations, but once a year our family would pack up the car and visit our relatives. I can't imagine how overwhelmed they were to receive so many guests at once, but in those days it was the thing to do. Relatives always covered your back, and without exception, they were there to help you out. I remember we were usually the ones to open up our home to my grandparents, aunts and uncles and their kids, and they were always welcome to stay as long as it took to get back on their feet again. It probably didn't help our finances any, but it did teach us the importance of family, and sharing.

Driving that day to my Aunt Fern's house, we talked about one of our longest and most memorable road trips from Sudbury to Thunder Bay to visit my Aunt Joan and her family. Dad was a carpenter by trade and he made this huge wooden carry all for the top of the car that must have weighed a ton. I'm not sure if the weight of that thing, or the fact that we had six kids affected the cars fuel consumption and car troubles, but this was definitely a trip to remember.

Everyone knew it would be a long gruelling trip because Dad said it was 1,000 miles from Sudbury to Thunder Bay. We sang, ate, and listened to his stories, which we had heard for the hundredth time. Whenever he would start telling one of them, Mom would interrupt and argue about the facts, which he seemed to change every time he told the story. Our eyes would glaze over and there was no escape. After spending so

much time in one position in the cramped sweltering confines of the back seat of the car, it felt as if we were glued to each other with sweat.

The hours seemed to crawl by and I was beginning to feel car sick. Dad was telling one of his scary bear stories, and as I looked around at my siblings, I knew that our only escape was in our minds. We looked out the window and dreamed of a better time or place to be. Tired, hungry and thirsty, Dad told us we would stop soon. He said that same thing over an hour ago. The only thing we had left was a warm can of Tab and we passed it around wondering if this would be our last drink for hours to come. There was nothing left to eat and we were only a little over half way to our destination, but I wasn't too worried about eating, as I fought back my nausea. All of a sudden my brother Jim said, "Hey Dad, look at that tire rolling right down the road."

My father calmly said, "Don't be silly Jimmy."

We looked around, and were wondering what he meant. The car went thunk, thunk, sparks flew, and instantaneously we knew Jim was right. The wheel had come off our car!

Dad pulled over cursing and swearing, just like Ralphy's father in "The Christmas Story." No one dared say a word, and we knew we were in for trouble. Just as he was ready to get out of the car Jim said, "Hey Dad what if there are bears out there?" Jim was teasing him as he often did and Dad said, "Don't be silly Jimmy." He quickly found the tire and put it back on the axel, ingeniously using one bolt from each of the remaining three tires to secure it. As he was screwing on the last bolt we heard two big bangs and out from the bushes came a big brown bear. Jim quickly rolled his window down and yelled, "Dad, a bear just came out of the bushes!!" Dad was getting a little angry with him at this point and I'm sure he was thinking, "You can't bullshit a bullshitter Jimmy." Glancing over his shoulder, just to be sure, he began to say, "Don't be si— hit!", as he locked eyes with the bear that was no more than 10 feet away. We never witnessed Dad moving so quickly in all our lives as he scrambled to get back into the car. The bear didn't stand on his hind legs, growling and pounding its chest like the ones in the movies, however, just the sight of it caused everyone to scream in sheer terror. It was interested in that rolling thing and he started sniffing the air. We were panicking and Mom was trying to calm us down before the bear decided to shift its attention on us. The beast slowly turned its big brown head towards the car and we screamed even louder. My brothers were laughing, probably due to the intensity of the situation, or their warped sense of humour. We tried to keep still and quiet so it would leave us alone. I am sure my mother was saying her prayers. It stopped and stood there looking at us for what

seemed a life-time before it ran across the road and into the woods.

We let out a huge sigh of relief. Just when we thought we were out of danger, the bushes beside our car rustled again! Out burst a hunter with his gun held high in the air. The only hunter I ever saw was Elmer Fudd and I was really impressed to see a real one. We rolled down our windows, pointed to the other side of the road and yelled, "He went that way!"

When all the fuss was over, we drove slowly to the next gas station praying hope against hope that the car would make it there. It wasn't too surprising to find out that there was something seriously wrong with the axel. Unfortunately it would cost more than my parents had with them. My father didn't have a credit card and there certainly weren't any A.T.M. machines around. All the money they had was in my mother's purse.

We went into the restaurant so my parents could come up with a plan, which was a real treat for us because we never could afford to eat out as a family. We had to order pancakes due to the fact that it was the cheapest way to fill up six hungry bellies. I ordered chocolate milk and everyone just looked at me in disgust, as if I was so stupid that I didn't realize we were in deep trouble, stranded in the middle of nowhere, without enough money to fix the car, let alone order chocolate milk. Dad was always so optimistic and I think he took pity on me and said I could have it. Looking back I realize that it was very selfish of me, but I was young, and yes I was very spoiled.

Dad convinced Mom to phone her sister Fern and ask her to lend us some money so we could get the car fixed. After hours of waiting we were on our way again. When we finally reached Thunder Bay, I wasn't feeling well and to add insult to misery, I ended up in bed for a week with the German measles. Dad had another good story to tell even if he did embellish it a bit throughout the years.

As we continued to drive to my aunt's house for the last trip Mom would ever make, the landscape began to change and we could see how the highway had been carved through thick walls of granite. Although it was our last road trip, I was glad that we decided to make it. We spent a great deal of our young lives growing up in Sudbury and the surrounding areas and I knew that I was taking Mom home, not just for her sake, but for mine too. Perhaps, if we went back to our roots we could make this nightmare we were living go away, even if it was just for a few days.

THE YOUNG ENTREPENEUR
IN PRAISE OF OLDER WOMEN
by Steven H. Stern

I WAS BORN SAMMY Starr in Timmins, Ontario, population, ten thousand, located about five hundred miles north of Toronto. I don't recall much about my life until I was six years of age. That's when I developed a pre-natural crush on an exceptionally outstanding seventeen year-old girl. She was our babysitter... occasionally. Yet, smitten as I was, I remember little of how she looked, her demeanor or her name. I can recall only two things... how delicious she smelled and the chocolate fudge she'd make after my mother and her sister, our Aunt Lil, left for their weekly bingo night at Trinity Church. The church was located a few blocks from the modest house we rented on Birch Street. At that time my dad was in his second year as a Canadian soldier stationed in Vancouver, British Columbia. We hadn't seen him since he left.

My seven-year-old brother and I loved to cozy up on the sofa on either side of that seventeen-year-old goddess and devour her chocolate fudge, secure and comfortable yet thrillingly terrified, listening to the weekly series on the radio, "Inner Sanctum" or "The Shadow." Both scary broadcasts were very popular at the time...1943.

My second greatest love was going to Saturday afternoon matinees. My mom worked at the theatre, so we got in for free. I liked that I could lose myself in the darkness of the theatre and transform myself into another world... I'd laugh and sing along moving my lips without projecting my voice so as not to humiliate myself should someone hear me sing out loud.

I did my real singing when I got home, and my mom was still at work and my brother was at a friend's. I'd sing all kinds of songs, but

rarely could remember the words, so I made up my own. Eventually I'd get bored and exhausted. I'd stagger into the bedroom, flop down on the bed and lie there thinking. When I felt sad or angry, I would have a dialogue with the "voice" in my head. He seemed to understand me, but, of course, I'd never tell anybody about it because they'd think I was nuts. But then the voice in my head started suggesting that my brother and I should be helping our mom around the house. "Times are tough," he said. "And when times get tough, the tough get going." He didn't stop there, he constantly berated me about helping. I eventually caved in. When my brother came home I definitely was gonna talk to him about us helping our mom. I was feeling real good about this now... real good.

A couple of weeks rushed by and I still hadn't talked to my brother, but I had developed this great idea. We would collect empty glass milk bottles and soft drink bottles and redeem them down the street at the variety store.

Before I decided to enter the variety store, I watched through the front window until the place was empty. Obviously I needed the owner's full attention. The lady who owned the variety store stood behind the counter and listened to me attentively. When I finished my pitch she gave me a big smile. I was thrilled. I think she liked me or at least my idea.

With a very thick French accent she told me she would be happy to accept all the glass bottles we could deliver and pay us cash after every transaction. She smiled and softly whispered, "You and your brother will make your mother very happy." I smiled back as I moved to exit the store. She wasn't finished yet. With an even wider smile she said, "You, young man, are going to be a real entrepreneur." This time I did a quick smile, waved my hand to her and exited the store.

What the heck is an "entrepren..." something? I couldn't remember the word or know what it meant but I planned to ask my mom when she came home from work. That evening she explained it to me...sort of: "An entrepreneur is a person who has vision and develops ideas to create businesses that become successful."

My response to that was: "Oh" and I went into the living room and turned on the radio. I was tired.

It was a new day and I was hoping to meet a girl I'd seen at school during recess on the yard. I'd been watching her watch the other kids playing. I had sauntered over to her, and said with nervous confidence, "Hi." She snapped her head towards me and just stared. I tried again, "Hi," I repeated.

"I heard you the first time," she said.

"Oh," I countered. She seemed bossy.

"I'm a second grader," she said. "What grade are you in?"

I stumbled, paused and before I could answer she continued.

"You in first grade? 'Cause I'd know if you were in second grade 'cause I know everybody in second grade and you're way too small to be in third grade, so you must be a first grader." She paused, "Unless you're in kindergarten."

I responded quickly and forcefully, "I'm in first grade."

I was pretty sure she was taken aback by my sudden take charge attitude. I countered, "How come you're not playing on the yard?"

She shrugged her shoulders, "I hate sports." Obviously she never played hockey. I loved hockey. It was the only thing I liked about winter. So I told her without offending her that I liked sports.

She pointed to the playground. "Then why aren't you out there?"

"'Cause I'm going to the grocery store. That's why." I was getting a little testy.

It was a late sunny afternoon as we approached the fruit and vegetable stands. Yes, I was finally able to convince her to come with me to the grocery store. I gazed across a massive variety of fruits looking for a red ripe plum like the one my mother handed me last week. I found one and offered it to my new friend. I'd hand-picked it from the box. Then I chose one for myself. But as fate would have it, when I lifted the plum to my mouth a hand stopped my forward motion and another hand snatched the plum from me.

Swiftly I looked up. It was the grocery man towering over us, my plum in his hand. He seemed angry.

"What do you kids think you're doing?"

In unison, without having to even look at each other, we said, "Nothing."

The grocery man gazed over to my new friend as she continued to eat the plum.

"Do you have money to pay for that?"

She was quick. While sucking the sweet, juicy plum she raised her hand pointing a wet plumy finger in my direction. "He gave it to me."

I was stunned. She ratted on me. I couldn't believe it. At least she got to eat her plum... well most of it. At that moment I knew our relationship was over.

The grocery man looked back at me. "Do you have any money?"

I shook my head no. He looked down at the plum he'd confiscated from me and did something I never ever expected. He handed me back the plum. Was this some kind of trick? What should I do? I took the plum. "Thank you," I said. My mom taught me to be polite.

"Okay, now you kids go home and don't come back without your mom or..." he paused, looking straight at me. "Are you one of the Starr boys?"

I responded quickly and I nodded, "Yes."

"Well, young man, your father's away fighting for our freedom, your mom's working two jobs to make ends meet and you do something like this. Shame on you...shame."

That crushed me. I felt as low as a garden snake. I didn't want him or my ex-girl friend to see me cry so I ran away as fast as I could. I was embarrassed... and ashamed. I knew I'd never forget what the grocery man said. NEVER.

With my new found humility, my brother and I began collecting empty glass milk and soft drink bottles, redeeming them at the variety store. We got two cents for each soda bottle and five cents for every milk bottle. We would give the money to our mom so she could go win a chicken at the Trinity Church bingo. She was extremely lucky at bingo. Almost a bingo professional, if there is such a thing. All I know is she almost always came back with something.

It was nearing a year since the plum episode and it was well behind me, but I needed to expand my entrepreneurial skills. I was seven years old.

While hanging out across the street from the high school I noticed that all the kids smoked cigarettes. Not on the yard but on the street corners. Most rolled their own. Some rolled the loose tobacco in newspaper...some used cigarette paper and some of the richer kids actually bought real cigarettes... "professionals" as we called them... store bought. I wondered how they'd got them. Probably stole them from their mom or dad.

Both my parents were heavy smokers... almost every adult I ever saw always had a cigarette in their mouth or between their fingers. Most adults had yellow teeth and permanent yellow stains on the two fingers near their thumb. Most kids wanted to emulate them. I was no different. Perhaps a little younger than most... but I had a plan. Here's how it worked. I would look for as many cigarette butts as I could find, starting at my home and friends' homes. I would empty the ashtrays into a paper bag. I would collect cigarette butts on the street, in the gutters... it didn't matter. I could fill the bag in a couple of hours. I would let the butts dry out and then rip apart the cigarette paper and let the tobacco fall into what would become a mountain of tobacco. Then I would "borrow" my mother's cigarette papers. (I would replace the "borrowed" cigarette paper from the funds I earned selling cigarettes at two cents each.)

My mother had recently purchased a new cigarette roller machine which made five cigarettes at one time. I was in full production.

My mother was amazed at how many bottles I was able to collect a week. I was getting a little worried she might be getting suspicious about where the "bottle" money was really coming from. I didn't want another plum situation in my life. While I was walking along the street one day picking up the better quality cigarette butts and throwing them into the bag (I was trying to upgrade the quality of my product at the same time as I was contemplating giving up the business) suddenly I heard something that was about to end my lucrative career as an entrepreneur... and begin an entirely new life.

It started as noise. I stopped to listen. At first I could hear the noise of automobiles, then music and people screaming through bullhorns. I looked up. Way up the street the sounds were getting louder but I still could not see anything. Then it happened. As the parade turned the corner, I could see swarms of people in cars and open trucks driving towards me. Crowds of people were laughing and crying, hugging each other, even kissing. They were all waving flags... British flags, American flags and flags I'd never seen before. Neighbors were rushing out of their homes, crying and singing, "O Canada." I wasn't sure why they were acting so crazy. I ran towards an old lady coming out of her house. I shouted, "Hey lady...lady... what's going on? What's happening? What's hap..."

Before I was able to finish my sentence her arms stretched out, tears in her eyes, she enveloped me into her arms.

"The war is over! It's over!! We won!! We won!!"

She kissed me all over my face. My infatuation with older women was over. I turned and started to run home. I ran and ran as fast as I could. I thought my heart would burst. My dad would be coming home and my life would change forever.

HOW I LOST MY BUDGERIGAR
by Phyllis Diller Stewart

DESPITE TENDER CARE, I can't keep a houseplant alive, so I have no idea what possessed Sylvia to give a bird for my birthday. Maybe she knew my apartment was too quiet and my heart was lonely. That I needed to nurture something that would love me back.

The care and feeding of a bird was quite alien to me, but I learned to enjoy my little budgie whom, scraping the bottom of my creative barrel, I named Budge. He had a striking green breast and yellow face, and hopped hopefully about his cage whenever I came near. He loved to sit on my finger, blinking his bright bird eyes while examining my large, uncaged world. Cocking his head to one side he'd make little budgie noises in my direction, waiting politely for me to answer in kind. I always felt he was mildly disappointed when I replied in English, idiotically repeating the same word over and over, hoping he might learn it.

Before long, Budge and I struck up a good relationship despite our communication disabilities. His muffled chirps reminded me to take the cover off his cage every morning, and each evening he gave me the hairy eyeball when I came to tuck him in. The poor bird had to suffer my moody silence as I filled his seed and water cups each morning but after I got home from work we relaxed together while I cooked dinner. Like a miniature jockey, Budge rode my shoulder, and he often twittered sweet nothings and nibbled my ear lobe for the sheer joy of it all. What more could a young woman like me have wanted in a man?

Budge had been part of my life for about four months when I came home from work one day to find the poor thing listing far to the

right, and clinging to his perch for dear life. I was sure he had suffered a stroke. In great distress, I called Sylvia who hurried over. She was horrified to see Budge in such bad shape and agreed with my diagnosis. Grabbing the phone book, she helped me search the Yellow Pages for a bird vet.

The next day I called in sick and went to the veterinary clinic instead, nervously entering the office, cage and crooked bird in hand. While I waited, I overheard conversations between the owners of other patients. They were apparently spending hundreds of dollars to look after their birds, ferrets, and reptiles. I was there to lay out $25 plus tax to end Budge's life.

The kind doctor advised me of treatment options that would prolong Budge's life, but I stuck to my guns and insisted on euthanasia. Budge's evening glares were nothing compared to this man's, but he did as I asked and, within minutes, I slunk back through the waiting room carrying nothing in my cage but a small cardboard coffin.

When I got home I surprised myself by crying, for I had grown quite fond of my little green bird. In honour of the wee fellow, Sylvia offered me a red velvet-lined box in which to bury him, and together we laid him to rest in a shallow grave dug in the ravine behind our apartment building.

It took well over a year until Sylvia had the nerve to tell me that a few days after the funeral she happened upon the red box, dug up, and no bird in sight.

I can only speculate, but I never did like the ginger-coloured tabby that lives on the ground floor.

HOW MUCH FOR THE MEMORIES?

by Urve Tamberg

AFTER FORTY SEVEN YEARS in the same house, my save-this-you-never-know-when-you're-going-to-need-it immigrant parents were emptying the nest with the requisite Saturday morning garage sale. Over the past few weeks, I had begged them to throw out the old margarine tubs, pleaded with them to ditch bags of fabric scraps from my mother's sewing ventures and implored them to scrap dozens of bent wire hangers and clothes not even fit for charity. Finally, they were ready to sell the rest.

At seven in the morning, I parked my car by the curb, got out, put my coffee mug on the roof then reached in and retrieved the ultimate garage sale accessory. I clipped a black nylon fanny pack full of loonies and toonies around my waist, adjusted it so it sat on my hips but knew looking cool was impossible. I caught a reflection of myself in the car window as I perched my Gucci sunglasses on my head. Let the sales begin.

I popped open the trunk of the van and dragged out a plastic castle and a basketful of plastic toys, the kind a future generation will find intact in five hundred years. I arranged them near the edge of the curb to entice people to stop.

The garage door was open and Dad had placed a tarp on the driveway to arrange his hardware and tools. I passed by a stack of Reader's Digest Condensed Books, yellowed magazines and our old kitchen table. I ran my hand over the table then shook my head. My husband wouldn't let me in the door if I came home waxing nostalgic over a Formica kitchen table circa 1958.

"Coffee, honey?" Dad asked as he headed toward the tarp with

an armful of wires and cords.

"No, thanks." I kissed his cheek and lifted my mug. "We should be done by noon, don't you think? I have a hair cut appointment. Where's Mom?" I sipped my coffee.

"Gone to her sister's place," Dad said. "She muttered something about salivating bargain-hunting vultures pecking at her good taste. She said if she had to bargain with them about paying fifty cents instead of a dollar, she would likely rip the item out of their hands and tell them to go... home." At the tarp, Dad knelt down to deposit his bundle. "Violence has no place at a garage sale. She'd probably end up on the front page of the local paper."

I just nodded. Since when did Reader's Digest Condensed Books constitute value and good taste? If we made a hundred bucks, we'd be lucky.

Dad walked into the garage and returned with one of his lamp creations. "Do you want this? I don't mind if you sell it. It's never been my favourite and it won't fit into the condo."

Dad made lamps out of wood. Driftwood, branches, anything with a shape that caught his fancy. He had an artistic touch but this was not his best effort. It stood about four feet high. Picture a debarked varnished tree branch sticking out of a hub cap at a forty-five degree angle topped with a lampshade from a thrift store.

I patted his shoulder, took the lamp from him and placed it next to a mountain of mason jars. "I'm sure it will find a good home."

Dad hovered over his collection of baby food jars neatly labelled with masking tape written on with black marker. Nuts. Bolts. Washers. Screws. ½ inch nails. ¾ inch nails. 1 inch nails. Old shoe boxes held bits of copper pipe, elbow joints, and lengths of wire. Telephone cord extensions, coiled and wrapped with string, completed the collection. It was like watching a child give away toys he still loved, but knew he was too old to play with. I blinked a couple of times and covered my eyes with my sunglasses. Who would buy used hardware?

By 7:15 a.m., three pick-up trucks had cruised by, windows rolled down. These serious bargain hunters scanned the merchandise from afar then stepped on the gas.

Annoyed, I rearranged the coffee cups, mismatched china and wicker baskets. Was our stuff not good enough? It had been good enough for my parents for almost fifty years.

I paced up and down the driveway while Dad continued his arrangement of hardware. A couple of cars parked by the curb. A man in jeans and a plaid shirt strolled up the driveway, his head turning side to

side as if he was watching a tennis game.

"Good morning." I smiled.

He grunted, twirled and left.

I turned my attention to the young woman in tight white jeans. "Hi, nice day, isn't it?"

She held up a coffee mug decorated with I LOVE NY.

"How much is this?"

I glanced at the sticker. "Seventy-five cents." I lifted the sunglasses onto my head.

"Would you take fifty cents for this?"

I let my eyes widen to let her know I was serious.

"No," I said as I took my time with the vowel. "It costs seventy-five cents."

"I'll give you fifty cents." She pulled a change purse out of her designer bag.

I bared my teeth into a fake smile. "It's seventy-five cents." Was she kidding? She was going to bargain over twenty-five cents? Pay up, honey.

"Oh." She dropped the change purse back in her bag. "No thanks."

Pearls before swine. I started back to the porch as Mom's words echoed in my ears. I began to feel like our dirty laundry was on display and people were judging my parents based on their castaways. Maybe I should join Mom at her sister's before I blew a gasket.

"How much for the lamp, honey?" A woman pointed a fat finger at my dad's creation on a hubcap.

Because she called me honey, I said, "Hundred bucks. It's one-of-a-kind. Hand-made. "

She harrumphed and wandered over to the pulp fiction section of the driveway.

An hour later, we had made $124.87 and there was more to sell. The toys were gone, someone had snagged the kitchen table and cars were lined up along the street.

"I need to go to the bathroom," Dad said as we stood on the porch. He leaned closer. "That woman has been looking at the mason jars for at least five minutes. Don't take anything less than two hundred dollars." He shook a finger at me. "They're worth a lot more." With that parting advice, he headed toward the house. A couple of steps later, he turned. "She looks like she does a lot of preserves. She'll pay."

Two hundred dollars? I would pay someone fifty just to haul them away.

A couple dozen cases of vintage mason jars along with packs of lids, probably from 1976, towered in the middle of the driveway. I eyed the woman. She circled the boxes like she was examining a bushel of heirloom tomatoes.

I decided to make a move. Sunglasses up, smile pasted on.

She acknowledged me with a nod, eyes still on the jars. "How much for these?"

"Two hundred dollars," I mumbled.

"Pardon me?" She leaned closer.

"Two dollars."

"Really?" I could swear her ears perked up, just like a cocker spaniel's.

"Each." I held my breath.

"Oh." Her ears drooped.

"The lids are extra."

"Oh." She opened her cloth bag, pulled out a worn wallet. "Would you take twenty dollars for all of it?"

"Twenty-five." It felt ridiculous to bargain but I feared my Dad's wrath. I could slip a few twenties into the fanny pack .

She counted out some bills and a handful of silver. "Done."

By the time I tucked the money away, she was half way to her car with a couple of cases. I hoisted two boxes and followed her to her Chevy. We loaded quickly. She probably feared I would change my mind and I didn't want Dad to swoop in for a price check.

I waved to her as she left, then made my way back to the porch. Three elderly men circled the tarp a few times. One bent down to sift through a box of copper pipe.

"Wow! Love the tacky lamp."

I turned around and looked down to meet the eyes of a woman with burgundy hair waving a bill at me.

"How much? I'll give you ten bucks"

"Two hundred bucks." I revealed my teeth in a fake smile. "It's vintage."

She cackled. "Are you kidding? Honey, you're dreaming." She waddled away.

I returned to the porch and my cold cup of coffee. A couple of seconds later Dad appeared.

"I told you she would buy those," Dad said as his eyes found the empty spot. "I know people." He puffed out his chest. "How much did you get? I should have asked two hundred and fifty for those jars. They had never been used."

"Yep, she paid... Oh, look, Dad.... Those men are looking at your tools and hardware."

Dad's eyes lit up and he ambled over to the three elderly gentlemen crouched around the tarp. I followed.

One of them thrust an open palm full of bits under my nose.

"How much I pay?"

"Dad, how much do you want for eight screws, three bolts, two washers of different sizes and a few inches of copper pipe?" I asked with fear this would launch us into a negotiation. I figured about six cents.

"Let me see," said Dad. "Exactly how many inches of pipe?" He came over to examine the goods before committing to this potentially serious financial transaction.

Over the next hour, another couple of men joined the group. All of them selected their purchases with care, comparing the size or length numerous times. Their palms overflowed with pieces so I fetched some plastic grocery bags from the house while Dad provided advice and opinions at this hardware love-fest. While Dad bonded with the do-it-yourself crowd, I sold almost everything that was saleable and scooped the rest of it into a box for the dump. I peeked at my watch. Almost noon. Then I noticed a pleasant looking woman loitering by the lamp.

"I love the lamp. How much?" She caressed the trunk.

"Sorry, it's not for sale." I picked it up under my arm like a mannequin and took it to safety in the back of the van.

I should have kept the kitchen table as well.

An excerpt from the novel "A Person of Letters"
WHERE DREAMS LIE BURIED
by R. G. Thompson

AFTER A COUPLE OF days in Paris to get over jetlag, we drove west to Normandy. We had booked a *gite* outside Bayeaux for a few days, so I could tour the beaches. Genny would find something touristy to do, and Chloe would get her choice of coming with me or going with her mom.

"What would we do, Daddy?" Chloe asked noncommittally, the night before my personal assault on the beaches. She has Genny's eyes and dark hair, and a not-very-good poker face she gets from me.

"Well," I said, rubbing my palms together, "we'll spend a couple of days, because there's so much to see. We'll walk around some old battlefields, where there are some wrecked pillboxes, and craters in the ground from bombing and shellfire. We'll take a day-long guided tour with a real historian, and see where the battles were fought! We'll go to some museums and see some old guns and uniforms. I'll show you where your Granddad came ashore in 1944. Maybe we'll even ride in an army truck. And if there's still time, after all that, we'll have ice cream!"

I threw in that last bit knowing from her expression that she would be spending the day with Genny on the trail of William the Conqueror in Falaise.

Next morning, safely on my own, I started off from Bayeaux, driving through stunningly beautiful pastoral country to the coast at Longues-sur-Mer, between Omaha Beach to the west and the British beach Gold to the east; I parked and walked along the cliffs to the concrete ruins of a massive German gun battery, destroyed by naval gunfire on D-Day. Then I drove east along the coast to Courseulles-sur-Mer, where I spent a couple of hours at the Juno Beach Centre, built to commemorate the Canadian

landings. Afterwards I sat out on the white sandy beach, feeling numbed and humbled, thinking about what it must have been like on the morning of June 6th, 1944. One of the guides had pointed out the ruined German machinegun emplacements, situated to cover that span of shore with deadly cross-fire. Men died out there, I thought – in front of me, and to the left and right – but the others kept coming.

A French family was picnicking on a blanket down close to the water; two adults with a baby and a little girl. The girl, a pretty child in a red swimsuit, jumped up now and then to run into the sea; she stopped in her tracks when her toes were covered, then raced out ahead of the gently lapping waves. She reminded me of Chloe at three or four. I paid her no more attention, thinking about the bodies that had stacked up here, and fallen there, and about the men who had kept coming through the withering fire. The first wave on Juno suffered fifty percent casualties. In total, there were a thousand Canadian casualties on D-Day; of those, three hundred and forty were killed. The Battle of Normandy would claim more than five thousand young Canadians; many more thousands would be wounded.

I looked around at the sound of a child's giddy laughter. Down by the water, the family had finished lunch. The little girl chattered to her parents as she dug in the sand with a plastic shovel. She filled a brightly-coloured bucket and ran to the water to wet its contents. With a shriek, she tipped and plunked the bucket onto the beach, pressing it firmly into the ground to form its contents. After a moment she lifted the bucket away to reveal her creation.

It was a smooth-sided turret, the very image of the ruined pill-boxes all along that shore.

At the sight of it I felt cold revulsion and anger. Young men died here, I thought. Right here, right where you're digging and building pill-boxes! How can you? Don't you know? Hasn't anyone told you? My eyes turned accusingly towards her parents.

But the dam of my resentment burst as quickly as it had filled, as I realized that no one can live in a museum or a graveyard – that life must reclaim its domain. And what had those men died for, if not for this: that a small child, an innocent soul, could build a sand castle on a beach. This was no show of disrespect, this child's excavation on Juno. It was an affirmation of life and a testament to their sacrifice.

I collected sand in a bag, wondering if any of their DNA remained in the particles of silica that sifted through my fingers. My father crossed that beach, although not on D-Day. He landed in July, a member of the then-green 4th Canadian Armoured Division. The front was thirty miles

inland by then, the Germans were resisting fiercely, and the Allies were desperate for reinforcements. His unit marshalled briefly on shore then moved forward. Within days he and his comrades were closing the Falaise Gap, bombarded by the enemy, bombed by their own air force, and facing counterattack from a trapped German army of a hundred thousand men still fighting with the collective ferocity of a wounded pit bull.

I drove next to Bernières-sur-Mer, a few miles east of Courseulles. This was Nan Sector, and there is a famous photo of the second wave of Canadians disembarking there, in front of the smouldering town. The ferocity of the fighting there, and everywhere on Juno, was comparable to that on Omaha Beach, where American troops were very nearly turned back into the sea; but the Canadians barged ahead, and by the end of the day they had advanced farther than any other Allied troops.

Canada, unlike its neighbour to the south, rarely trumpets its achievements. There will never be a *Saving Private Ryan* made for our modest nation.

It was getting late in the day, but I had one more stop to make, the cemetery at Beny-sur-Mer, a couple of miles inland, where two thousand Canadians are buried – those who died in the initial assault or in the weeks of hard slogging to establish and consolidate the beachhead. They include a hundred and fifty infantrymen taken prisoner on June 7th and shot by the Nazis, and fifteen airmen downed in support of their brethren on the ground.

It is an idyllic setting, greenery everywhere, bucolic French countryside peaceful with birdsong, and thousands of markers set with monumental precision on an impeccably landscaped lawn.

I walked past a finely-edged stone carved CANADIAN WAR CEMETERY, through a colonnaded entrance, along a path lined with trees whose leaves whisper in *their* lost voices; to the Stone of Remembrance, a wide plinth of Portland stone engraved with a simple motto: THEIR NAME LIVETH FOR EVERMORE.

Beyond this lay the graves, row after row, hundreds of identical stones. A limestone cross stood in their midst, profiled against the sky in the direction from which they came, that day, to the beach – and ultimately here.

If that sight does not cause your gut to clench, your throat to constrict, and a manly tear or three to blur your vision...

If a sob does not escape you, if your face does not collapse in grief for these your countrymen who lie beneath foreign soil and a fluttering flag they did not know...

If while you act as though a speck of dust has blown into your

face, or while you fiddle with your camera, or pretend to look for a notebook in your pocket, buying time until you can furtively wipe your eyes – if while confronted with this sight you are not humbled, if you are untouched by the presence of those dead youngsters, if you are unmoved by the vision of that beautiful, peaceful place where hundreds of dreams lie buried, where life's potential was snuffed before youth's passion cooled, before life's inevitable failures broke their spirit...

If.

If they had earned a reprieve, if they had lived – if a shell had not landed where it had, or if it had not exploded because the Jewish slave-labourer who assembled its fuse did not arm it, as she did not arm the next one she made (in defiance of those who would later incinerate her); if a bullet from a Mauser had not transited at that precise millisecond through the exact geographic coordinates and at the specific elevation above the ground where a young man's beating heart, coursing with vitality and adrenaline, was also transiting, resulting in a fatal collision of matter, the dimming of consciousness and the end of dreams; if he and the others had made it off the beach, over the barricades, through the town, and ultimately home – if they had lived, would they have accomplished anything greater than what they accomplished in death?

If on that September morning in New York, I had not made it down the stairs, past the ascending firefighters, out of the burning tower and into the noxious soot-covered street and settling ash, and ultimately home, would the world be any different?

Confronted by the graves in the cemetery at Beny-sur-Mer you must question what you are about. You must ask what you have done with your own life.

I was running out of time, the sun's rays were lengthening, but these men would know no succour that night, no hot meal, no pint of beer, no glass of wine, no hugs from a beautiful woman nor kisses from a tired child. They were here for all time, these soldiers, on eternal parade for me – for all of *us* – and I could not walk one row and pay homage to a few while ignoring the rest. I could not turn my back on a single one of them. So I walked down every row, not reading every headstone but not hurrying past. Past Private Robert Neville Cooper, age 22, Canadian Scottish Regiment. Past Private Adrien Leo Roussel, age 23, Le Regiment de la Chaudiere. Past Rifleman John Gordon Martin, age 21, Queen's Own Rifles.

And all the others.

There were Canadian flags on most of the graves, not official ones but the small paper kind that come on a white cardboard stick on Canada

Day – citizen tributes from people with the compassion and forethought to bring a dead stranger a gift. And on the graves of the Regina Rifles, someone had placed another modest paper flag, this of green and gold, emblazoned with a prairie lily. Saint Andrew's cross sprouted from the graves of the dead North Novas, Manitoba's Red Ensign from the graves of the dead Winnipeggers, and so on, our strange specimen of a dysfunctional federation, good-hearted at its core, demonstrating its unwavering pride in its fallen boys, there in Beny-sur-Mer, so far from home.

That night, when I related my day to Genny and Chloe, my eyes brimmed again at the memory of that field, those graves, those men; and with the wisdom of a ten year old, Chloe silently gripped my hand.

SALLY, LOU AND THE RED GNU
by Linda Torney

SALLY AND LOU'S FIRST camping vacation came about because of high interest rates and a low Canadian dollar.

One rare warm Sunday afternoon in April, the two women sprawled in lawn chairs on Lou's balcony, drinking a bottle of Pinot Grigio. Actually, it was their second bottle; they had already polished off the one Sally brought and were starting on Lou's supply.

"I've got to get some vacation this year or I'll be totally insane by the end of summer," said Lou, "but I can't afford to go anywhere. That loan payment is killing me."

"You've got a shiny new car to show for it," said Sally.

"The bank's got a shiny new car. All I have is a headache."

"Yeah, I know what you mean. I wish I hadn't let myself get talked into that Caribbean cruise last winter. The price looked good, but I forgot about the exchange rate. Why does everything have to be in U.S. dollars? All I got to show for that was a temporary suntan, and I'm still paying off my Visa."

They reflected on their moneyless state in silence for a few minutes. In their thirties, both women should have been further ahead financially, but Sally had recently achieved her Master of Social Work, and was clawing her way up the obstacle-ridden path of the provincial civil service, while Lou struggled to keep her monetary feet in an under-funded social service agency. She bought the car to visit clients, but was beginning to wish she had continued to haul her leaden briefcase on public transit.

"I have an idea!" Sally leaned forward, almost knocking over the wine bottle. Lou rescued it just in time.

"We could camp! You have a car now. We could split the cost of gas. Campsites won't cost much."

"I haven't camped since I was a kid."

"Me neither but it isn't that hard. It will all come back to us."

When Lou had last camped, she'd been twelve and her parents had done all the work.

"What about equipment?" she asked.

"Don't you have a sleeping bag?"

"Yeah."

"And an air mattress?"

"Well, yeah. But what about a tent, cooking utensils, one of those stove things?" Lou pumped her arm as if she was priming a cook stove.

"I have my dad's old tent," said Sally, "and we don't need special cooking utensils. We'll take stuff from our own kitchens. I have an old pot and a frying pan I don't mind getting battered."

"I have a picnic cooler," remembered Lou. Excitement began to stir in her chest.

"This calls for more wine," she said, eyeing the half-full bottle. She trotted into the kitchen, returning with more Pinot Grigio plus a pen and paper for list-making.

"Where shall we go?"

"How 'bout N'Brunswick?" said Sally, her words slurring. The wine and the unseasonable warmth were having an effect. "You c'n meet my family. We could stay with my cousin for a few days. That wouldn't cost us anything. She has a gu-nu."

Lou, who had only heard 'gnu' spoken aloud on an old record of the British comedy team Flanders and Swan, could feel her brow fur-rowing as she struggled to make sense of this non-sequitur. Her hearing must be as impaired as Sally's speech. She searched her memory for what she had been told about Sally's cousin Emma. She was a scien-tist of some sort; taught at the university. Was it botany? No, zoology. That made sense, but why would she have a large African animal at her home?

Sally had noticed Lou's silence.

"She'd let us borrow it," she said.

Lou's brow furrow deepened. Her eyes narrowed and her lips pursed as she tried to think through this last bit of information.

"Why would we do that?" she asked finally.

"Well," said Sally, "we could take it down to the river and mess

around with it."

Lou's mind filled with the image of the two of them frolicking in a reedy river shallows with a large cow-like, horned creature, and her jaw dropped.

"What's the matter?" asked Sally.

"You, uh, want to play in the river with a gnu?"

Disbelief, comprehension and mirth washed across Sally's face in quick succession. "Canoe, you idiot. I said 'canoe'!"

They collapsed into shrieks of laughter, tears streaming from their eyes. Lou held her aching sides. "Thank heavens," she gasped. "I thought you'd lost your mind."

"You should have seen your face," said Sally. "Sort of like this." She parodied Lou's expression, sending both of them off again.

"A 'gnu' look," said Lou, when she had caught her breath, establishing an inside joke which would resurface many times between them, even after their camping holiday was over.

Emma's 'gnu' was a pretty little cedar boat, painted red. It was old, but in very good shape, and Lou fell in love with it at first glance. Whether she would know what to do once she got in it was another matter. She hadn't been in a canoe in more than twenty years.

"Maybe it comes back to you, like riding a horse," she thought. But one glance at the swift-running Saint John River told her she'd best find another body of water to practice on.

Sally, whose paddling skills were equally rusty, concurred. They borrowed Emma's car, which had roof racks, and set off in search of quiet water.

They found a meandering, tea-coloured stream winding through cow-studded fields and mixed hardwood forest, and pulled off at a wide spot in the road. Between them, they managed to lug the heavy canoe to the water's edge.

"Do you remember how to get into this thing?" asked Lou, puffing with exertion.

"They're tippy," said Sally. "Let's push it in a little ways and then we can get in from opposite sides."

They shoved the canoe's nose into the stream. Lou cast a dubious look at the murky water. As designated bow paddler, she would either have to shed her sandals or ruin them.

"What's the bottom like, d'you think?"

"The bank's sandy here," said Sally, "so I'd guess the stream bed is, too."

Lou tossed her sandals into the boat, grabbed her paddle, and

waded in. Two steps and the bottom squelched up between her toes.

"Yuu-uk. I've hit bog. Let's get aboard this thing before I sink."

They scrambled in. The canoe rocked dangerously, but stayed upright. Lou thrust her paddle into the water and pulled back. Nothing happened.

"Uh... I guess we'll have to push it in a little farther," said Sally.

Lou looked around. The stern of the canoe was planted firmly on the creek bed.

"I'm not climbing out into that stuff again," she said.

"You won't have to," said Sally. "Your end's floating." With a sigh, she shed her sandals and inched her way out of the boat. She gave a shove, and the canoe slid into the middle of the stream.

"Hey, hold it!" she yelled.

"I'm trying!" Lou flailed about with the paddle, struggling to reverse the boat's forward motion. Finally she thrust the paddle straight down until it connected with the stream bed. The canoe shuddered to a halt.

"Come back in a bit," called Sally.

"How?"

"Never mind."

Lou could hear sloshing as Sally made her way to mid-stream. The boat tossed violently again as she threw herself over the side and landed in a panting heap. Lou withdrew her paddle, and they began to drift downstream on the gentle current. Sally sat up and seized her paddle. For the next quarter hour they cut a drunken wake through the water. At last they settled into a tentative rhythm and were able to keep the nose more or less straight.

"It *is* like riding a horse," called a delighted Lou.

For a while they paddled in dreamy silence, the sun warm on their shoulders. Placid black and white cows raised their heads to stare at them as they drifted past. The terrain changed. They left the fields and slid into dappled woods. The stream narrowed and the moving water picked up speed. Lou, lulled into a near-trance, did not see the overhanging limb until one of its branches thwacked her on the forehead.

"Ouch," she cried, barely managing to hang on to her paddle.

"Watch out for that branch," said Sally.

"Gee, thanks."

The canoe shuddered to a stop.

"What's that?" asked Lou.

Sally peered over the side.

"The water's too shallow. The bow's grounded. See if you can

push us off."

"I'm trying, I'm trying."

The canoe swung around broadside.

"Damn it, now my end's stuck as well," said Sally. "This isn't passable. We'll have to go back."

"Yeah," said Lou, "just as soon as we get the boat facing the right way."

They exchanged looks. Sally tittered. Lou joined her. They doubled over their paddles, their laughter echoing through the woods.

"The farmers will think there's a hyena in here," gasped Lou.

"To go with the gnu," said Sally, "which is too heavy with us in it. We'll have to get out and turn it around."

Lou peered down at the obscured creek bed. "What do you suppose is down there?"

"Not much water, that's for sure."

"What if it's quicksand?"

"Hang onto the canoe."

"Or broken glass."

"Put your shoes on then."

Lou thought about the cost of her new sandals. "I'll take my chances."

They began to ease themselves out of the boat. It listed heavily to one side.

"Careful!" yelled Lou. "This would not be a good time to tip over."

"Ick," said Sally, as her feet hit bottom.

"Double ick," replied Lou. "What is this stuff?"

"Primordial ooze."

"Fabulous. That means it's had lots of time to digest dead bodies."

They turned the boat and guided it several yards downstream, the gooey muck sucking at their feet and ankles.

"Try to rinse the mud off when you climb in," said Sally, mindful of Emma's well-cared-for canoe.

Cleaning the first foot worked well enough. The second foot was more problematic. Lou knelt on one knee, her left leg straddling the gunwale, trying to swish the goop off without tipping. She kicked backward, trying to dislodge a tenacious clump of muck.

"Hey," called Sally.

Lou glanced back. Some of her mud had caught Sally squarely in the middle of her once white t-shirt.

"Sorry," Lou giggled.

"You are not."

They settled themselves and began to paddle.

"I didn't think the current was this strong," panted Lou after an hour.

"Neither did I," said Sally.

They paddled for another thirty minutes.

"I can't go any further." Lou's arms were shaking with fatigue.

"I can see the road," said Sally. "Let's pull out here, leave the canoe and get the car."

"We're in the middle of a cow pasture," said Lou, "complete with cows."

"They won't hurt you," said Sally. "They're herbivores."

"Yeah, and suppose the ladies have a nice protective boyfriend in here somewhere?"

They mulled this over.

"Well, it's a potential bull versus certain exhaustion," said Sally at last.

"Yeah, I guess."

They hauled the canoe out, and half-carried, half-dragged it through the field.

"Hurry up, they're getting curious."

They picked up their pace, ignoring the heaps of cow dung.

"We'll have to give the canoe a bath," gasped Sally, as the keel slid through another cow patty.

"After we have a beer," said Lou between gritted teeth.

They reached the fence, and hauled themselves and the canoe over just as the first doe-eyed bovine ambled up. Leaving the canoe on the grassy verge, they began the trek. By the time they spotted the car, Lou had begun to think they were on the wrong road.

An hour and a half later, they pulled into Emma's yard.

"Did you have a good time, girls?" asked Emma, eyeing her dung-spotted canoe.

Sally and Lou looked at each other and grinned.

"Yeah, we did," said Lou.

MEDITATION ON A MK IX
by David Tucker

THIS IS A STORY about a car, but it has nothing to do with horsepower and carburetors. It makes no reference to engine types, gearbox ratios, performance upgrades, tune-ups or other mechanical concerns that men and boys often like to obsess about. Nor is it about rallies, club news, or parts for sale on-line. Rather, it is a meditation: a search for meaning amid the mileage, along roads too well travelled.

In the early Sixties, at age fifty, my father decided he wanted a Jag — a just reward, he believed, for years of toiling as a professional engineer with Ontario Hydro. Being a practical-minded individual, Dad wanted to find a good used example and decided to test drive a MK IX, a large, heavy saloon model that had recently gone out of production. I was just eleven when I accompanied him that fateful day to the downtown Toronto dealership. The Queen Mum, as it would subsequently become referred to, made an instant and lasting impression. Although still barely old enough to reach the windows of this stately Pullman-like coach, I was dazzled. The car resembled an old Bentley that had just returned from a day at Ascot. I opened a rear door and was overcome by acres of gleaming wood and the intoxicating aroma of rich, red leather. It was love at first sight and sense.

My father hesitated; he had had something sportier in mind. However, since I would be the one spending most of the time in the rear and was mad about the back seat's folding picnic tables, I had no choice but to intervene. After days of constant nagging, my poor father and mother were left no option — the needs of a rather spoiled only child won out and

the Queen Mum arrived at our doorstep a mere week later.

Despite breaking down on her inaugural run, the Queen Mum quickly had our family under her spell. No matter how many times she broke down on long trips or had to be ignominiously towed off to a garage for expensive repairs, all was forgiven in the end.

My mother taught me to become a clean freak and the Queen Mum quickly became my object of choice. With acres of lacquer paint, mountains of chrome, forests of walnut and fields of leather, the MK IX was an obsessive-compulsive's dream. While my father tinkered under the bonnet, I would labour for hours, waxing and polishing away in a Zen-like trance. This constant care and feeding soon imbued the car with a special aura that few other cars possessed: in short, she looked loved. With the passing of time, her brothers and sisters began to fall by the wayside, and as my ever-frugal father searched junkyards for spare parts, more and more MK IXs forlornly began to rust away, waiting their fate with the wrecker. Of course, I wanted to save all of them, to give them the same pampered life our own fêted feline enjoyed, but I came to accept that not all cars are created equal.

As the years sped by, the MK IX assumed many roles: daily driver, father/son hobby, companion, pet, sculpture, icon, and, eventually, repository of family memories. Today, my parents are long gone but still the Queen Mum lingers in the garage, my one and only extended family member.

Reyner Banham, a noted British design critic, once wrote that cars are part of a disposable aesthetic that fades as the technology that drives them becomes obsolete. He described how tailfins went out of fashion in tandem with the decline of their flathead engines and drum brakes. As a Modernist, he argued that any piece of industrial design that outlasted its time and function is rendered a forlorn piece of fine art.

Certainly, from a design point of view, the MK IX is now a faded Forties relic, a fetishized piece of Art Deco sculpture—all form and little remaining function. Once routinely used for grocery shopping, the MK IX has become revered art, displayed at car shows, fussed over at gas stations and swarmed in restaurant parking lots like some old-time movie star. Her flamboyant, autocratic styling makes no concession to present day aero-dynamics or fuel economy; her mechanical aesthetic of polished aluminum is now so archaic that young mechanics flee on sight, as if confronted by a rotary phone in a Blackberry age. With her acres of exquisitely matched burled walnut and leather hides, the MK IX has grown strangely exotic, like some rare orchid.

It is now over fifty years since the Queen Mum rolled off the as-

sembly line and forty-seven years since she first joined my family. Like me, she has witnessed the passing of everyone around who was dear. She has, like me, outlived her time and yet, while I age before the mirror, the Queen Mum retains her youthful complexion, thanks to the hours of polishing and preventive maintenance routinely lavished on her. Ironically, she will likely outlive me. I sometimes worry if she will be able to adjust to a new owner after so many years and fret about how she will get her spa appointments when I become too frail. Yet, I have also come to appreciate that we possess nothing in this life, we merely pay to borrow things for a little while. As well, thinking in cosmic terms, even a MK IX will eventually become ashes to ashes, rust to rust.

What then does this pampered piece of tin ultimately represent? Or more specifically, what does it mean to me after so many years? It carries the reassuring echoes of my parents' words, the warm slobbers of the family Labrador, the chatter of school friends long gone, the sounds of Expo 67, the laughter of forgotten girlfriends, the reassuring warmth of the sun beaming down through the windows on a spring afternoon. Unlike myself, who is beginning to experience life as a series of losses, the Queen Mum defies time, her leaper looking ever-confidently forward, unimpressed with the impatient technology that tries to pass her on the highway, as she grows evermore vibrant with each compulsive cleaning, repair and tune up. Gazing at my greying hair and deepening lines, I realize that I have become the picture of Dorian Gray while the MK IX, in contrast, basks in the Fountain of Youth.

MURDEROUS AMBITIONS
by Edwin Vasan

HE PULLED UP ON the driveway of the landlord Mr. Sinha's secluded house, noticing the absence of the van that was used by the servants to perform some of their household duties. It was a Sunday and Mr.Sinha had given the household staff the day off to go to the city and spend their hard-earned wages. Good! A wonderful day for revenge.

He came to a stop and walking to the rear of his truck took out the bundle of vegetables that he carried to the front door. Putting the bundle down, he knocked on the door and waited as he always did, albeit, never on a Sunday. There was no response so he knocked again and waited patiently. Still no response. Very slowly he turned the knob on the door expecting it to be latched. To his surprise it wasn't and he was able to open the door. Cautiously, stepping inside he called out softly "Saab? (Sir)"

Not a word. He decided to walk in a little further towards the staircase that led to the upper floor when he thought he heard a scuffling sound above.

Suddenly there was a loud sound like a gunshot. He ran up the stairs and reached the upper landing area. Looking ahead he saw a door slightly ajar and walked towards it. The sight that greeted him stopped him in his tracks. Inside the room a large safe door was ajar and bundles of currency notes were visible within as well as scattered on the floor below the safe. He walked into the room and couldn't believe what he was seeing.

The landlord stood over a man's body on the ground with what appeared to be a bullet wound to the head. There was blood flowing from

the body and the victim was dead.

Very dead!

The landlord, who was a very small man, abruptly turned around, gun in hand and yelled

"This bastard was trying to kill me! Look!" he pointed to the floor, "he even had a length of rope in his hand. What the hell are you do-ing here anyway?"

A dead man, money and lots of it and a length of rope.

Perfect.

"Saab, let me get something from my truck to help you clean up this mess," he said and rushed back to the truck.

He had a pair of old canvas gloves that he would need. He knew there was a typewriter in the house.

Inspector Pillai surveyed the scene that faced him while his men were busy working the house. The dead man on the floor worked as a secretary for the man that had been brought down after he was found hanging. It seemed obvious that the secretary had waited while the rest of the staff left for the city before he had come in here to rob the landlord and then murder him. He would still have had ample time to leave and disappear among the millions of human beings that made up the popula-tion. That much made sense to the inspector.

What didn't make sense was the apparent suicide of the robbery victim. If he had killed a man in self-defence then he would surely be cleared notwithstanding the procedures of law.

Why weren't these things as simple as they appeared to be?

The other big issue was the half-empty safe. He was told by the other servants that the dead landlord stored millions of rupees in hard cash in that safe. What he saw in there certainly didn't come close to that.

One of his constables entered the room and approached Pillai.

"Sir, I think you need to come down and look at something."

"What is it constable?"

"A suicide note sir."

"Yes, I've already seen that. Sinha left that here."

"No sir. This one's another suicide note. It's downstairs."

"Let's go."

They walked briskly down through the hallway and into a cor-ridor that brought them to the staff's living quarters. The consta-ble led the way and entered one of the rooms. Pillai looked around quickly and noticed a photograph on the wall of a smiling couple. The man in the photograph was the same man who had been shot up-

stairs. This must have been his room. Another constable who had been waiting in the room handed him a note. Pillai took it and read it, his expression changing from anticipation to one of surprise.

"My God. This is amazing."

"That's what we thought sir."

"Have the movements of all the staff been checked out?"

"Yes sir. They were all out of the house and we have proof of that."

"So that means that there was a third person here."

"I would say so sir," said the constable. "We already questioned all the staff about that. They said that the only visitor here on a weekend might be a farmer bringing produce for them to take to the city on Monday or for consumption for the household here."

"Well?"

"Nobody asked any of the farmers to bring anything this weekend."

"Would the farmers have known that the landlord was alone this weekend?"

"It was common knowledge that he allowed the staff to take the Sunday off and head for the city in a van he provided for deliveries. This Sunday would have been no exception."

"Let's go talk to these farmers right now."

The farmers were sitting in groups around cheap wooden stools and sipping tea and coffee in the only food stall in the village after a hard days work in the fields when they saw the police jeep pull up and some police officials step out towards them.

"Namaste (good evening). My name is Inspector Pillai. Your landlord, Mr. Sinha, was found dead in his house last night and I'd like to ask you all a few questions."

There were exclamations of surprise and nervous apprehension as they all began to slowly stand up and face the officers.

One of the men slowly spoke up.

"This is terrible news inspector-saab but what has that got to do with us?"

"Nothing so far but I have some routine questions."

That seemed to appease them slightly and the same man who had spoken responded.

"How can we help you then?"

"Were any of you at the landlord's house yesterday for any reason at all?"

They looked at each other and in a jumble of voices he heard that

they weren't.

"Is there any one among you farmers who isn't here this evening?"

"Of course, some of the other farmers are in the city visiting relatives or shopping for supplies but they left last week."

"Alright. Was there anyone here on the weekend who isn't here tonight?"

There was a pause before another man spoke up.

"Well, there is someone but he rarely comes here in the evenings to join us. Tells us he is too busy studying English in his house. Wants to be a teacher and get rich, he says."

There was a wave of cynical laughter around the gathering.

"Ever since his brother hung himself last year after losing his job at the landlord's house he stopped coming here to join us."

"Where can I find him?"

"Oh... probably in his house down that lane." One of the others pointed the way.

"House 54B" he added.

"His name?"

"Navin Kumar."

Pillai turned to his constables and said, "Let's go."

They got into the jeep and quickly drove over. Walking to the door of house 54B, one of the constables knocked. It wasn't long before a reasonably well-built man wearing a pair of faded old jeans and a vest opened the door.

"Yes?"

"Navin Kumar?"

"Yes. What is it?"

"We'd like to ask you a few questions Navin."

"What is it regarding, please?"

"Your landlord was found hanging in his house yesterday."

"So the old man killed himself did he?" remarked Navin.

"I don't recall mentioning suicide. Where were you yesterday Navin?"

"Right here as I usually am on Sundays. With my books trying to improve my English. I have no family and nowhere else to go."

"Is that your truck outside?"

"Yes it is."

"May we have a look inside the truck?"

"Yes, please do. It is not locked."

Pillai walked over to the truck and examined the truck bed at the

back. Nothing there except a couple of tomatoes, reasonably fresh. Just like the bundle of tomatoes they had found outside the door of the landlord's house.

He opened the passenger door and looked inside. A stained notebook and a pair of dirty leather gloves. He picked them both up and opened the pages of the notebook. There were entries for each day. Monday, cucumbers and onions, Tuesday, chillies, capsicums and corn and so on.

There was a single entry for Sunday. Tomatoes.

He raised the gloves and showed them to Navin.

"May I borrow these for a few days?"

Navin seemed to tense up a little but nodded his head "Of course."

One of the constables who had quietly entered Navin's house stepped out, looked at the Inspector and nodded.

"Navin Kumar, I believe you were at the landlord's house yesterday. I'd like you to come with us to the station and tell us exactly what you were doing there."

Navin looked angry and surprised. "How dare you call me a liar?"

"There's something you should know Navin."

"What the hell should I know?"

"Most of the servants at the landlord's house knew that he was having an affair with his secretary's wife. The only one who didn't know was the secretary himself. But he found out. We're not sure when. He probably overheard the servants talking among themselves. It doesn't matter. What matters is that he hid in the house when the servants left for their Sunday outing and went to the landlord's room where he found him counting his money. He had a gun that was kept in the house for security but the landlord shot him with his own gun that he kept in the safe."

He continued, "We suspect that you entered the room just after the landlord shot him and strangled the landlord. You are a much bigger man and lifting his body up to make it look like suicide would have been fairly easy for you."

"You are lying inspector! Where did the rope that the landlord hung himself with turn up from? How could you know all this from two dead men? More importantly, you have no proof that I could possibly be involved."

"The answer to your first question is quite simple. The secretary was going to hang himself after he killed his master. You see Navin, we

found his suicide note in his bedroom. He knew he had lost his wife to another man, his boss, and he was an object of shame among the staff."

"What else?"

"You missed the secretary's own gun. It was right under his body on the floor."

"How the hell does that make me the guilty party?"

Pillai nodded to the constable standing behind Navin. He was holding a cloth satchel.

"You either get paid a heck of a lot more than the other farmers or..." The implications were obvious.

"We also found the rest of the money you had taken hidden under your bed. I believe if we check the landlord's account book inside his safe and add the money that we just found in your house it will come pretty close to the total shown in the book."

"You were bent on avenging your only brother's death one way or the other without any witnesses Navin Kumar."

Navin was silent.

"Oh, a couple of other interesting facts," continued the Inspector.

Navin had a disdainful smile as he looked up.

"If indeed the landlord, Mr. Sinha, committed suicide his fingerprints would have been on that rope. The only identifiable prints on the rope belonged to the dead secretary. The gloves you wore covered yours. On the other hand," he paused for effect, "there was a fresh fingerprint on the inside knob of the front door that didn't belong to any of the household. I suspect we can prove it was yours."

THE STAFF
by Herb Ware

THE IMPORTANCE OF SOME things just does not click in an active youth's brain. A brain like Caleb's. A brain that could fixate on just about anything but what his master was telling him.

Like the day Master Moncrief told Caleb that he was not yet ready to own a staff of power. It was a nice summer-sunny day, a sweet counterpoint to the storm brewing in Caleb's mind as he watched — for the umpteenth time — Moncrief first use his staff to set the outdoor cooking fire blazing then to move the iron cooking pot over the coals.

Caleb hated that Moncrief was diminutive — make that tiny — a wizened, skinny, old, gray-bearded sorcerer who was hardly taller than a dwarf. Caleb, at 15, stood six gangly feet tall and was expected to grow to the size of those giant humans who became warriors for hire.

It wasn't size per se that upset Caleb. When mini-Moncrief caught him doing something wrong, out would come the staff, and towering Caleb would be flipped into the air to hang helplessly upside down like a carcass in a butcher's barn. If Moncrief deemed the offense sufficiently bad, he might then drag Caleb along the edge of the barberry shrubs. There was never any discussion. Always Caleb saw the punishment as the unfair tactic of a tyrannical father figure.

So he watched Moncrief. Carefully. And asked questions. Carefully.

"How did you know to pick that particular stone for your staff," he asked as his master stirred the fire.

"Certain stones when properly dressed can contain and

concentrate the natural energy around us," was Moncrief's answer.

"How do you know which stones?"

"Witch stones are different, you silly boy," was Moncrief's answer. "This stone, however, would melt a witch stone." He raised the staff so that the stone was level with Caleb's eyes. "Note the finished shape; a hexagon tapered to a point. I cut and polished it myself."

Looking with fascination at the gleaming jewel, Caleb asked, "did you have to make it yourself? Couldn't you just get the jewel master to fit one up for you?"

"Then the soul of the stone would bond to him, not me. That is why I had to make the whole thing myself. You ask too many questions," Moncrief said, emitting a tiny pop of light from the stone that sent Caleb flailing blindly until he tumbled into the barberry bushes.

One evening after dinner Caleb asked, even more carefully, "I remember Master Tan's staff. It was a different height than yours. Does the length of the staff matter?"

"Of course it matters," Moncrief said from his chair by the fireplace. A spark from his staff lit the shredded leaves in his pipe. With the smoking pipe snugged between his teeth, Moncrief raised the staff over his head and spun it like a baton. "The length is tuned to the owner's height, using the golden mean to balance the energy in the stone with the natural vibrations of the earth and the heart of the owner. It's all in the books behind you, if you could only read, you illiterate child."

"Master, If I could read as well as you have been trying to teach me, would the books tell me why you used hickory for the shaft?" Caleb asked, watching in fascination as Moncrief's staff spun faster and faster.

"This is more than a wand. I also need a sturdy walking stick that assists me when I climb the hills to the mines. When I venture onto the paths full of highwaymen, it must double as a fighting staff. You ask too many questions," Moncrief said, then showed Caleb how a fighting staff worked. As Caleb leaped from the room the staff whacked his butt and tagged his ribs. Through the doorway he ran, flailing wildly at the staff until he tumbled over the barberry bushes.

Throughout the following months, Caleb diligently pored over Moncrief's arcane texts, finding bits and pieces that nearly all made sense of some sort. From those bits and pieces, he secretly assembled instructions for constructing his own staff. He gathered the materials, squirreling them into places he knew the master would not ferret out.

He had problems. One time, Moncrief walked into the sitting room unexpectedly and, complaining about the "damp cold that could

chill an old man's bones," he dumped a small pile of broken sticks onto the fire grate. With his staff he set the pile ablaze.

Caleb knew something was not right. The master never gathered wood.

"Nothing like a fresh blaze to warm a body, eh, Caleb?" Moncrief rubbed his wizened hands together, enjoying the fire. "And the aroma of that wood — reminds me of my early days as an apprentice. Used right, the smoke from this wood could cure meat. Of course, as a willful apprentice, I was trying to do something different with the wood. Master told me not to. But I was strong-headed. Nearly killed myself."

An aromatic curl of smoke evaded the chimney updraft, made a path under Caleb's nose. Hickory!

Caleb excused himself, hurried outside and fell into the barberry bushes while trying to retrieve a hickory rod that was no longer hidden there.

It took six long months to cut new hickory, shape and cure it, and three months of guarded work mining then shaping the copper sleeve and its flawless gem, using the incantations built into the instructions he had created for himself.

Finally, he only needed to assemble the pieces and test it. That proved to be a problem. Moncrief had him working harder than ever as if some deadline were impending. He began to teach Caleb spells to ward enemies; he taught him how to set and unset the magic traps protecting their cottage.

Then one fine morning Moncrief declared, "I have been invited to a Wizards' Gathering. I will be gone two weeks." He looked around. "This is the first time I have left this place since you came four years ago. I have taught you everything I can about the protections for this place. Remember them well. And don't do anything I have told you not to."

Two emotions welled up in Caleb; the fear of not having the master to protect and care for him, and the joy of being on his own, in control his own life. The latter took over.

With a light spring in his step, Caleb hugged the tiny wizard and handed him his carrying bag and staff. "Be well master and enjoy your trip. I promise not to leave this place. And I will remember the spells."

He waved until Moncrief was out of sight.

Then Caleb set about gathering up the parts for his staff: the straight, cured hickory rod stood nearly seven feet tall, perfect for a youth still growing; the jewel he had shaped into a hexagon the same thickness as the rod — a little larger than recommended but the larger the stone the greater the power it could hold, he had read. He unpacked the wax, glues,

copper sheathing and other fine bits of metal and lacing and spread everything neatly across his bed.

Assembly took all day and part of the night. With only placement of the stone to go, Caleb collapsed in exhaustion onto a chair, jewel still in hand.

He woke with a start as the late morning sun touched his face. He looked around trying to remember where he was. He jumped up, feelings of guilt flaring in him as he realized what had happened. Part of the instructions included: "...focused concentration without a break during assembly." He wondered what effect that would have on the power of the staff.

He looked around. The stone lay on the wooden floor by the chair where it had fallen from his hand.

Shaking, he gingerly picked it up and checked for cracks or chips. The gem was still flawless.

Eagerly, he moved to the bed and finished the assembly.

He raised the staff and focused. A small light glowed feebly from the center of the stone.

He did it!

He had his own staff and his own power! He looked around, eyes stopping on his bed pillow. He focused his energy and pointed the staff. With a muffled poof, feathers flooded the air as the pillow exploded.

Caleb ran into the kitchen area and pointed the staff at a jar of lizard eyes. A sharper, more satisfying explosion sent eyes and preserving juices spattering across the room.

Suddenly his knees buckled. His head began to spin. It was all he could do to flop onto a kitchen chair. "Too much energy used," he thought. On the table beside him was a loaf of bread and Moncrief's favorite jam preserves.

He ate the whole loaf and nearly emptied the pot of preserves.

The whole time, his staff was propped next to him against the table. Now he could feel the pull of its energy, the bonding with him. Caleb wanted to use the staff again. But he could not afford to just spend his own energy. "That is what Moncrief was afraid I would do," he thought. "But I understand now. I will be very careful with my experiments and learn to build my energy before I use it."

Using his staff for support, Caleb went outside to relax in the afternoon sun. He lay down on the ground and closed his eyes, staff angled across his chest. The sun's heat beat down, warming him, massaging his tired muscles with its energy. He drowsed. Then the heat was gone. He opened an eye to see what had happened. A dark, screening

cloud greeted him. He opened both eyes and gazed at the sky. A summer storm was brewing.

"Oh to have that energy," Caleb thought. Then he remembered watching Moncrief standing in a storm one night chanting an incantation.

Caleb sat bolt upright, knocking the staff off his chest. "Of course!" Caleb hollered to the world. "Moncrief was gathering energy from the storm!" He remembered the sudden brilliant flash and accompanying boom as lightning had struck Moncrief's staff. He remembered running half blind to the end of the porch expecting to see a pile of ashes. But there had stood Moncrief, arm outstretched, hand wrapped around the staff that was anchored on the ground. Caleb remembered that the stone in Moncrief's staff had been pulsing with light, and had continued to glow for several days.

"I could do that," Caleb thought as he eased himself off the ground and onto the porch. Huge rain droplets began to spot the dusty earth. A promising thunder grumbled vaguely in the distance as the warm summer wind picked up. "All I need is the incantation that Master Moncrief was using."

The droplets turned into shattered sheets of warm water, raising the smell of the damp earth to his nostrils, the same living-earth smell he recalled from that night. Suddenly he remembered the words Moncrief had chanted.

Caleb stepped back into the rain, staff gripped tightly. He went to the spot where his master had stood and began the incantation. The power of the storm rose around him. He could feel the energy swirling around his staff. He stretched his arm out and lifted the staff to the sky.

A huge lightning bolt ripped the air and slammed into the crystal. Thunder exploded as the air clapped together to fill the void. The force of the bolt shot Caleb's rod skyward onto the fork of a young oak. Of the apprentice, little was left but a pile of ash which quickly became a gray slurry that washed into the thicket of the barberry bushes.

An excerpt from the novel
THE DEVIL'S STONE COOK
by Joyce Wayne

BY THE TIME FREDERICK returned from Tintagel, the night after the Ladies Brigade arrived, I was propped up on silk pillows, Polly beside me,
reading in her perfect honeyed tones from George Eliot's *Middlemarch*.
Earlier in the evening, she and the ladies had dispensed with the medi-
cines on the sick table next to my bed and replaced them with a gramo-
phone. Caruso's singing "Ich liebe dich" played over and over again, with
Polly rising each time to crank the handle on the contraption. "I love thee
now and for eternity " was playing when Freddy burst into the room.

As usual, Frederick was intruding on any small moment of happiness I might experience. My husband was wearing his pinstriped waistcoat adorned with a flowered yellow cravat. "Leave this room, whoever
you are," he shouted to Polly, who gracefully gathered her needlework
and her book to exit the room.

"It's my friend, Mrs. Polly Turnsey," I said, surprising myself with
my own detached tone.

"Your friend. I don't give a monkey's..."

"Yes, my friend. There are some people who enjoy my
company."

"I see," Freddy said sitting down beside me on the quilt. His face
was changing expressions faster than a West Country storm heading toward Shebbear. "Your friend, yes, I see." Frederick held his head in his
hands.

"You must be terribly lonely, Cordelia!" he whispered. Then suddenly without a dram of guile, he asked, "What have I done to you, dear

girl?" From his pocket he pulled an elegant silver flask.

"When did you start drinking?" I asked. "Fabians don't drink. What would Mrs. Webb think?"

Frederick swallowed a large quantity of the clear liquor. "She swills more champagne than a French can-can girl."

It had been such a long time since he'd actually looked me straight in the eye and spoke to me with anything but complete disdain that I was taken aback.

"What next?" I said, not daring to believe that he'd changed his tune.

"We've made a great mess of things, haven't we? Don't suppose we might sort it out? I only wished to protect you, my dear, to save you from what would happen if anyone deduced it was you who was spreading typhoid."

"Oh Freddy, we don't know that for certain. It might just appear that way to you since you are always so eager to apportion blame. What if I'm innocent? In my entire life, I've never purposely hurt a fly. What if you're wrong about me?"

My husband rose from the bed to begin pacing the room. I didn't believe it possible for us to see eye to eye on this matter. How could we, when my own man saw me as a murderess, intent on killing every time I stuffed a fowl for roasting?

"When we married, I believed if I could keep you out of harm's way, protect the county and not perish of the disease myself, I would ascend to heaven a happy man," Frederick said sanctimoniously, clasping his hands together in the act of prayer. " But when William passed, every bit of goodness went out of me and I can't force it to return. I can't love you with the same pure devotion, Cordelia, not after what you have done."

Although I'd become accustomed to closing my ears to my husband's outbursts, I did understand what he said about William's death. Since losing my boy, I could feel virtually nothing accept indignation. Why should anyone be happy when William had suffered so? If Frederick was right about me — and with Polly confirming his suspicions — why would I bother ever getting out of bed again if it wasn't to rain down evil on the world? But I needed to remind myself that no one, not even Polly, had actually proven to me that I was responsible for people dropping dead of typhoid.

Ultimately Frederick's confession was like throwing water on smoking oil. "What *I have done*," I shrieked. "He was born deformed — and it wasn't the fever. It wasn't me, Freddy, *it was you*," I said pointing

my finger up at his incredulous face. "You never bothered to inform me, but this malady runs in your family. Only after William passed did I hear the old hag Bullbrook gossiping with the parlour maid, describing your brother who expired of the very same disease before you were born. She said he had a big head, filled with water and a bent spine, just like our boy! "

Frederick shook his head in disbelief, pretending I was the mad one and he was the perfect English gentleman — and that was it! That was the precise moment my marriage collapsed. I wished to be free of Frederick's constant surveillance.

If I could, indeed, kill by cooking, then why shouldn't I do it at will and how and when I wished without a husband who was watching for the fatal mistake, the missing piece of evidence that would slip the noose around my neck? Why shouldn't I discover the thrill of knowing it was my work that turned the screw? Killing wouldn't bring my boy back, but I might find the justice and retribution I required to regain my equilibrium.

Naturally, I wished this disastrous discussion to be over, but Frederick continued in his ponderous manner, tying his cravat tighter around his thickened neck. He'd not shaved for days. His waistcoat was stretched over his belly and he was sweating profusely.

"For all those years, I thought if we waited until the end of your monthlies, when you were the cleanest, it would be the most opportune time to avert the plague. You must know by now that I would have bedded you each and every night. My precautions were hygienic. I was trying to stop you from passing the plague along to any innocent child we might create."

"*It was you*," I cried. "*Not me.*" I couldn't imagine trying to pull the wool over on something as important as this.

"As usual, you are evading the truth..."

"You are a fraud, Frederick," I said cutting him off coldly. "If you'd confessed to me I might have freed myself from the burden of believing that it was all my fault that William was maimed from birth. You made me feel that way, you counted on it, endorsed the filthy unfounded lie that I was a witch with black powers..."

After a very long time, sitting on my bed without moving a muscle, he said pitifully, "If only the boy had lived, I only wished for him to grow up, to walk straight, to talk, to smell, to taste, to realize how much I loved him."

"William knew how much you loved him...he knew everything."

Frederick just sat and wept. But I could not join him in the easy release of tears. My rage and bitterness were well beyond that.

"You must see that it is over," I said at last. "Between us, I mean."

He looked at me suspiciously, his eyes bloodshot from tears and drink. "You could stay on at the manor," he said beseechingly. "We could confine ourselves to separate rooms — permanently. I won't lay a hand on you, I give you my word as a gentleman."

As always, Frederick had gotten it all wrong. What I wanted was a husband who desired me and for reasons that were bursting with magnanimity and free of suspicion.

"Besides," Frederick went on, "you ought not to risk another confinement. I mean, you wouldn't want to create another..."

"Another monster?" I demanded.

He drew back, wary of my tone. "Yes... I mean another... little William."

"Like mother, like son, you might claim."

And then I finally did break down into tears. Had I been able to make William whole, I would have put my head on the chopping block. But since I could not, it was the rage burning inside me that would win the day.

I knew, then, I shouldn't stay with Freddy no matter what he promised me, under any circumstance. My mind was made up in the split second I realized that he truly thought me guilty all those years of purposely spreading the plague and damaging our son, but I answered him sweetly, "I require time to consider your offer, Freddy... If you'd allow me to hold a dinner party, invite your friends, perhaps that would lift my spirits." Butter wouldn't melt in my mouth.

Frederick stammered, paced about the sick room anxiously, perused the expression on my face and, putting his best foot forward, agreed with a great heaving sigh. "Whatever you wish, dearest."

Frederick believed he could save his skin by burying me alive in Holsworthy. Most likely the dolt was fearful that I'd spread the news to the entire West Country about his sickly brother; everyone who mattered would learn that it was *his secret* and not mine that turned William into the crooked back he'd been. What if his blessed Fabians found out? Where would Frederick stand among them with all their fine ideals about aiding the poor and the hard done-by? Well *I was the poor and the hard done by* and it was Freddy who'd done me.

Assuring myself that I could concoct a plan for Frederick and his mates — with consequences more ingenious than he could possibly suspect — I shouted for Polly (who I surmised was listening on the other side of the keyhole). She'd be more than pleased to assist me in devising the

menu for my last supper at Wendice Manor; and so we set to work, Polly and me, that very night as Frederick scurried off to his study to record our conversation in one of his wretched notebooks.

Inside I was seething. Even today, I can't imagine why Frederick wished me to remain at the Manor as his wife. This was the man who'd forced me to don a collar whenever we were intimate; he'd placed all the typhoid deaths in Devon at my doorstep; and he'd even blamed me in some insane way for William's deformity.

When you are a woman who is married to a man who assumes she is a murderess, but lusts after her all the same, she feels dirty deep down inside. The dirtiness stays with her night and day so no amount of good deeds or proper behaviour can erase the filth from her soul. If she's like me, and I'd wager that she would be, she'd choose to behave any which way that suits, since neither good nor evil make a difference when a woman is attached to a man like Frederick Wendice.

DEMONS
by Saniya Zahid

I SAW HIM FOR the first time in my parent's drawing room. I had already been informed that his family was coming over for a visit for 'special reasons.' I remember entering the room, feeling shy and reserved. My heart was pounding in my chest, I could hear my own breath, could feel my hands shaking. I was nervous.

I still remember his face, the way it looked when I gathered enough courage to raise my eyes, the straight nose, the big eyes, the elegant glasses, the short hair, the grey suit and the red tie. Whenever I close my eyes, the same image still crosses my memory.

The encounter that day was short and formal. There was nothing extraordinary about it. He saw me, I saw him. We already knew the essential details about each other. I was a recent college graduate and he was a well-established doctor in Canada. My friends always told me that I was pretty, a walking-talking Mughal doll. When I saw him, I thought that I was meeting a Greek god in twenty-first century; well educated, charming, handsome and well established. I couldn't have asked for more back then but now I wish I had. He liked what he saw and I liked what I had heard about him. The arrangement went well, and we married a month later on 1st March, 2008.

I sit in my new bedroom, on my wedding bed. The smell of roses makes me anticipate the next few hours. We haven't talked again after the first time we met. He didn't make an effort and it was not customary for me to do so but the celebrations tonight have given me courage to wait for him as his bride. I sit here, waiting for my husband to meet his

charming bride. He knocks on the door and enters with a bouquet of flowers. He sits beside me and holds my hand.

"I gather that you are as nervous as I am. I might be a decade older than you but I am still behaving like a teenager." He joked to make us both feel comfortable.

"Thirty two isn't that old or I hope it isn't," I replied with a twinkle in my eye.

"I hope I am able to prove you right." This time he laughs while slowly pointing to the bed with his eyes.

"Mahnoor, we are starting a new life. We are both in this together. We were both in two boats before but now we have to merge them together."

"I am ready to jump aboard yours!" I cut him off.

He stared at me and continued. "I hope I fulfill your dreams. I will be a faithful husband and a good father." He didn't say more that night.

He did fulfill all my dreams but I never even asked him his.

It's been two months since I married. I am very happy and very content with life. Mehr is a loving husband, considerate and caring but sometimes he seems more like a teacher, lecturing about life. I am fascinated with his opinions, his thoughts, his concepts, and his views. I always anxiously look forward to see him. He always has something extraordinary, something different to teach. I think I am a great student as well, listening intently, following his every word, every move without interruption. But it bothers me when he sometimes goes silent, seems bored with our relationship. It seems like he puts up a great effort to make me happy, to keep the relationship working. I am happy with him but I ask him if he is happy with me. He nods silently, smiles at me and says that I am a great wife. I think I agree with him, I AM a great wife, but I don't know whether this is my own opinion or is it another one of the things he has taught me slowly.

Last night he behaved a little strange. He was silent and lost in his own thoughts. Although he looked at me and talked to me, it seemed as if his words were directed at someone else and his gaze searched for another face. He took me to the beach in the middle of the night and asked me to leave my shoes in the car.

"Close your eyes, hold my hand and walk with me."

I was scared but I trust my husband with my life. I did what he asked me to do.

We walked along the shore. He didn't say a word for a long time and then quietly whispered in my ear, "Meet yourself tonight. Awaken your senses, talk to your inner self."

I thought he was going crazy, I could hardly hold my laughter but then my feet touched the icy cold water. A shiver ran up my spine and I started following his instructions.

"Feel the sand between your toes. Let the water tingle your soles. Feel the breeze, the cold, the chill. Feel the silence of the night and the crushing noise of the waves. Smell the ocean salt and light breeze. And now feel my warm hand caressing your palm. I will always be there for you, will let my warmth seep into your body even if the contact is as small as the touch of our hands."

Then he pulled me in his arms with great force.

"I love you Mehr," I managed to whisper.

He suddenly stepped back and stared at me speechless.

"I-I-I think we lost track of time, lets walk back now," he replied silently.

I am dressed up, waiting for Mehr to come home. I want to surprise him or maybe 'seduce' is a better word. He is already home. He stares at me like a wolf would stare at his prey. He takes off his coat, I ask him to come have dinner.

"I will directly shift to dessert tonight." He laughs aloud, steps forward, picks me up smoothly and head straight to our bedroom.

I can feel his bare skin touching mine. His mouth is travelling all over my body. He supports my neck, and his lips touch mine. My world is spinning. I cannot think. Nothing could be more heavenly, more sweet than this. BUT he suddenly pulls back, breaks the spell. He is sitting on the edge of the bed, panting, out of breath. He looks at me. I can see the passion in his eyes. I smile at him and slowly run my hand over his back. He turns around, caresses my cheek with the back of his hand.

"I am sorry angel if I were too fast. I think I lost control"

"I want you to lose control."

He smiles sheepishly and returns to me.

Mehr has night shift today. It is late at night and I miss him. I enter his study room to find myself a book. I find a book sitting on his desk, *By the River Piedra I sat down and wept*, by Paulo Coelho. I open the book. It is not a book but someone's journal. "I don't know why Mehr would change the cover of his journal." I say to myself.

Feeling curious, I open the journal and start reading the first entry.

Dated: March 1st 1998. The first time we met:

Mehr and I are like two boats. Both self-sufficient, hard working. We don't need someone else in life but something has drawn us both

together. He didn't want a relationship in life and neither did I but we both ended up together. We merged the boats to go down the stream, together, neither of us leaving our own. Feeling happy, feeling contented. Feeling like two individuals yet being one.

Stunned. I flipped the pages.

Dated: May 15ᵗʰ 1998.

I have been with Mehr for more than two months. He is an amazing guy, very caring, very kind. But sometimes I feel something is missing from our relationship. I think he is like a good puppy that learns fast and remains obedient. I am like a toddler, who gets bored with the puppy after some time.

I feel like I am a teacher and not a lover. I am the one always making the decisions, the moves, the efforts to bond.

Sometimes I wonder if he even understands what I am saying. I know I am a bit different but I really wonder if he will be able to touch the deepest cord of my soul.

I took him to the beach last night. It was a starless night. I asked him to take off his shoes and I did the same. I asked him to close his eyes, hold my hand and walk with me for as long as I say. I asked him to feel the water tingle his toes, to feel the sand grains putting pressure on his sole. I asked him to feel the cool water between his toes. I asked him to breathe the sweet smelling air. I asked him to raise his head and feel the breeze caress his hair. I asked him to feel the pleasure of the water-cooling his feet. I asked him to humm sweetly and let his voice merge with the wind. I asked him to feel himself. I asked him to talk to his sensual self, feel the pleasure, admire it. That's all I asked.

He opened his eyes after fifteen minutes. He broke the spell. He laughed at me. He splashed water at me and asked me to wake up. He told me to live in reality. It was getting cold and we might end up catching flu.

"I am hungry. Lets go to McDonalds" That is all he had to say when I was trying to show him my soul.

Dated: May 22ⁿᵈ 1998.

It happened today. He came to my room. We were sitting on my bed and talking. He moved a little bit closer and stared directly into my eyes. I could anticipate it coming. He asked me, "Can I kiss you?" I want-

ed to know how it felt. His mouth on mine, lips touching lips. The most intimate contact. I wanted to know. I nodded.

His mouth was on mine in a few milliseconds. His hand was supporting my neck and his lips were moving fast. Very fast. I didn't imagine it to be so intense, so full of passion. Was he expressing his love?

But then why was my world collapsing at the same time? Why did I feel like a piece of meat being devoured by vultures? Why was I screaming in my head but completely silent at that moment? Why were his eyes closed and mine wide open? Why was I only feeling the wet saliva and texture of his tongue and mouth? Why do I only remember the physical details but cannot associate any emotions with that act?

I pulled back. He supported his head with both hands, "WOW! Is your world spinning as fast as mine?"

I had no answer for him.

I quickly turn to the last page, desperately trying to figure out the mysterious author who is present in my world even when absent. The last entry is a letter. With shaking hands I start reading it slowly.

Dated: September 11th 1998.
DEMONS.

My dearest,

I have decided to disappear from your life as silently as you crept into mine. I have decided to leave you with all the memories, so you can think about us as I thought about us when I wrote them. I am leaving my journal for you.

You are the kindest, sweetest, most caring person I have ever met. My friend says that if I leave you then I would be the most thankless person of the world. I think she can't see things from my perspective. You are the best pragmatic solution to companionship. Well-educated, kind, caring, loving. From love to money, you have all you can offer me as a husband. But pragmatic solutions have the negative connotation of 'compromise.'

I would never be able to forget you and I don't want you to forget me either. Walk down the memory lane, and find me again and again.

Meet me at the beach, meet me at a starless night, meet me with the touch of lips, meet me with the intensity of your gaze, meet me in the folds of your sheets;

meet me but don't await me.

I will always be there, close your eyes or open them wide, I will

always be there.
    LOVE YOU ALWAYS!!
    Your angel.
    Saira.

I was still staring at the page with wide-open eyes. I took a step back. My elbow hit the vase on the table and it smashed in a thousand small pieces!

THE STORE
by Karol Zelazny

TODAY MY OLD FRIEND Ygreek came to see me at the store. I hadn't seen him in a while and maybe calling him a friend is an overstatement since I'm still in possession of a knife which I had to pull out of my back after one of his previous visits. He is a great entertainer, deeply set in his weasel-like ways. I could see through his evil designs immediately though, but it was hard not to warm up to him quickly.

The originality of his expressions always delighted me. He would usually start with a salutation that could make you scratch your head for a long time. This time he spat out a greeting, "May the wisdom of a four-year-old child be your guiding light."

"And Merry Christmas to you," I answered cheerfully, knowing full well that the current date pointed to the middle of July.

"I have an offer for you. I want to buy your store," he continued. "What do you sell here anyway?" he asked, speculation in his voice.

"You realize, this is not a regular store," I responded. "Thousands of people leave here happy every day, when allowed to purchase various, usually very expensive merchandise. I don't advertise, and I don't have any marketing strategy. I don't carry any brand name products and you know how far it is to the highway from here. It would take too long to describe what I sell here, but I can give you a short summary of what I don't carry," I finished.

"Spill the juice," said Ygreek, disappointment in his face.

"We don't sell pizza. I'm allergic to cheese."

"There must be something more," insisted Ygreek.

"Ok, here is a full list: potatoes, dresses for bulimic and fat women, neutral emotions. I don't sell any municipal politicians, empty phrases, broken hearts and absolutely no cleaning supplies of any kind."

That seems reasonable, Ygreek was thinking. "How much do you want for the store?"

"It is for sale," I remarked, with little empathy.

"I'm not rich," lied Ygreek (his wealth was legendary), "but I can still manage to borrow a few thousand."

"Don't insult me," I said firmly. "A store like this can not be bought for money. Give me a few words that will resonate with my heart, one or two deeds that will heal my primordial wounds, or even better, find the key that opens the door to this store. That's my price. I haven't been outside for centuries because I don't have the key. The price is really very low."

Ygreek looked around. "There are no doors here! How did I get inside?" he wondered, surprised and suddenly fearful.

"Exactly. However, the absence of the door does not make your assignment for finding a key any easier," I answered.

We stopped talking. Our attention had been drawn to a tall, long-legged blond from the third row, near the window. I approached her, touched her warm skin and asked with a voice that vibrated with anticipation, "Do you need me for anything, number 1125?" She answered me with one of her enchanting smiles, stretching like a sleepy cat. She threw her arms back, exhibiting a well developed body. Her breasts attempted to break free from the embrace of a bra, reminding me of exotic animals. Curious and afraid at the same time, she smiled at me provocatively. I lost my head. I pushed her against the wall, and began ripping off her clothes. "Bend over," I mumbled through my clenched teeth. A few minutes passed, poignant with vocal expressions of   pain and pleasure. "How do you like it?" I yelled to Ygreek. "It is a good cardio exercise that keeps the product fresh and attractive, not to mention other fringe benefits."

"Could I also... with her?" he inquired meekly.

"Unfortunately that is not allowed. This form of exercise is forbidden before the final purchase by the customer, for health reasons. It is also against fire regulations. Read here." I opened a book that was thicker than a locomotive. "A customer is not allowed to use any merchandise in a manner that produces friction, before purchasing."

"There is a lot of friction here; it seems that everything is so well oiled, but in reality there is friction," I explained. "There is also good news: When you become the owner of this store, you will be able to exercise them all." I smiled at him lightly.

Looking around with a keen trader's eye at hundreds of women placed throughout the store, I felt proud of myself. I always skillfully managed to sell older models, sometimes taking a bit of a loss, in order to make room for new merchandise.

"I own an exquisite collection. Tell me your preferences and I will probably have something to your liking. If you want for example an almost new model that is around 165 cm in height, average breast and legs, not too thin, a bit of flesh here and there, small brain, attractive nose, full lips, long fingers and eye lashes, pleasant to the touch skin, not too dry, green eyes and hard nipples — then there is a high probability that I have this in stock. Choice, quality, novelty, freshness: This is my store's promise to you. Now give me your offer," I said to Ygreek, "and don't be cheap. Penny pinching, figuratively speaking, could prove dangerous to you."

"I have no idea what offer to make," mumbled Ygreek.

"I advise you to give me your offer now," I said, assessing his features. "This store has a rule. You can't back down from making an offer. If you do that, you will become a product yourself. You do look good. I could place you on the main display." I gave him a warm smile. "There is nothing wrong with that. Long ago I was a product myself. I was bought and sold, I changed owners, I was pushed,   put aside and then I was thrown out. Look at me now. I'm the master of this world. I'm the one who gives and takes. I rule. I'm a higher being with unlimited patience. Time is at my service. I give orders, I destroy, I hang, I give life."

"You don't have much time left before you become part of my stock but I will give you two more average size moments. When I raise my hand you had better start speaking, or do something that will move my heart. There is a sound..." I couldn't speak anymore. I had never heard this sound, but I knew from old scriptures that it existed. Oh, how I yearned to hear that sound. I had high hopes for Ygreek. He seemed very capable. He just needed a bit of persuasion.

And then he started speaking. In the beginning his words were naked, shapeless, squeaky, like an old boot, but soon he found a rhythm. His voice gradually became strong, tranquil, clear. It made the sound of a bronze Greek vase, touched by a woman's finger nails. I recognized in it new tones, and a full pallet of pastel, transparent colors. Finally, his voice started flowing like a mountain stream, touched by the wing of a butterfly.

The sound — I remembered it! I realized this sound had always been with me but I had never heard it before. My body absorbed the sound. My sick shop keeper's mind became alive. Suddenly, I was free! I looked around. The walls of the store had disappeared and I could see

for miles; valleys, mountains, streams, blue sky. I felt for the first time the sun on my shoulders. I breathed deeply, slowly, deliberately, the first real breath of air in my life. I had known it would happen. I had read about it in old books sold at my store.

I turned to leave the store and walking along the river's edge, I stepped onto the soft surface of the water. I felt it sag a bit, but it held its tension. I walked on water and reached the other side. Across the river and....

TRIBUTE TO GRAND MOTHERS
by Zohra Zoberi

HAPPY AS A LARK sometimes, I'm just a sorrow sparrow. It's that bird's eye view in my heart that's a killer. Contrasts I constantly observe, that disturb me. While in the North West the sun may be shining bright, in the South East the view is ominous with a dark cloud constantly lurking.

Amidst the musical clutter of the Royal Doulton china, over high tea they relax on a patio, sipping Earl Grey tea and Jasmine Delight - the Grandmothers of North America. Rejoicing, boasting about their gifts from God, ecstatic at the sight of smiling innocence, how they describe the warm cuddles of their grand children! Like fresh petals their beauty unscathed by the roughness of life.

Latest achievements of these children they compare, each Grandma outdoing another. The first word Jason spoke, or how 'my Amanda has now learned to crawl.'

"Did we enjoy our own children as much?" one of them wondered.

"Not really, we were too busy just raising them."

"How fortunate, as grandmothers, we all are! While our children must deal with dirty diapers, bag packs, cribs and strollers, boxes of books and tons of toys, we finally get to relax for these are our golden years," remarked another.

"Now that we're no longer entangled into mashing potatoes and preparing formulas, we deserve to have the luxury of this pleasure at our leisure."

"Once upon a time we too paid our tolls for the blessings be-

stowed," proclaims one of them.

"Ah, but don't we still continue to extend our helping hands, constantly contribute to nurturing?"

"But... enjoyment has now become our rightful blessing! Play with them — then hand them over. After all we're the modern grandmas. We need time for our weekly blow dry's at the salon."

"And what about the opera or theatre we mustn't miss!"

I say, "Whatever time we spend with our grandchildren should be highly appreciated by our children. So, here's a toast to all of us Grandmothers," with confidence, she stands up to propose a toast.

Everyone cheers, but one becomes sad, and sorrowful — it's that sparrow with a bird's eye view in her heart! Her throat choking, she dares stand up to say:

"Do you know who we should be proposing a toast and paying the highest tribute to?" Everyone suddenly becomes curious and attentive.

"Just think, an entire generation has been wiped out from the surface of the earth! So, let's not forget about those Grandmothers who have lost their off-springs to a Monster, that deadly virus!" Her throat chocking she continues.

"Wrinkled women with aching limbs and fatigued bodies are now landed with the responsibility of raising these 'left over' children."

Takes a sip of tea and continues.

"Not to mention the burden of grief they carry. From two miles away, they must fetch water for those naked orphans with pot bellies whose lives are void of toys! How vulnerable and prone to disease they are."

With respectful awe and awareness, everyone stands up to propose a toast and repeats after her.

"We do salute you and pray for your strength, as you are truly Grandmothers!

The Grand 'Mothers' of Africa."

PART TWO
POETRY

SONNET: RECKLESS HEARTS
by John Ambury

Up, up, away, a Russian shuttle jets
With Guy Laliberté in purchased berth
A clown-nosed circus stunt, no ropes or nets
And as per script he comes back safe to earth.

All systems go, on rockets' fearsome thrust
Columbia lifts; the earthbound watchers cheer
Exhilarated trav'lers soar in trust
Not knowing there's a damaged tile to fear.

The roller-coaster thrills on plunging tracks
But firmly clings, to climb the further peaks;
Icarus flies on feathered wings of wax
Too high, downed by the very heat he seeks.

In love we feel the rush and seize the crown,
Take flight with reckless hearts, and don't look down.

SONNET: MAKING LOVE
by John Ambury

Before the touch, the kiss; before the kiss
The words: hot verbs, bold adjectives, raw nouns
Exciting syllables that steam and hiss
Arousing turns of phrase – our mating sounds.

Between the words, unwanted clothing flies
Exposing flesh in Eden nakedness
We need our touches bare, without disguise:
The searing burn, the tender cool caress.

Our mouths breathe wet sensations in like air
We're savages in tune with primal beat
The jungle cries of coupling fill our lair
Till, spent at last, we melt in panting heat.

Romance brings wondrous music to the soul
But only passion's fire can make love whole.

TO EARTH
by Elizabeth Barnes

your uncle
who had farmed the land
all of his life
one day in late summer just
as the trees were about to flare
walked   like a great bedraggled heron
his tattered greycoat
flapping about his calves
            into the field of drying dying corn stalks
he drew his coat over his head
            and huddled against rain and sun and sky
and turned from living dying flesh
into a rock   a solid bulging granite rock
            dominating his beloved fields
the sun sparked pink and green and golden flecks
off his grey sides

his sister
who had farmed with him all those years
weeks later
thin as a thin stick
and as brittle
reached up towards the gathering winter clouds and
dressed in green and gold
became a trembling aspen
looking over him
as she had looked over him all his life.

INSTRUCTIONS
by Elizabeth Barnes

give into gravity
it is not beneath you

leave time alone
to mind its own business

walk, eyes down, mindful of each step,
but seek not enlightenment

sit in pleasurable idleness
and trace the patterns in the neighbour's brickwork,
veins across the back of an ancient land

watch and feel the suck and swirl of the incoming tide
grasping, releasing, grasping, releasing

douse all lights as darkness falls

recite a Shakespearean sonnet
but only the bits you remember

sleep long and drift,
with no mind for the night wind

dream only your own dreams
mindless of the dreams of others

THE LANGUAGE OF TREES
by Kathleen Burke

Trees speak to me.
Their fresh green voices whisper all things;
Secrets of the blissed and the blessed
With centuries old harmonies and stories so old,
as to have become the sound of laughter
during the wind time.

All transformed into countless invitations
to ponder the burning theologies
of a supernatural subculture
mystical auras revealed
in the fleeting moments
before sleep.

EQUINOX
by Kathleen Burke

My mother's heart grows in my body
She swims through all time
in rhyme and rhythm
sharing the power songs
of all we have been,
shall be and are
condensed and ground to finest dust
then spread far and wide

All in preparation for the dramatic deepening
that catches you unaware
monday next.

FINDING PLUTO
by Maurus Cappa

Frozen orb like an arctic snowball.
So remote, ever so faint,
uninviting and barren.
But, Clyde Tombough, spotted you
in a 1931 sky.

Astronomers proclaimed you
the ninth planet from the Sun.
You were honoured and feted.
Scholarly journals around the globe
wrote of your majesty. You took
your proper place in the solar system.

But now, some astronomers scoff,
say you are too small.
You can not be a planet.
You do not measure up.
Let the naysayers be gone, I say.

I saw you once on an ebony evening
in a lonely black sky.
With averted vision in a powerful scope,
a few photons of your light
from three billion miles away
reached my incredulous eyes.

You will always be the ninth planet to me.

MESSIER RACE
by Maurus Cappa

Charles Messier, with
primitive telescope
discovered and catalogued
one hundred objects.
He called them nebulae.

Galaxies, star clusters, gas clouds
beckon us to behold the heavens--
God's creations.

From M42, the Great Orion Nebula
to M45, the brilliant sisters,
to M97, the elusive Owl,
all worthy and breathtaking.

Astronomers world-wide seek
to observe these discoveries.
Some may be observed in a lifetime,
Some in a single, long night.

I have viewed over ninety
from our light polluted, murky skies.
Will I make it to one hundred?
Or will the night sky be extinguished
by the encroaching city lights
before my race is over.

TILL WE MEET AGAIN
by Dolores B. Carfagnini

My darling you are safe back home, recovering with wounds,
from this awful war. I miss you.

I too now am shoulder to shoulder, mortar to mortar,
socks so cold, soaked through.
I can barely feel my toes.

The courage and strength I gather from you will help
me battle on.

My hips are weakened,
my knees won't hold me,
these wet boots are weighing me down.

Icicles of tears stick on my red chapped cheeks,
making it hard to smile.
Why would I?
No pink nail polish for me.
My hair is dirty, matted, under my helmet,
with no beautician in sight.

Alone, my mind plays tricks.
I feel you standing beside me.
Your warm hands, melting the ice on mine,
it is difficult to write now.

I am so weary, I lay my head back on what's left
of a frozen barren tree.
My eyes won't close, lashes are frozen.

I dream of you once more, with the warm sun on your
smiling handsome face. As you placed the ring on my finger.

I see our son laughing, and jumping in his playpen,
a runny nose from a cold.

"Thank you mom!"

I search for these memories to keep me alive,
among the dead, and the noise,
from cracking artillery around and beyond.

Besides God, guarding me now,
the only buddy left for miles,
its' frozen strap....
Keeping it upright in the snow, like a monument
to the soon to die, and the dear departed.
My buddy, my rifle, frozen, stands on guard beside me.

Again, I dream of you, placing a poppied wreath on my father's grave.
I think soon it will be Christmas.

'Hug my mom"
Kisses to you and our son.
Send me scribbles from him.
Buy him toys just from me.
Show him my picture, over and over, and over.

Merry Christmas. Till we meet again, I'll dream.
Remember I love you.
Your dol, Bambi

REMEMBRANCE DAY
by Dolores B. Carfagnini

Remembrance should be every day,
of the men and women at war,
and back home where the children safely play.
With bruises on their little faces,
knees skinned all over the place.
There is shrapnel in the soldiers back.
A grenade went off.
Because of these soldiers, the children played safe.
They played war games,
with toy rifles, helmets, grenades.
Then off to bed, their war games were over,
but not the case of the warriors, our soldiers.
Christmas was coming, but they won't be there.
There will be toys and wrapping paper,
placed by their chairs.
In the kitchen sits a turkey stuffed,
with bread, wine and chesnuts,
and cooling their favourite, minced meat tarts,
bowls of Clementines, candies, and all kinds of fruit.
To be part of this picture,
they would give up their boots.
Remembrance should be every day,
of the men and women at war, and back home,
where the children safely play.
Their bruises faded, skinned knees healed,
but not the case of the absent soldier.
The pain is deep, the shrapnel remains.
Remembrance should be every day.
Remember, remember.
Lest we forget.

THE GREAT DEPRESSION
by Jasmine D'Costa

Savings painstakingly augmented over the years
A centime here, a centime there,
Put into a hollow pink plastic pig with a slit on its back
standing on his shelf basking in the occasional sunshine
that creeps in through the slats of his blinds.
Deprivation, frugality, an exercise in self-preservation

The pig, smug with nurturing, bursting with coins is emptied
into sub prime investments of various kinds;
diversification to cut the risks

Until the depression

Unforeseen spirals of sub prime investments
In people long forgotten, crash downwards
Leaving him alone, impoverished, aged, ailing, seeking redemption
He sees the pig, a gaping hole on its back, as it sits on the shelf
and drops a dime in.

A CARDINAL IN THE CEDARS
by Josie Di Sciascio-Andrews

a cardinal in the cedars
is such a wonderful thing

a dash of red
against drab, winter foliage

life calling out
with unabashed boldness

as if to spite the marbled tomb
of cold, nebulous skies

a glimpse of fleeting passion
short lived, fearful
lover's lust

so bold, so true
so swiftly gone

BALLOON MAN (MEXICO CITY)
by Josie Di Sciascio-Andrews

Was this his mother's dream?
Was it his own?

A man standing in black pilot uniform
a dark stem
blooming pastel helium dreams.

His gaze is far away
from where he stands
waiting for balloon buyers.

Such paltry remuneration
a few small coins for a man
in the center of this Aztec city
conquered with pride and blood.

His austere, masculine profile sprouts
from a bouquet of inflated plastic petals.

From his strong, tanned hands
dangle strings of satin ribbons.

You can swear you've seen him before
somewhere. You almost know his name
as he fades into a background of pale light
on a street you walked through in a dream
when you caught a glimpse of who you were
once, before you became yourself.

SILENCE
by Emily Dunn

Silence is the loudest sound.
Ringing.
The congestion of thoughts
Weaving a web of neurons.
Too many questions
With over analyzed answers
That in the end doesn't change anything.
Stimulation from grasping the unidentifiable,
The unimaginable shooting through the mental logic,
Begin again... asking.
Building up until the metaphorical membrane is breached,
The voices stop but all is not yet silent.

GOODBYE
by Emily Dunn

It lifted off
The sun was bright as it rose,
Blinding.
The light stung my eyes,
Tears rolled down my cheek,
As I smiled and lifted a hand
It fell back to my side
And I could feel the same movement deeper within.
The warm arm of summer seemed cold,
Time had stopped for just a moment,
I could feel the last touches,
But as I stood alone
The pavement's stretch reaching far past my sight
And the blaring sun stole my last glance.

HELIUM-HEADED LOVE
by Iddie Fourka

Sticking to each other like barnacles,
our shiny bodies glossed with evaporation,
Poikilothirmaly absorbing sauna heart,
while singing Beatle anthems,
and sneaking kisses between every chorus.

Then when our bodies kettle over,
out of that wooden cabin we run out,
to jump into the cool & cleansing,
Panache-lake water;
the home of loon calls of the night.

We float with limbs spread out and overlapping,
resembling Davinci's Cartesian men.
You mumble something,
my hair oscillating, up-and-down like algae
my water-clogged ears blocking all waves of sound.

And then my body goes into a thermal shock,
quickly dispersing like electric jolts,
as temperature transitions from boiling to cool.
My spinning-mind, swirls stardust into impressionism,
which gets my soul & body high,
Vincent Van Gogh diffused across the sky.

Then helium-headed, I emerge upon uneven rock,
where we remain awake nocturnal owls,
Whispering our secrets on that special spot
as I curl your nape-hairs, damply sticking to your neck.

THE LOST PAPER CRANE
by Iddie Fourka

Signs hidden in the misty air
accumulated in the clouds for too long
plummet like dense-raindrops from the sky.
Splattering tiny treasures,
upon the ground and Earth,
later excavated for my guidance.
      The guidance of a paper crane;
white-speck on vast and murky water,
these compass-signs with their magnetic fields,
they guide through turbulence and sunny-rays,
even on rising water.

The signs—they guide and guide,
even when I don't notice,
until I've reached my destination-shore,
until my nose has caressed your warm, soft face,
and I've landed gently into your embrace.

A CURVE OF MEMORY... THROUGH UPPER SWALEDALE
by Mary Craig Gardner

It used to be a green hill crowned with a Norman castle.
The keep looking grand and forbidding still stands
in the middle of the cobbled public market place.
A surrounding black iron railing removes it from the hustle and bustle
    of life.
A strange, misplaced alien. There's no way in.

Saturday morning. I'm at the weekly market.
Dales' people are buying hardware, crockery, eggs, cheese
and farm tools from the stalls pitched on the cobbled stones.
Clustered round the market place old houses and shops
stand half crumpled by centuries of wear and tear.
And beyond this nucleus - the suburbs.
I'm in Richmond, Yorkshire - a small town through which runs the River Swale.
Every summer before World War 2 my father drove the family
through this market place, usually on a Sunday morning,
on the long journey from our home town
to a small village eighteen miles west of Richmond.
Reaching Richmond we stick our noses on the windows
hoping to get there faster.
The road now narrows.
Room only for one vehicle in each direction.
The gradient increases and the little Morris chugs as we climb up onto the
    moors,
Hedgerows and stone walls come closer.
Then we arrive.
A small village.

Memory funds everything.
Childhood holidays seared in memory are the gold coin of that realm.
Day after day, in this small village,
I and my small sister live under blue skies, enfolded in August's hot
    summer roundness.
Earth's great beneficence taken for granted.
Each day is an endless stretch of play and fantasy.

Memory, a long distilled brandy that I now drink slowly meditatively,
bit by bit retrieving glimpses of every day life in the dale -- miniatures
     as it were,
burnished with a sheen, a pastoral patina,
the adult city dweller's idyllisation of rural life.
Beneficence is the right word now. Not a child's word.
Other words arrive stinging the mind with the intensity of these early
     experiences.
At the time it was the enough to be alive in dazzling sunlight all day.
Always in memory the days are sunlight bright.
The colours of video, photograph, print and television are rejected.
All lack sunlight's actuality.
Childhood -- everything matters -- red campion in the hedge, a bend
     of the road, the deepness of the river,
a flat topped road side wall on which we can walk --
are suspended in memory's palette of light particles -- a pure sensorily
     refracted sunlight.

And now.
Like Hubble's telescope revealing the past through captured light
memory gives it all back to me.
Not as something simply recorded.
No. Something impregnated with the warmth of life itself,
shaped by memory's own index and garnished with adult dreams and
     desires.
The shades of Proust surround me.
I now know what drove him.

Suddenly I catch myself up. An inner voice says, 'Hey, this is England.
There must have been rain sometime.'
That's right. The adult's editorial hand intervenes.

I remember the rainy days and reassemble
the picture -- voluminous grey pillows hide the moors.

We watch through blurry windows the gloppy fat rain drops elongating
     themselves
down the smooth slippery glass.
Other raindrops stot off the ground. Then steadily aggregate into
     pools.
'Stot' -- North country onomatopoeia -- for a raindrop's vertical bounce.

By evening the clouds, back in their proper sky place, shroud only
  the hilltops.
Wind sheers away all wetness from flag stones, roads, walls, roofs.

We go out. A matter of family importance to inspect the beck
  (local stream).
Full – stepping stones across the stream invisible under rushing water.
'Good lot of rain that was', says someone sagely.
 We walk down the road to where the beck joins the River Swale.
A due sense of awe overtakes us – the river's brown muddy water is
  leaping along
in driving muscular swirls. Fierce. A mad, yet contained force.
Like a bunch of race horses coming round the last bend.
Next morning we see the purple heather on the moors again.

CAN YOU REMEMBER
by Zita Hinson

Come my friend, now tell me the truth
Can you remember the hopes, the dreams, the expectations of our youth
Can you remember our youthful escapades, the giddiness, the joy,
    the laughter
How we believed all that, and more were ours and would go on forever
    after

Can you remember running thru the falling rain in youthful
    abandonment
Soaked to the skin, hair dripping, face beaming with unabashed
    enjoyment
No thought of discipline, disapproval, or punishment
For the world was our oyster and we could taste the excitement

Thru pain and disappointment thru confusion and turbulence
Can you remember the spirit that could not be broken, the pride that
    stiffened our spines
That youthful resilience
We believed that tomorrow would always be there for the taking
And nothing absolutely nothing could keep us down for long
For there was always a new conquest, always a new adventure, always
    a new song

Can you remember on our journey to success, the pain, the disillusion?
For we discovered that the road to ease was but an illusion
Yet we continued to believe that there was no mountain too high
No valley too low, no river we could not cross
But thru much tears, and many prayers, we mellowed thru the years
Yet our dreams burn fiercely on, not like a raging consuming fire as it
    was so long ago
But as a steady flame that would not be quenched, and that my friend
    is the truth.

I, TOO, AM CANADIAN
by Jasmine Jackman

Born in local hospital in Toronto close to my home
I play hockey, cricket, tennis, rugby, and basketball
Drink beer, wine, Jamaican rum, double lattes, and schnapps
Love to go to operas, watch Bollywood movies or simple stroll
    through the malls
I play mah-jong, chess, dominoes, cribbage and craps
The beautiful mosaic of rich cultures,
religions, and languages spoken make Canada so unique.
Each day is like taking a trip around the world but you need not board
    a plane
To see people from Somalia, Nigeria, West Indies , South Africa,
    India ,Thailand Italy
Russia, Portugal, the Middle East , New Zealand, China, Brazil
    and Spain.
Accents of my forefathers may be different than those of the first
    settlers,
But even the accents of people from Alberta,
Quebec, PEI and Newfoundland are not the same.
And of our native inhabitants where are they today
most killed off and now hidden away.
Are they not the landlords of this pristine country we have
    adopted and cherish?
So please do not take my accent or the darker hue of my skin
For mistaking me to be any less Canadian

LEADERSHIP
by Jasmine Jackman

Not like a dog on a leash
But like two friends walking down the street
Fulfillment is found by collaborating with others
Driven by desire to realize dreams
Rather than from fear
With warmth and cooperation
Find your passion, make your way
 Make a difference, find your place
The stars are the limit for which you should strive
Share your plans with all that will listen and aim for the sky
Improve on problems and move ahead
Never allow your passion and vision to end up dead.

I WANT
by David Kimel

I want my voice heard from afar,
My words chiseled in bedrock,
My fire should ignite the stars
Lighting ever through epochs.

I want to leave a mark behind,
Create paths that never were
To guide the needy like a blind
Out of woods of dark despair.

I want to build a bridge to you,
Helping you find me, my thought,
To taste, to touch, to see my view
And feel my love, when I'll be not.

ALYSSA
by David Kimel

You're the little girl I love
Matching me like hand and glove
And for you I can't refuse
Anything, find an excuse
That I'm old, too busy, sick,
Worn-out playing hide and seek.

You're the girl who taught me laugh,
Made me play and played me tough
You're so soft and softened me
And you're warm and made me be.

When you dance, you dance with me
Sing along and watch TV,
We read stories from kids' books,
Painting drawings for best look

Now you grew, I grew with you,
Learned your tricks and tricked you too
But the most of all above
You taught me what means to love.

WHERE ALL THE JOHN WAYNES HAVE GONE
by Ashley Maniw

I like blue because it's your favourite colour.
    "What's your favourite colour?"
Mine is purple.
What's yours?
    "Blue."
Then you kissed me.
    "Sorry I asked you that."
Don't apologize.
You've given me a story.

I like dark hair and blue eyes on a man.
I want them tall,
with rugged hands and bitten nails.
In faded blue jeans and plaid shirts.
The smell of cigarettes in their jackets.
Creativity buried in their bodies.
And I want them with their hair long.

I like men who look like my father
with dark hair and light eyes.
He's a man who wonders where all
the John Waynes in the world have gone.
Finding a real man is like searching for sea-glass in the sand.
Tedious. Though not impossible.
I want to love so hard my soul hurts.

I like blue because it's the colour of your bed sheets.
December's morning light bled purple into your room
when a headache woke me up.
It was a sinus headache,
the kind of pain that sears your eyes
and numbs your nose.
It was a headache caused by the cold outside.
But you were holding on close.
And I was warm.

TIME HEALS!
by Jatin Naik

You cannot reverse back in time,
'Cause it's already beyond and out of sight,
In trying to look behind and back,
You might fall down in your forward track,

Time is the healer, don't hold on to the past,
Let go off the things that have gone by fast,
Look ahead for better times,
Keeping in sight of what's in the line,

Since what's gone cannot come back,
You might miss what's ahead and lack,
Its no use crying over spilled milk,
Save what's left behind of the half glass filled,

What's happening is for the good,
You cannot resist it with a forlorn mood,
'Cause if you manipulate the outcome,
It will be no good in the long run to come,

With the new times you need to accept change,
And openly embrace that what has to pain,
'Cause as the graduating class has already dispersed,
You need to move on without keeping any terms!

For a lapse of moment or two in time,
Nothing seems to be moving in sight,
Yet as time goes on without waiting forever,
Often there are changes positive all over and over!

THE CLOWN
by Jatin Naik

He makes them laugh when they are laughing,
He makes them laugh when they are crying,

He makes them laugh when he is laughing,
Though inside he might still be crying,

He wears a mask when he is clowning,
To prevent others see his suppressed frowning,

So people be one like that clown,
And help others when they are feeling down,

Do come forward to do some clowning,
Else it could be the whole world drowning!

APPOINTMENT
by Deena Kara Shaffer

What was it for you
The wait
Her: slowed shoes
You: onto her pause

To have a cool doc's
Warm hand, brace
She: clear-cut
You: remediless

Your bones onscreen
Slowed time, louder
She: explaining
You: slumped

The wintry clinic
Moirae's revolving door
She: apologetic
You: done for
             and waiting again

ON UN-MAKING CONTACT
by Deena Kara Shaffer

I deleted
From Facebook
Your friendship
No more
Picture stalks
Update scans

A non-continuation
Half retaliation

You're off
My Skype
No more
Late night
Calls, scripts

Part self-protection
Contact obliteration

But if
You requested
Online re-acquaintance
I'd accept
Delete, accept
Like always

PETALS WITHIN LEAVES OF A BOOK
by Sheila Tucker

Like a dried, flat flower
Found in a book—
You discovered me...
A wallflower.

You watered me
watched me become
three-dimensional.

I will bloom for you
forever.
May my newfound fragrance
saturate your dreams.

CEMETERY
by Sheila Tucker

The Teddy Bear says it all
sitting to attention, soaking wet and faded by sun,
but with bright, wide eyes
and arms outstretched
waiting for a hug that never comes.

In this small cemetery I stumble upon
I do not need to read
the gravestone, to know
that a child lies here.
Child, interrupted.

I think of the parents, interrupted,
bringing this Teddy, some time ago,
and these flowers, freshly cut.

I think of them
remembering a babe with
bright, wide eyes.
I see them walking home
with broken hearts,
with shoulders hunched,
longing for a hug that never comes.

Ah, Teddy.
Little stuffed toy leaning on a slab.

Ah, Teddy.
You are the Sphinx sitting by your Pharoah.

Ah, Teddy.
You are a sentry guarding your precious charge.

You are silent, yet you say it all.

APOLOGY
by Sarah Zahid

Morning Prayer
Numbers.
Dupont analysis
Data
Trends
In midst of all this
I have been thinking about her
Alone afraid in pain
Probably in morning she is like me
Vulnerable
Sullen
Sad
Standing on the prayer mat
Asking the divine.
All the whys in her life
Probably she also wears white when she is happy
Smiles on your meaningless jokes
Laugh at the tingle of your eyes
Probably she is also like chai to you
addictive?
I wonder if she fights with you..
Argue on useless things
Weep on your shoulder
Play with your hair?
Does she talk in the late hours of the night?
How does her hair look on the pillow?
Is she a frightened woman like me?
Does she long and desire for you?
I think about her in all ways
I draw a portrait every morning after my morning tea
I rub it again for the next morning
Sometimes I feel naked, vulnerable and painful
Thinking she knows
What I know
Where desire ends and pain starts

And then I think about writing her a letter of apology
Thinking that my reassurance of a dead love
Might calm her nerves
Make her a bit happy?
She might realize that in this game of desire
All the sunk costs were mine
I was the one without any gains
I have the word loss written on balance sheet of life
She might realize that I was no one
In this story
But when I sit down to write it
I don't know
How to write an apology for love

BIOGRAPHIES
OF AUTHORS

VALERIE ALBEMARLE spent many years in Russia, England and the US before settling in Canada. She has worked as a translator, a university professor of philosophy and the humanities, and currently earns her bread as a veterinarian specializing in cats. She marvels at her good fortune to live in a century when such women are no longer burned as witches. This story is her first published foray into non-academic writing.

JOHN AMBURY is a technical writer with a number of operating manuals and project proposals to his credit. While he has posted genre fiction on-line, his first published work appeared in Canadian Voices, Vol. 1. He is also a freelance editor and proofreader, a technical speaker, an amateur photographer, and a part-time professional actor. John is a member of the Writers and Editors Network and the Canadian Federation of Poets.

ELIZABETH BARNES is a poet, writer, and an active member of the High Park Writers' Group. She was shortlisted for the Writer's Union of Canada short story contest for her story entitled The Yellow Dahlia in 2002. Elizabeth had two poems published in the first volume of Canadian Voices. She works for the City of Toronto facilitating a creative writing and a fabric art group at a women's resource centre.

DAHN BATCHELOR was a nationally syndicated newspaper columnist and TV talk show host during the 1970s and 1980s. He has had several short stories published along with a number of articles and he is the author of several essays in business and medical journals. At 76, he is now working on his memoirs.

SHARON BERNAS fell in love with writing at the University of Toronto. Inspired by prose, she completed a program with the LongRidge Writing Institute. She has published short stories and magazine articles and is currently working on her third manuscript, a fun, fantasy romance.

MAYANK BHATT Immigration to Canada in July 2008 changed Mayank's life for good. Although he was a writer in India, he began writing fiction only in Canada. His short story -- The New Canadians -- was published in TOK 5: Writing the New Toronto (2010). Mayank has completed a course in Canadian Journalism at Sheridan College (2009) and has completed a creative writing program at Humber College (2010). He is working on his first novel and writes two blogs -- Generally About Books (www.generallyaboutbooks.com) and My Immigrant Adventures for Canadian Immigrant magazine (www.canadianimmigrant.ca/immigrantstories/mayankbhatt).

JESSICA BORGES is an award-winning advertising copywriter who has lived and worked in Mumbai, Dubai, Muscat and Toronto. A poet, story-writer and illustrator, she received the Montblanc-Emirates Woman prize for her novella *The Gulfie Wife* in 2007 in Dubai. A people's person, she also enjoys conducting creative writing, interactive story-telling and media literacy workshops in Toronto schools.

ALISON E. BRUCE started writing stories at the age of twelve and hasn't stopped since. Copy writer and editor since 1992, she started working toward publication of her fiction at the insistence of her terminally ill sister, Joanne. Alison is a member of the Writers and Editors Network and Crime Writers Canada.

MARY HARRINGTON BRYANT taught school in the 1930s and 1940s, wrote and produced the first English Primer for arctic schools. She is a botanist, naturalist and artist and has put those skills to use in several publications ranging from museum books, government technical publications and recently in several self-published books about her experiences.

SILENE BUMBACA is a grade nine student from Mississauga, Ontario with a passion for reading and writing. Silene has received several awards in English, Public Speaking and for several poems she has written. She loves travelling, competitive swimming, and is working on various literary pieces which she hopes to publish one day. Silene plans to pursue her passion for literature and make it a part of her future career choices.

KATHLEEN BURKE has been writing and daydreaming all of her life and is new to the publishing scene. A long time community arts and social service advocate she believes passionately in the arts as a catalyst for empowerment, healing and change. She loves the sound of the wind, the smell of the ocean, rocks (including husband Tony), sparkly stuff and still believes in magic.

ALTUG CAKMAKCI is a member of High Park Writers Group and he is currently working on a novel. His two novels in Turkish, Simdiki Zamanin Tarihi/History of Present Time and Renkli Taslarin Siyah Golgesi/Black Shadow of Coloured Stones, were published in Turkey. One of his short stories had been published in Canadian Voices Anthology, Volume 1.

MAURUS CAPPA writes specifically on the topic of astronomy, his childhood hobby. He was the first to spot Halley's Comet in Toronto in 1985. After retiring from IBM as IT manager, he turned poet. His poems are published in the Vaughan Poets' Circle anthology "Earth to the Moon."

DOLORES BAGNATO CARFAGNINI is a chartered member of Writers and Editors Network. She started creative writing courses at Humber College (1986) and memoir classes (1996). Delores is improving her skills in workshops with guest authors, and member authors of WEN Network. Her publications include Outreach Connection, 2005, poem titled *How Long*, and in Verse Afire with T.O.P.S., poem titled *Heaven Awaits You*. Dolores' passion for writing includes poetry, short stories, and memoirs. Her continued interest for poetry of war is inspired by the memory of her father, Sergeant Bagnato, WWII.

JACK CAULFIELD is a writer, actor, visual artist, poet, and independent filmmaker. With the cooperation of Black Creek Pioneer Village he successfully wrote produced and directed a short period piece entitled *Surfacing* all while earning his degree at York University. As Features Editor for his college paper Mac Media, he published a controversial article entitled *The Extinction of Art*.

SHAHEENA CHOUDHURY moved to Canada from Bangladesh three years ago. She has a Masters Degree in English Literature and also an M.S in Education from the University of Pennsylvania. She taught English and ESL for over 20 years. She has published several articles in numerous academic journals. Exploring the world of creative writing, she hopes to publish a book on memoirs and short stories.

CHRISTINA CLAPPERTON is fascinated with the human mind and uses story to depict her observations of human nature. An excerpt from a longer work appeared in the first volume of *Canadian Voices* and her short fiction has been recognized in writing contests and published on WriterAdvice.com.

L. J. CLARK has a doctorate in English literature and has taught writing courses here and overseas. She has published essays, articles, reviews and short stories, one of which was given the Award of Excellence by the Ottawa Independent Writers' Association (2007). She is now working on the third in a series of children's books published by Baico Press.

DAYLE CLEVELAND lives in Toronto and is known for being creative in many ways, according to those around her. She has written stories throughout her life, and much of it is based on her own experiences. "Ghost from the Past" is Dayle's first publication. She is working on her first novel/ memoirs/collection of short stories.

CASSANDRA CRONENBERG HUNTER is a writer and visual artist living in Toronto. She has written for Eye Magazine, has two BA's in East Asian Studies and Psychology, has worked as an Assistant Director in Feature Film for 10 years and this is her first published work of fiction.

JULIET DAVY was born in Clarendon Jamaica. She is an author, actress, a facilitator in Special Education and Professional Development. Her short story Treasured Moment was published in the Food for Thought anthology. Her work The Path to Transformation and Forgiveness was nominated for a top ten award in Dream Weaver Writing Competition. Juliet also co-wrote and performed in the play *StreetHearts*.

JASMINE D'COSTA is an accomplished Toronto author. Her recent publications include a collection of short stories *Curry is Thicker than Water* by BookLand Press. Jasmine just completed her first book of poetry *A Million Pieces of China* and currently working on her novel *Saving Ali*. From banker to writer, her mind is one large whirl of words and stories waiting to be written.

SUSAN DESVEAUX is a health care/medical research worker and Reiki Master, born and raised in Toronto. She has a background in theatre performance, production and design and has written poetry, plays and short stories. Susan is currently working on her first medical mystery novel.

HEATHER DICK is an actress, stage director and the Founding Artistic Director of the Sirius Theatrical Company. The Company focuses on creating multi-disciplinary theatrical performances that fuse dance, music, poetry and traditional text. She has written several one-act plays and short stories and co-authored the full length play *StreetHearts* that premiered in Toronto in 2006.

SALLY DILLON is a freelance writer residing in Toronto, Ontario. She has had her short stories published in *More Memoirs Around the Table* and *Canadian Voices, Volume One*. Sally is presently working on a book portraying her memoirs about growing up in a small Ontario town. In her

time out from writing Sally enjoys gardening, swimming and practicing the martial art of Taoist Tai Chi.

JOSIE DI SCIASCIO-ANDREWS was born in Italy an emigrated to Canada at the age of 13. She studied Italian and French Literature at the University of Toronto. She has a Masters Degree in Education and pursuing a Masters Degree in Italian Literature. Josie won several prizes for her work in both Italian and English.

EMILY DUNN is currently a student in Biomedical Toxicology at the University of Guelph. In her spare time she enjoys writing poetry. She has had two poems published, one in the Hamilton Gazette titled I Remember, and Bring Me Home was in the in the local Humane Society newsletter. Emily has done readings at the Burlington Art Center and the local chapter of CFP. She is thrilled to have this opportunity and hope it will open more doors.

MICHAEL ROBERT DYET is The Metaphor Guy. Novelist, closet philosopher, chronicler of life's mysteries all through the lens of metaphor. He is the author of *Until the Deep Water Stills*: An Internet-enhanced Novel – traditional print novel with a unique, optional online companion – which was a double winner in the 2009 Reader Views Literary Awards. Visit Michael at www.mdyetmetaphor.com.

FRAN EDELSTEIN was born in Montreal and raised in Toronto. She studied Creative Writing at Ryerson College. Her feature articles and monthly columns appeared in major newspapers and art and antiques publications. Her first book, *Set to Music*, a collection of seven short stories launched in 2009, is being enjoyed worldwide and soon to be followed by her first novel. Fran is married, a mother and a grandmother. Please see website: www.franedelstein.com.

JUDE PAUL FERNANDES was a Creative Director at McCann-Erickson in Mumbai and now heads Sulekha.com in Toronto. After a Writing workshop at Humber College, his mentor suggested that he could explore writing about the Goan community from Goa, India. He then went on to write a couple of stories that got published in Anokhi Magazine. He is currently submitting his first book of short stories titled *Not Truly Canadia*n and when time or insomnia permits is working on a novel called *The Keeper of Secrets.*

IDDIE FOURKA has a degree in English literature & Creative writing, and was raised in Ukraine, Italy and Canada. In between her writing rampages, she audio engineers and composes at Euphonic Sound, writes music articles, and acts in films, music videos & movies. And, just like Bob Dylan, she believes that art is always flowing, moving and changing – this reflects in her experimental & ever changing poems!

FRANCES FROMMER is a writer, artist and librarian and the author of *Surviving & Thriving Solo: Options When You Live Alone*. She contributes book reviews to Personal-Development.com and has published articles in *I Love Cats* and *Cat Talk*, and stories in *Cats, Cats, Cats and More Cats* and *Wordstruck.*

MARY CRAIG GARDNER was born in England and immigrated to Canada in her late twenties. She is a graduate of the University of Toronto. Mary's work has been published in *Reflections*, a UK poetry book, and also in the Canadian Authors Association's book of essays and short stories, *Winners.*

MARILYN GARSHOWITZ is the author of the feisty, non-fiction book *The Brutal Truth*. It delves into the issue of bullying and misuse of power— whether one is talking of bullying in the schoolyard, workplace harassment or misuse of power from judges or lawyers, or otherwise. Ms Garshowitz is also the founder of *The Brutal Truth Organization* established to continue the work initiated within the book and to establish herself as a writer, speaker and educator on the subject. She has also been co-published within a psychology journal with professors and is currently working on her second book. Visit www.thebrutaltruth.ca for additional information.

JEFFERSON GUZMAN is an actor, writer, and director. Film/TV acting credits include Mouth to Mouth, Queer As Folk, and DOC. Stage acting credits include Bad Acting Teachers and Sofie & Leo, (also written by Guzman). Playwrights Canada Press published excerpts of his first play Playing in the Leaves in Gay Monologues and Scenes, An Anthology. His articles have appeared in Xtra Magazine. Jefferson wrote and directed the short film M-F, which received a worldwide distribution deal.

JOHN R. HEWSON: The "human condition"— novelists examine it, physicians treat it. The synergy is obvious. No surprise then that, sooner or later in their lives, a number of people with a medical education (e.g. Anton Chekhov, Arthur Conan Doyle, W. Somerset Maugham, A. J. Cronin,

Vincent Lam) have chosen to embark on a career of writing serious fiction. So it is with John. After decades of ICU practice, he took up writing. Now honed by ten years of intense apprenticeship in the world of fiction—no less than he devoted to his medical training—he will soon offer the full manuscript of *Corbett's Daughter* in which he examines the meaning of our lives and the values that propel us.

ZITA HINSON lives in Toronto, Ontario. She has written many poems to inspire and help women. Zita is the author of the book *Woman Reach For Your Destiny* published by her Church.

STEVEN JACKLIN published his first book of short stories, A Slight Kink in 2010 and has also recorded them as an audio release. Currently he is writing a series of children's stories, *The Giggleopolous Zoo* as an audio release. His first novel, *The Adventures of the Dwarfgiants* (an adventure fantasy, ages 12+) will be completed in 2011.

JASMINE JACKMAN is a mother of two boys, business woman, writer, actress and teacher who dedicates her free time to volunteering on community boards and working with underserviced youth. Jasmine writes poetry, children stories and has also written two plays *Junior* and *Sisters*. She is currently working as a United Nations research volunteer.

MANNY JOHAL is a chiropractor from Vancouver B.C. This work is his second published excerpt from his non-fiction manuscript *Breaking Through the Bull; How God Works*. It illustrates a personal, burgeoning spiritual journey from a scientific and Sikh perspective.

FATMATTA KANU was born and raised in Freetown, Sierra Leone, West Africa. She attended Boston University where she obtained her Master's Degree. Now retired, Fatmatta has written an autobiography Through the Calabash (2008). She is also a contributing author to three anthologies: *Memoirs Around the Table (2006)*, *More Memoirs Around the Table (2008)* and *Canadian Voices, Volume One (2009)*.

DAVID KIMEL is a newcomer to Canada from Eastern Europe who strives to deliver a message of peace and love through his poems. He is the author of the poetry book *Simple Seeds* published by Author House in 2008 and is currently working on a biographic novel *Shrouded Dawns*. David also writes for several Romanian newspapers.

DONNA KIRK is an Oakville writer who concentrates on non-fiction. Reese Matthew, her special needs son, is the inspiration for *Finding Matthew*, a book length memoir. Soon to be the next best seller? Donna, who has a fashion design back ground, is a dreamer of big dreams. She is encouraged and mentored by the Fiction Highway Writing Guild, her critique group, her husband and family. Being published in *Canadian Voices* is the biggest thrill of her writing career.

ENXHI KONDI is an author previously published and currently aspiring to publish a fiction novel. Writing started out as a hobby for her, but after her first publication she realized she could take it further. She is an active volunteer for Cosmyc Vybes fitness as a yoga demonstrator and often uses yoga to aid in creating moods in her fiction.

MARY ELLEN KOROSCIL operates a public relations business, creating a "Buzz" for her clientele within the media. Over the years she has written reams of press releases and decided it was high time to try her hand at writing short stories. This is her first published work. She originally hails from Moose Jaw, Sask., and has lived in Calgary, Hamilton and in Toronto. For many years she now calls Mississauga her home.

KAREN LAM is currently studying Radio and Television at Ryerson University. She is an advocate for literacy and accessibility. As a writer, editor, and producer, Karen believes our greatest asset is the power to influence change. Oranges are her motif. Visit www.amidnightmuse.com for writing, multimedia, and more!

PETER LISINSKI has been an ordained minister of the Evangelical Lutheran Church in Canada since 1986. He and his wife, Rosarie, have four adult children and currently reside in Brampton, Ontario. This is his first published story and was submitted at the suggestion of a congregant who heard its original oral presentation as a narrative sermon.

JOHN MAAR is a writer from Croatia who now lives in Toronto, ON. He is the winner of 2009 Canadian Aid Literary Award Contest. His fiction novel *The Drums Cried* will be published by BookLand Press in 2010.

VICTORIA MACDONALD is a retired special education teacher who currently spends her leisure time writing, volunteering and singing karaoke. She was born, raised and continues to live near High Park in Toronto.

DAVID MANDEL is an aspiring freelance fiction writer with experience in multiple genres for multiple mediums. A recent graduate of The Institute of Children's Literature Writing Program, he hopes to publish his first novel for middle-grade readers, *Flotsam*, sometime in 2011 and secure compatible literary representation. In nearly ten years, he has completed four feature-length screenplays, three novels, a comic book and several short stories.

ASHLEY MANIW graduated from York University in 2009 with an Honours Bachelor of Arts degree in English and Creative Writing. Ashley has had a passion for writing and telling stories since she was in grade school. Along with prose and poetry, she writes screenplays and has recently sold a five minute short to a small production company based in Los Angeles. Her inspirations include literature, blogging, pop culture, television, film, and Robert Downey Jr.

MARIA PIA MARCHELLETTA is a quadrilingual poet, writer, editor and translator. She is Vice-president of the Writers and Editors Network and Chair of the Toronto Bayview Chapter and of the Italo-Canadian Writers Chapter of the Canadian Federation of Poets. Her full collection of poetry *On the Wings of Dawn* was published by In Our Words.

LOUIS MASSEY is an Assistant Professor at the Royal Military College in Kingston, Ontario and a retired Canadian Air Force senior officer. As a Computer Scientist specializing in Artificial Intelligence, he is a published writer, with articles in various specialized journals. In addition to his interest in science and technology, he has been passionate about visual arts and fiction writing since childhood. He is launching his literary work in fiction with his debut short story *The River: Car ton bras sait porter l'épée* in this volume.

CORINNE CAST MCCORKLE began her writing career with the class play in Grade Three. She has won awards in business communications, and is a freelance writer, editor and publication designer. She also enjoys crafting poetry and fiction. Corinne holds degrees from Northwestern University and University of London Royal Holloway. She grew up near Chicago, lived in Germany and England, and now resides in Mississauga.

CASSIE MCDANIEL regularly attends the High Park Library and Soft Spot for the Universe writers groups in Toronto. Her writing includes both fiction and poetry and often features the Texan landscape. She is

currently editing her first novel, also set in Texas. Find more of her latest shenanigans, including updates from her blog, Two Thick Thumbs, on www.cassiemcdaniel.com.

BRAZ MENEZES is a Kenya born architect and urban planner, studied Creative Writing at George Brown in Toronto. Previously published by the World Bank, his new work appears in *Canadian Voices* (Bookland Press) launched November 2009, and *Goa Masala* (A Plus Publishing), Toronto, February 2010. Braz is currently working on a full-length novel. He lives in Toronto.

MICHELLE MONTEIRO is currently a student at St. Joseph Secondary School in Mississauga. She was given an honourable mention from the Young Authors Awards for her short story, *Lively. Serendipity* is her first published work.

YOKO MORGENSTERN has worked as a writer, editor, and translator in Japan, Europe and Canada. Currently she is pouring all her energy into her historical novel. Also, she is playing important roles in forthcoming projects such as a museum or a think-tank, taking leading roles in two Toronto projects: a think tank of internationally-trained writers and a children's museum. Yoko lives in Oakville,Ontario.

JATIN NAIK lives in Toronto, Ontario and works in the field of journalism and web publishing. He is a member of the Writers and Editors Network. Jatin has a passion for writing and visual arts. He has contributed his time and volunteered for many not-for-profit organizations.

PETA-GAYE NASH is a short story writer whose work has appeared in the *Jamaica Observer Literary Magazine*, the *Bearing Witness Anthologies and Bookends.* A graduate of McMaster University, she teaches English as a second language and is working on her first book of short stories. Born in St. Andrew, Jamaica, she resides in Mississauga, Ontario with her husband and four children.

BRANDON PITTS co-hosts a monthly Prose and Poetry reading at the Prana Coffee Bar in Toronto's Beach and is currently working on his novel, *The Gospel of Now*. He has been published in *Quick Brown Fox* and *Conceit Magazine's* anthology of short fiction, *The Bracelet Charm*. His song writing credits include the lyrics for Roselyn Brown's, *The Siren*.

WAHEED RABBANI was born India and obtained his undergraduate degree from Loughborough University, England, and master's degree from Concordia University, Montreal. While an engineer by profession, Waheed's other love is reading and writing English literature, which led him to obtain a Certificate in Creative Writing from McMaster University and start on his fiction writing journey. His first historical fiction novel, *The Azadi Trilogy, Book I: Doctor Margaret's Sea Chest,* was published, by Youwriteon-Legend Press, UK. More information is available on his website: http://home.cogeco.ca/~wrabbani

ELANA RAE is the pen name used by Debbie Rolfe. Debbie's stories have been published in *Canadian Woman Studies, Touched by Adoption 1 &2, Canadian Voices, Volume One,* and *The JCB Voice.* She lives with her family in Scarborough, Ontario.

ELIZABETH CARINA RAMOS started writing in English language at the High Park Writers' Club. A mother of two, a permanent learner with a positive spirit, Carina never stops seeking opportunities to grow. That energy flows in her writing with the simple and bold style she has developed working as a journalist for 16 years in the Argentina print media.

ANU RAO works in the Information Technology field and lives in Mississauga, Ontario with her husband who is a perfume designer. She has always had a passion for writing and has published a few poems, children's stories and articles in various publications. She eventually hopes to become a full-fledged novelist.

LARRY RODNESS lives in Toronto with his wife, Jodi and their 3 children, Adam, Jonathan and Erin. Both Larry and Jodi have been professional singers for over 30 years. Larry has written professionally for musical theatre and has had 3 screenplays optioned to date. His first novel of fiction, *Today I am a Man,* was published by Savant Books and Publications in February 2010.

PHILOMENA SALDANHA was born and raised in Bombay (she refuses to call it "Mumbai"). She came to Canada in 1991 from a familar world to a whole new experience. An accountant by profession, she was nudged into the writing world by a close friend. Her first story, *A Perfect Evening* was published in *Canadian Voices, Volume One.*

MEL SARNESE is a writer and poet living in Toronto. Her short story, *Torn Seams*, was featured in *Canadian Voices, Vol. 1*. Mel's poetry and short stories have been anthologized and broadcast in Canada and abroad. She has recently edited a book of poetry, *The Healing Rose,* from her work as writer-in-residence at the Markham Stouffville hospital. Mel facilitates poetry workshops for the Canadian Mental Health Association.

SUZANNE SCHMIDT is a writer, poet, teacher, and active member of the Writer's Circle of Durham Region and the Ontario Poetry Society. The short story presented in this book is an excerpt from her memoir *Till We Meet Again*. Her work is inspired by her loving mother's display of optimism and strength after given only two months to live, their incredible journey, and the special bond they shared and hilarious life long adventures.

DEENA KARA SHAFFER is a poet, teacher, business owner, and perpetual student, completing the Certificate for Creative Writing at the University of Toronto. Her forthcoming first poetry collection, *The Grey Tote*, takes death and dying as its aim. Avoiding cliché at all costs and hovering between the stark and the light, Deena's poetry entwines freshness, insight, empathy, and threads of humour.

STEVEN H. STERN received his degree from Ryerson University in Toronto and began his career at the CBC. He worked in every aspect of the Canadian entertainment industry for many years. Steven has directed over 60 motion pictures, many of which he also produced and/or wrote. His films have been shown and won awards at film festivals around the world.

PHYLLIS DILLER STEWART is a secretary in a busy Emergency Department, a fertile field for character observation. Once home she morphs into a writer and has been developing her craft ever since a Durham College course challenged her to move from dabbling to serious writing three years ago. She has been encouraged by recent publication successes and is currently at work on her first book, *The Rock Wall*.

URVE TAMBERG is a writer and consultant specializing in health care. After years of writing business and marketing plans, she has overcome her tendency to use passive voice and now enjoys writing fiction. She is working on her first historical novel set in Estonia in 1941. She is a member of CANSCAIP and the Canadian Author's Association. Her short fiction has been published in print and on-line.

R.G. THOMPSON was born and raised on the Prairies. Early in his career, he trained as a naval officer on Canada's west coast (where his novel, *The Wind from All Directions*, is set), and served as a CUSO development worker in Africa. He completed graduate studies in Toronto and England, and subsequently worked as an economist, consultant and investment banker before turning to writing. His Voices contribution is adapted from his second novel, *A Person of Letters*. He lives in Toronto.

LINDA TORNEY worked as full time staff in the labour movement for 30 years, culminating in her election as the first woman president of the Toronto and York Region Labour Council, a position she held for thirteen years. Early retirement afforded her the opportunity to pursue a life-long desire to write fiction. She has completed one novel, and is currently working on her second. Her short story, *Seeing Red*, was published in a Writers and Editors Network chapbook, and her short story, *Swirling Leaves*, was published in *Canadian Voices, Volume One*.

DAVID L. TUCKER is a Gemini award-winning documentary filmmaker who operates a small production company in Oakville, Ontario. In addition to his work as a television writer, producer and director, David is a media professor at Ryerson University and has served as both an academic chair and associate dean. He has a Masters Degree in Interdisciplinary Fine Art. To expand his interest in creative storytelling, he recently began life writing.

SHEILA E. TUCKER is an editor and designer for an international professional firm; as well, she studies English part-time at the University of Toronto. Sheila first started writing poetry and short stories as a hobby several years ago and recently began submitting work to contests and publishers. She won first prize in a Mayor's poetry competition and has been accepted into three Canadian anthologies, including U of T's *Vox*. Sheila is an active member in local poetry groups in the Toronto area.

EDWIN VASAN was born in India and completed his engineering degree at the prestigious Indian Institute of Technology in Madras (now known as Chennai). He has lived in Ontario for the past 25 years in the Durham Region. Edwin is the author of his debut novel Kanishka.

HERB WARE has worked as a journalist and business writer for most of his career. He recently moved into the fiction field and is now concentrating his efforts on this genre. Herb is also a member of an allied group of

professional writers and editors who conduct writing workshops, and provide critiques and editing services that help authors improve their work.

JOYCE WAYNE is a writer, editor and educator. A recipient of the Fiona Mee Award for Literary Journalism, she has written extensively about authors and their books. Wayne has worked as the trade editor at Quill & Quire and the editorial director of non-fiction at McClelland & Stewart. She is also the founder of the Canadian Journalism for Internationally Trained Writers program at Sheridan College, where she teaches cultural and diversity studies to new Canadians.

SARAH ZAHID was born and raised in Pakistan. She is trained in art of number crunching. Sarah is a graduate of Carleton University Ottawa. She believes that lyricism is a universal language. She writes short stories and poems.

KAROL ZELAZNY is an author, philosopher and transformational speaker. His book *Walk on Water In The World of Symptoms* is now available at Chapters. Karol is a certified hypnotherapist who specializes in Past Life Regression/Exploration and Spiritual Healing. He is a Silva UltraMind ESP seminar instructor. Karol has a genuine thirst for knowledge. He plans to create a 'True Knowledge Center' in Ontario in the near future. Karol is also a program director at the Radical Health Center.

ZOHRA ZOBERI writes drama, poetry, and fiction in English and Urdu. She is the founder of Bridging the Gap with a mission of Enlightenment through Entertainment which is reflected in her stage plays *Window Shopping... for lasting love* (2007 Finalist Award) and *Questionably Ever After* (Emerging Performing Arts Award for 2008 from the Mississauga Arts Council).